Publisher
www.bhutan-switzerland.org

Editors:
Ernst Reinhardt, chief editor, research and management
Ueli Rüegg, arts and design, research assistance
Peter Moser-Kamm, design and desktop publishing

German summaries: Thomas Biland
French translation: Dominique Guenat

Translation and editing:
Peter Rainer, Innsbruck
Birgit and Eric Reinhardt, Birmensdorf
Tshering Wangda, MoHCA, Thimphu

Portraits of Pema Wangchuck, Chenkyab Dorji, Gembo Tenzing, Jampel Ngedup, Karma Tobden and Ugyen Dorji
by Dorji Wangchuk, Chenzig Communications, Thimphu

Printed in Switzerland

ISBN 978-3-9523611-1-5

Printing and delivery:
Wolfau Druck AG
CH-8570 Weinfelden
wolfau-druck@bluewin.ch

Far apart and close together

Bhutan and Switzerland – Partners in Development since 1950

society
switzerland-bhutan

Let this be our tribute to the visionary leaders, late Majesty, 3rd King Jigme Dorji Wangchuck and his son, the 4th Druk Gyalpo, King Jigme Singye Wangchuck, the 5th Druk Gyalpo, King Jigme Khesar Namgyel Wangchuck and late Fritz von Schulthess, the architects who shaped the Bhutan-Swiss friendship.

The beginning of a friendship-inspired co-operation has stood the test of time. It stands as solid as the Alps and the Himalayas. At present, the area of co-operation has diversified and matured. Bhutan and Switzerland share tremendous good will and friendship and stand as equal partners in the community of nations.

Society Switzerland-Bhutan /
Bhutan-Swiss Friendship Association

We acknowledge sincerely the financial and technical support of Helvetas, Swiss Development Cooperation, the family von Schulthess, the members of the Society Switzerland-Bhutan, the Bhutan-Swiss Friendship Association. We would also like to thank all those who have contributed texts, photographs or given interviews or helped us with relevant information.

A very special word of appreciation goes to Thomas Biland for his informative, concise german summaries.

And last but not least, we would like to thank Dr. Saamdu Chetri for his endeavours to compile the information on numerous projects.

Contents

དཔལ་ལྡན་འབྲུག་གཞུང་། Royal Government of Bhutan
བློན་ཆེན། Prime Minister

7th May, 2008

Foreword by His Excellency Lyonchen Jigmi Yoezer Thinley, Hon'ble Prime Minister, Royal Government of the Kingdom of Bhutan

It gives me immense pleasure to note that the Bhutan-Swiss Friendship Association is bringing out this publication highlighting the friendship and cooperation between the two countries with its many proud achievements. It is gratifying to note that this book is dedicated to the introduction of Constitutional Democratic Monarchy in Bhutan even as it commemorates the Centenary Celebration of the Monarchy and the Coronation of our beloved Fifth King, His Majesty Jigme Khesar Namgyel Wangchuck.

The foundation of this friendship was laid in the early 1950's through the personal ties of friendship between the Late King, His Majesty Jigme Dorji Wangchuck, and Mr. Von Schulthess, an eminent Swiss industrialist. Their personal friendship developed into meaningful cooperation in 1975, when Helvetas assumed the responsibility of coordinating Swiss Development Cooperation in Bhutan. With this transition of personal ties into a bilateral development initiative, Switzerland has been an understanding and a reliable development partner for Bhutan.

Today, the fruits of this partnership are visible everywhere in Bhutan. Badpalathang in Bumthang, in particular, is a traditional Bhutanese village with Swiss features – pine forests, wooden houses set in rich pastures, Brown Swiss breeding farms, cheese making, workshops for heating stoves and farm machinery and bee keeping to name a few. Over the years, the Swiss support has diversified into other important areas to include health services, education, culture, and research and training in agriculture, forestry and environmental conservation. The RNR Centers in Lobesa and Zhemgang and the Paro College of Education are some of the outstanding examples of Swiss support for Bhutan.

The development philosophy of Gross National Happiness propounded by the Fourth King is the guiding principle of our development process and we are committed to achieve this goal for the happiness of our people. As we jointly mark and celebrate the Centenary of the Monarchy and the Coronation of our Fifth King, let us seize this opportunity to deepen and add new dimensions to our long established bonds of friendship for mutual growth and advancement.

I am happy that this book, while guiding the reader through the genesis of the extraordinary Bhutan-Swiss friendship, articulates our mutual desire to further strengthen our ties and cooperation. I wish to commend all those who were involved in bringing out this commemorative publication for their contribution to the cause of friendship between our two countries.

I wish the Bhutan-Swiss Friendship Association great success in its noble endeavors.

Tashi Delek!

(Jigmi Y Thinley)

1 Prime Minister Jigmi Yoezer Thinley

Schweizerische Eidgenossenschaft
Confédération suisse
Confederazione Svizzera
Confederaziun svizra

Federal Department of Foreign Affairs FDFA

2008-02-28

Foreword by Ms. Micheline Calmy-Rey, Foreign Minister of Switzerland

Nice stories always have a personal dimension. The long lasting friendship between Bhutan and Switzerland is no exception to it, as it started with the friendship of the daughter of the King of Bhutan and the daughter of a Swiss industrialist in the 1960's. The many similarities between Bhutan and Switzerland – small size compared to its neighbours, mountainous, large forest area, landlocked and endowed with limited natural resources – are also favouring such ties.

2 Micheline Calmy-Rey, Federal Councillor, Foreign Minister

Since the 1960's, the Swiss industrial family von Schulthess, then Helvetas and later the Swiss Agency for Development and Cooperation (SDC) have accompanied Bhutan in its unique development story. Bhutan has a lot to teach us. Its "Gross National Happiness" principle (balancing out economic growth, preservation and promotion of cultural heritage, conservation and sustainable natural resources management, and good governance) has gained interest of a lot of development specialists and has proven very successful in Bhutan. In the last 50 years, Bhutan has gone through an impressive development and is well on track to achieve most of the Millennium Development Goals.

On the political side as well, Bhutan is successfully managing a smooth transition. The year 2008 will be remembered as its culmination with the creation of political parties, elections, adoption of a constitution and the creation of a new parliamentary democracy. The ability to respect traditions and at the same time adapt to the globalization is remarkable.

On the occasion of the 100th anniversary of the Wangchuck Dynasty and the coronation of His Majesty the 5th King Jigme Khesar Namgyel Wangchuk, I wish the Bhutanese people, its government and all Bhutanese friends all the best in the future development of their country and a long lasting friendship between Switzerland and Bhutan.

Micheline Calmy-Rey
Federal Councillor,
Swiss Ministry of Foreign Affairs

Gross National Happiness

3

The Philosophy of Gross National Happiness

by Jigmi Y. Thinley, Prime Minister, former Minister for Home and Cultural Affairs, Keynote Address at the 7th UPE International Conference, 2007, Bangkok, Thailand (excerpts)

1

Conceived by our King more than thirty years ago, it serves as the beacon for Bhutan in its search for greater well being and advancement of the Bhutanese people. But such an aspiration does not need to be that of Bhutan alone. We are, therefore, heartened by the growing circle of people in the world who see flaws in our purely materialist way of life and how it is structured, by design, to trap human life in an unending circle of desire and self gratification.

Propelled by this yardstick, the world has changed and continues to change. Most of us have become richer economically and will continue to aspire for greater accumulation of wealth. It is thus, only natural and reasonable to assume that countries which have become very rich should be in a position to share with the lesser developed countries their knowledge and insight into the true nature of material success. But can they?

How happy are the rich people and how unhappy are the poor? Is there truth in the belief that to be wealthy is to be happy? And as human beings become richer and acquire greater material comfort, is the world becoming a more sustainable, peaceful and happier place?

Such questions should compel honest introspection and may lead to the conclusion that, as human beings, we are bound together in a common journey. We are all hands aboard ships in a vast uncharted ocean.

What will our legacy be for future generations? What kind of society and environment will we bequeath to posterity? What is our collective future? Are there options?

Just as the dark future will be of our own making, it is within the genius of mankind to make it bright and hopeful. What we need is wisdom. We need wisdom and courage tempered by the truth that our way of life is not sustainable and that its promise of happiness goes no further than the illusions on TV screens and the bright billboards. The change must, of necessity, come from a fundamental departure from all that we have strived for and come to live for. It will require social, political and cultural reorientation. It must result in stronger environmental ethics and a new kind of economics.

GNH may be viewed as an option for such a change

GNH is founded on the conviction of our philosopher King that the purpose of development is happiness. It stresses that the legitimacy of a government must be tested on how well its policies and actions support this goal. It is based on the belief that the realization of happiness lies in the judicious balance between pursuing material and spiritual needs of the body and mind. Thus, while the GDP based economic model promotes only economic growth for the comfort of our body, GNH offers a holistic paradigm within which the mind receives equal attention.

It is important to note that GNH does not discard GDP completely. Rather, it assigns this indicator to its rightful place, which is to measure the sum total of goods and services produced and consumed in a country at any given time.

How is the philosophy applied on the ground in Bhutan?

We see the responsibility of the state as being twofold:

The first is to promote conscious pursuit and internalization of happiness by the people rather than letting it remain in the deeper recesses of the subconscious mind. This is done mainly through advocacy and ensuring that all public documents and statements serve to remind the public. School curricula, in particular, are a powerful medium in this regard.

The second is to create and maintain enabling external conditions for the attainment and enjoyment of happiness. To this end, public policy and expenditures must be directed to address the collective happiness of the people.

The Royal Government, in discharging this sacred responsibility, has adopted a four-pronged strategy to fulfill these responsibilities. It is popularly referred to as the 'four pillars' of GNH and comprises the following:

Sustainable and equitable development

The first condition of **sustainability** prescribes that human development must be pursued as a timeless process benefiting not only the present populations but all future generations for all time. It is the moral responsibility of each generation to ensure that its comforts do not come at the cost of lesser opportunities and resources for future generations. This consideration questions the nature and purpose of economic growth and supports research findings which dispel the fallacious belief that having more results in more happiness. There is no doubt that, once the threshold of basic needs is crossed, the correlation between income and happiness becomes less and less true. The principle of sustainability urges moderation of consumption on the basis of real need and cautions against the cancerous nature of mindless and limitless economic growth that is simply not sustainable.

The second condition of **equity** is followed just as seriously in Bhutan. Despite the forbidding features of our geography and the scattered nature of our population distribution and hence, the extremely high cost of socio-economic service delivery, the benefits of development must be equitable across all sections of society at the regional and community levels. This is not only in respect of equity in a quantitative sense, but also in terms of quality.

2

Cultural preservation and promotion

In its widest sense, this pillar holds up the spiritual needs of the individual and society. Seeing culture as a set of tools that define our values; shape our identity and expressions; and guide our behaviour, relationships and practices, it is recognized that there are aspects of it which are timeless in their relevance and those that must yield to innovation. Yet, culture has been a principal victim of the corrosive effect of consumerist ethics. The rate, at which our value frameworks are being questioned and dismantled or abandoned, compels one to wonder whether humanity in reality, is caught in a downward spiral of decivilization and dehumanization.

In the ultimate analysis, happiness is about relationships more than anything else. It is about having family and friends to share precious moments of joy and not having to grieve alone. It is about caring and sharing and knowing that you are not alone.

3

Environmental conservation

Having spoken of the two pillars of the material and the spiritual, the third pillar represents the dynamic space in which we live. It is within the natural environment that the mind and body receive nourishments to grow. Our way of life should thus, be conditioned by nature. But believing in our supremacy over all other forms of life and nature itself, we have shown little respect for the laws of nature. Of late, however, saner voices appear to pave the way albeit, ever so slowly, for man and nature to abide in harmony.

For Bhutan, the health of the environment is an every day concern. The awe-inspiring majesty of our mountains, the sublime beauty of our glacier fed lakes and the torrential rivers that flow through valleys and narrow gorges command our respect and humility. Blessed with an amazing range of biodiversity within its small territory, Bhutan is recognized by wild life conservationists as a biodiversity hot spot. At the same time, we are extremely mindful of the fragility and vulnerability of our environment. Being located in the folds of the high Himalayas, our geology itself is unstable, compelling caution whenever any action that could alter physical environment is to be taken. These include road construction, irrigation channels, and land conversion for agriculture or urban development.

Unless right technology and measures are employed, nature reacts with wrathful vengeance. For these reasons, HM the King established stringent conservation policies long before environment advocacy became fashionable. While hydropower generation in Bhutan actually promotes conservation and has become our biggest foreign exchange earner, exploitation of our forest resources is carried out with extreme care. Likewise, many potentially polluting mineral based industries have been prevented from being established. As a result, Bhutan is among the few countries where green cover is expanding against demographic growth and increasing human activity.

4

Good governance

The role of this pillar is pivotal. It is good governance that must ensure the strength and capacity of the other three pillars and, in turn, be strengthened itself to hold up the architecture of happiness.

The erection of this pillar has received the highest priority of HM the 4thKing since the time of His Coronation in 1974. Deeply convinced that the fate of Bhutan must not depend on the accident of birth or providence, HM has worked methodically against popular will to transfer the absolute powers of the ruler to the people. In so doing, he stands as a rare leader who has worked hard to distance and separate himself from the centre and source of power.

It is the wish of our King that the future of Bhutan be safe and prosperous under the guidance of leaders who will be chosen by the people on the basis of merit and whose accountability will be directly to the people through the ballot.

3b

Happiness Index

In a world where quantity and measurements govern all aspects of life, and indeed decision-making, there are many who argue that anything that cannot be quantified is not worth being taken seriously. Furthermore, where tax money is involved in promoting happiness, politicians need to be able to explain how much more happiness has been and can be enhanced through tax expenditures. It is obvious that academics, economists, politicians and, should I add, urban planners, seldom dare to break out of the box of conventional wisdom. Therefore, there is the danger that unless a set of indices are developed, GNH may be forgotten at the expense of human well-being.

Bhutan Development Index

The Royal Government has now commissioned a research institute (Center for Bhutan Studies) to develop GNH indicators to bring the sublime, as it were, to the reality of the consumerist world. In this regard, I should report here that several indicators have already been developed by GPI Atlantic of Nova Scotia in Canada to measure elements that affect quality of life and human well being. But an aggregate indicator for happiness has never been attempted.

The indicators that are presently being developed by the Centre for Bhutan Studies comprise the following:

- living standard
- population health
- education
- cultural vitality
- time use and balance
- emotional well-being
- community vitality
- eco-system vitality and resilience
- good governance

Together, these will form the Bhutan Development index. If and when accepted, the index will be integrated into policy framework. It will become the principle basis for planning, monitoring and evaluation processes.
Meanwhile, we are quite satisfied with the results of the National Population and Housing Census of May 2005, which revealed the following happiness levels in Bhutan:

Happy =52%
Very happy = 45%
Not very happy = 3%

Now, what will a country or a world that pursues GNH be like?

It would be a peace-loving democracy; harmonious and united in noble ideals and guided by high principles. Its people would be trusting and trustworthy. They would be understanding and believe in dialogue and conciliation as the way to resolve problems. They would be tolerant and subscribe to the principles of peaceful coexistence, cooperation and good neighborly relations.
Such a country would not spend precious resources on weapons. It would face neither terrorism nor instability and would believe in the virtue of multilateralism. It would be mindful of and feel responsible for the well-being of generations unborn. A GNH guided country would place the happiness of its people as the highest national priority. In this sense, GNH is a utopian idea. At the very least, it provides a glimpse of the world that ought to be.

In Kürze

GDP – Gross Domestic Product – zu deutsch Bruttosozialprodukt: Das ist die gesamte Wertschöpfung einer Volkswirtschaft, ein Index an dem gemeinhin der Wohlstand eines Landes gemessen wird. Der König von Bhutan hat dem schon vor 30 Jahren sein Konzept der GNH – Gross National Happiness entgegen gesetzt, in der Überzeugung, dass Glück das Ziel jeder Entwicklung sein müsse. Der Zustand von Glück liegt im klugen Gleichgewicht materieller und spiritueller Bedürfnisse von Körper und Seele. Die Philosophie ruht auf vier Pfeilern: Keine Generation darf ihre Entwicklung auf Kosten kommender Generationen vorantreiben. Kultur und Tradition sind die ersten Opfer einer materialistischen Ethik, sie sind entsprechend zu schützen. Der Lebensstil muss Rücksicht nehmen auf die Natur. Und schliesslich hat gute Führung dafür zu sorgen, dass jede staatliche Tätigkeit auf Nachhaltigkeit ausgerichtet ist. Die Regierung hat ein Forschungsinstitut beauftragt, welches Messgrössen für einen „Bhutan Entwicklungs-Index" zur Messung von Glück entwickeln soll. GNH – das wissen auch die Buthaner – ist eine utopische Idee, die aber immerhin den Blick auf eine Welt ermöglicht, wie sie sein könnte.

En bref

GDP – Gross Domestic Product, ou PIB (produit intérieur brut) en français : c'est la mesure de la richesse créée par une économie nationale, un indice généralement utilisé pour mesurer le niveau matériel de bien-être d'un pays. Voici plus de 30 ans, le Roi du Bhoutan proposait la notion de Bonheur National Brut (BNB), étant convaincu que le bonheur doit être le but de tout développement. Le bonheur résulte d'un équilibre subtil de satisfaction de besoins matériels et spirituels du corps et de l'âme. La philosophie est basée sur quatre piliers : aucune génération n'a droit à un développement se faisant aux dépens des générations suivantes. La culture et la tradition sont les premières victimes d'une pensée matérialiste, elles doivent par conséquent être protégées. Le style de vie doit prendre égard à la nature. Et finalement une bonne gouvernance doit assurer que toute activité de l'Etat prenne en compte les principes du développement durable. Le gouvernement du Bhoutan a créé un institut de recherche chargé de développer des indicateurs pour un indice de développement destinés à mesurer le bonheur. Le BNB – les Bhoutanais le savent bien – est une utopie, mais elle a le mérite de permettre un regard sur le monde tel qu'il devrait être.

4

Leaders

by Dr. Pema Gyamtsho, Minister for Agriculture, former Dy-Resident Co-ordinator Helvetas until 2007; attached to Helvetas projects since 1970

The chronicled history of Bhutan began with the visit in 747 AD of Guru Padmasambhava, the great Buddhist master from India, who introduced Tantric Buddhism in Tibet and Bhutan. He is today revered as the second Buddha and patron saint of Bhutan. Before the advent of Buddhism, people practiced an animistic faith known as Bon that is still followed in parts of the country during the celebrations of local festivals (Pommaret 1997).
The second watershed in the history of the Kingdom was the visit of Shabdrung Ngawang Namgyel, a great Buddhist Master of the Drukpa Kagyue Sect in Tibet. He came to Bhutan in 1616 because of a strife in his ancestral seat of Ralung in Tibet and soon consolidated the country under a unified power adopting a dual system of governance combining temporal and religious authorities. He built the grand structures known as Dzongs that serve as monasteries, fortresses and administration. He introduced for the first time in the country a theocracy, an administrative system and a code of law. This dual system of governance continued for nearly 250 years.

However, internal struggles among regional warlords began to divide the country towards the later part of the period and political instability threatened the survival of the country around the time British India was gaining power in the region.
It was against this backdrop of political instability that Jigme Namgyel, the Governor of Trongsa, emerged as a powerful leader to hold sway over all the other chieftains and paved the way for his son Ugyen Wangchuck to be enthroned as the first King of Bhutan in 1907. The establishment of the monarchy unified the country under one central authority and brought about an unprecedented period of peace and progress to the people of the country. The Second King, Jigme Wangchuck (1926-52) continued with the process of consolidation and initiated engagements with the outside world, mostly with British India and signed the important Indo-Bhutan treaty in 1947 following India's independence.
However, it was not until the reign of Third King Jigme Dorji Wangchuck (1952-1972) that Bhutan really began to emerge as a modern nation and shed centuries of self-imposed isolation. The Bhutanese political system has evolved rapidly in the last forty years. Jigme Dorji Wangchuck is hailed as the father of modern Bhutan when he ushered in many reforms in the fifties and sixties.
He instituted the National Assembly in 1953; the Five Year Development Plans in 1961, the Royal Advisory Council in 1965, and the High Court in 1968. Most importantly, he guided the country's accession to the United Nation's Organisation in 1971. He was instrumental in cultivating the goodwill of the Government of India and obtaining its support for implementing its development plans that included roads, schools, hospitals and agricultural development. He was also responsible for laying the foundation of Swiss assistance to Bhutan through his growing friendship with the Swiss industrialist von Schulthess. He made a profound impact on the shape of the administration and governance policies of the country.
The Forth King Jigme Singye Wangchuck, who had to take the reins of government at the tender age of 17 due to the untimely death of his father, rapidly transformed the country from a medieval setting to a modern nation now. He not only consolidated the initiatives taken by his father but also introduced many major changes. He decentralized most of the functions from central government to dzongkhag (district) level government in 1980 and then from district to geog (sub-district) level in 1992 in an effort to bring governance and services closer to the people and empower people to take responsibility for their own development and well-being. In 1998, in an unexpected move, he dissolved the hitherto appointed cabinet of

5 Guru Padmasambhava

6 Shabdrung Ngawang Namgyel

7 HM Ugyen Wangchuck

ministers and replaced them with a new cabinet, members of which were elected from the National Assembly members through a secret ballot. The new cabinet was entrusted with most of the responsibilities for governance that till then were in his absolute power.
His political reform culminated with the sudden and unprecedented announcement to transform the country from monarchy to a constitutional democracy and abdicated in favour of his eldest son, the present king.

In 2006 His Majesty Jigme Khesar Namgyel Wangchuck became the new King of Bhutan. After completing his basic education in Bhutan, Prince Jigme studied at the Cushing Academy and the Wheaton College in Massachusetts USA. He graduated from Magdalen College, Oxford University, England, where he completed the Foreign Service Programme and the M.A. Programme in Politics. He also completed a course at the National Defence College, New Delhi, India, in 2005. He has officially represented Bhutan in several high level international events. A keen sportsman, he is an icon for the Bhutanese youth. In 2008 he will be formally enthroned as the fifth Druk Gyalpo and will be the first constitutional monarch of Bhutan.

In Kürze

Bhutans Geschichte beginnt im Jahre 747 mit dem Besuch des Guru Padmasambhava, der den tantrischen Buddhismus nach Tibet und Bhutan bringt. Im 17. Jahrhundert gelingt Shabdrung Ngawang Namgyel eine erste Einigung des Landes. Er errichtet das Netzwerk der Dzongs, die Kloster, Festung und administratives Zentrum in einem sind. Schon bald flammen die Kämpfe zwischen den einzelnen Kriegsherren wieder auf. Erst mit dem Auftauchen der Briten in der Region gelingt es dem stärksten unter ihnen, dem Gouverneur von Trongsa, sich durchzusetzen und im Jahre 1907 seinen Sohn Ugyen Wangchuck zum ersten König von Bhutan zu machen.
Der 4. König, Jigme Singye Wangchuck, führt das Land in die Moderne mit einer Verfassung, dem Wechsel zur konstitutionellen Monarchie, der Auflösung der Nationalversammlung und der Ankündigung allgemeiner Wahlen. Ende 2006 verzichtet er auf den Thron. Sein Sohn wird als nominelles Staatsoberhaupt keinen direkten Einfluss auf die Regierungsgeschäfte mehr haben.

En bref

L'histoire du Bhoutan commence en 747 avec la visite de Padmasambhava ou Guru Rinpoché en langue tibétaine. Il a introduit le bouddhisme tantrique au Tibet et au Bhoutan. Au 17ème siècle, Shabdrung Ngawang Namgyel réunit le pays pour la première fois. Il fait construire un réseau de dzongs, forteresses réunissant monastères et centres administratifs. Toutefois, les combats entre les différents chefs de guerre reprennent peu après. Ce n'est qu'à l'arrivée des britanniques dans la région que le plus fort des chefs de guerre, le gouverneur de Trongsa, parvient à s'imposer. Il fait de son fils Ugyen Wangchuck le premier roi du Bhoutan en 1907.
Le 4ème roi, Jigme Singye Wangchuck, mène le pays vers la modernité, avec une Constitution, le passage à une monarchie constitutionnelle, la dissolution de l'Assemblée Nationale et l'organisation d'élections générales. Fin 2006, il renonce au trône. Son fils en tant qu'autorité suprême du pays, n'aura plus d'influence directe sur les affaires du gouvernement.

8 HM Jigme Wangchuck

9 HM Jigme Dorji Wangchuck

10 HM Jigme Khesar Namgyel Wangchuck, HRH Prince Namgyel Wangchuck; HM Jigme Singye Wangchuck

A timeline of political changes since 1950

1953
The National Assembly was established by His Majesty Jigme Dorji Wangchuck, the Third King of Bhutan. It comprised 150 members of which 115 members were directly elected by the people.
During the reign of the Third King, His Late Majesty Jigme Dorji Wangchuck, the National Assembly enacted in 1953 the first comprehensive codified laws known as the Thrimzhung Chhenmo, or Supreme Laws, which contain almost all modern categories of criminal offenses and their penalties.

1965
The Royal Advisory Council (RAC) was also proclaimed by the Third King in 1965. The nine-member council, comprising representatives of the Government, the Monastic Body and the people, became the highest advisory body in the Kingdom.

1968
The High Court was established in 1968 with judges representing the Government, the Monastic body and the people .

1970
Under Royal Decree, the Royal Audit Authority was instituted as an independent agency on 16 April 1970.

1972
His Majesty Jigme Dorji Wangchuck, the Third King, suddenly passed away at Nairobi, Kenya on 23 July 1972. His Royal Highness Jigme Singye Wangchuck, Trongsa Penlop and Crown Prince acceded to the throne as the Fourth Druk Gyalpo.

1974
His Majesty Jigme Singye Wangchuck ascended the Golden Throne with formal coronation on 2 June 1974.

1975
His Majesty propounded the concept of Gross National Happiness as the development philosophy of Bhutan.

1981
The Dzongkhag Yargay Tshogchung (DYT) or the District Development Council was instituted in all 20 Dzongkhags/Districts and the members elected by the people of the Dzongkhag.

1991
The Gewog Yargay Tshogchung or the Block Development Committee was established in all 221 Gewogs (blocks) in Bhutan and its members were elected by the people of the block.

1998
The Lhengye Zhungtshog or the cabinet was dissolved for the first time in August 1998.
A new Council of Ministers was elected by the National Assembly for a five-year term and the minister obtaining the highest votes assumed the role of Prime Minister for one year on rotation. His Majesty the King devolved executive powers of governing the country to the Council of Ministers and the Cabinet.

2001
A drafting committee comprising 39 members with the Chief Justice of Bhutan as Chairman was formed to draft the first written constitution of Bhutan .

2002
The 80th Session of the National Assembly enacted in July the revised Gewog Yargay Tshogchung Chathrim (rules & regulation) and the Dzongkhag Yargay Tshogchung Chathrim.

2003
Under the direct command of His Majesty the King, the security forces launched a successful military operation and expelled all militants from India from the forests of Bhutan.

2005
26 March 2005: The draft Constitution was ready and officially released nationwide for public comments.
29 October 2005: Public consultation of the draft Constitution was initiated by His Majesty the Fourth King and the Crown Prince in all twenty Dzongkhags beginning from Thimphu Dzongkhag.
17 December 2005: His Majesty suddenly announced his decision to step down and hand over the reign to the Crown Prince at the National Day address to the Nation from Tashi Yangtse Dzongkhag.
31 December 2005: His Majesty decreed the establishment of the offices of the Anti-Corruption Commission, the Election Commission and the Office of the Attorney General.

2006
9 December 2006: His Majesty the King Jigme Singye Wangchuck hands over the responsibilities as Monarch and Head of State to Crown Prince Jigme Khesar who assumes full responsibility as the Fifth Druk Gyalpo.
17 December 2006: His Majesty Jigme Khesar, the Fifth King, addressed the nation on the occasion of the 99th National Day at Changlimithang, Thimphu.

2007
Bhutan and India sign in New Delhi the updated friendship treaty of 1949.
21 April 2007: A nationwide first mock election was held in preparation for the general elections in 2008.
28 May 2007: Second mock election held.
27 July 2007: The National Judicial Council was established to streamline judicial reforms, strengthen the institution, and to ensure effective and efficient delivery by the justice system. This was constituted according to the provisions of the Judicial Service Act enacted by the 86th Session of the National Assembly. It is a mandate for the judiciary to embrace the future in keeping with the change in the governance of the country.
July 2007: Seven of the ten Cabinet Ministers resigned to join political parties.
The Election Commission announced that the 20-member National Council election would be held on 31 December 2007.

2008
The General election for the 47-member Lower House (the National Assembly) was held on March 24, 2008.
In 2008, Bhutan will celebrate the following landmark events:
- 100 years of the Monarchy
- A newly elected Government with a two-party Parliament
- A written Constitution
- Formal Coronation of the Fifth King.

The Constitution of Bhutan

Bhutan is among the few countries where all reforms have emanated from the monarch, ironically, despite the strongest resistance from the people.

In the words of His Majesty Jigme Singye Wangchuck: "If the lessons of some democracies are not encouraging, it is not because the concept of democracy is flawed. It is because of mismanagement and corruption by those who practice it."

His Majesty Jigme Singye Wangchuck commanded the drafting of a written constitution for the country. A 39-member Drafting Committee headed by the Chief Justice, including the Speaker of the National Assembly along with 20 people's representatives, one from each Dzongkhag (District), all the members of the Royal Advisory Council and representatives of the government - was formed in November 2001.

The draft constitution was distributed to every citizen of the country in Dzongkha and English. His Majesty, the Fourth King and the then Trongsa Penlop and Crown Prince traveled to different districts of the country to listen to the views and clarify every issue of concern.

Bhutan has perhaps the first Constitution in the world that has been launched on the Internet for open discourse. The Constitution of Bhutan will be adopted by referendum, as has been the practice in Bhutan for all important issues, and then enacted in the National Assembly.

Some highlights of the Draft Constitution

- The Druk Gyalpo is to hand over throne to Crown Prince/ Princess at the age of 65
- Abdication of King through resolution passed by a joint sitting of not less than 3/4 of Parliament, followed by national referendum.
- The government is to ensure that 60% of the country remains under forest cover for all time
- Explicit normative values with reference to the pursuit of Gross National Happiness, inclusiveness and compassionate society
- Promoting equitable distribution of public facilities among people regardless of where they live
- Provision of free education for all children up to tenth standard
- Free Access to basic public health services and guarantees security in the event of sickness and disability or lack of adequate means of livelihood for reasons beyond one's control
- The National Council as one of the houses of parliament with 20 members elected directly by the people in the 20 dzongkhags and five eminent persons nominated by the King. The Council would act as review body on matters concerning the sovereignty of the country and the interests of the people that needed to be brought to the notice of the King, the Prime Minister, and the National Assembly.
- The government would fully fund the political parties through the Election Commission to ensure the integrity of the electoral process in Bhutan.
- Unlike other countries where persons holding constitutional positions appointed by a King, a President, or a Prime Minister, thus compromising their objectivity, the position holders in Bhutan would be nominated jointly by the Prime Minister, the Chief Justice, the Speaker of the National Assembly, the Chairperson of the National Council, and the Opposition Leader would be appointed by the King.

Establishment of Constitutional Offices

Taking a significant step towards a Democratic Constitutional Monarchy, the appointments to the first three constitutional posts – the offices of the Attorney General, the Election Commission and the Anti-Corruption Commission – were created by Royal Decree in 2006. All three incumbents are interim appointments made in preparation for the general elections in 2008.

Source: Window on Bhutan 2007-08, Royal Bhutanese Embassy, New Delhi

Far apart and close together – Bhutan and Switzerland

11

Bhutan and Switzerland

by Dr. Pema Gyamtsho, Minister for Agriculture, former Dy-Resident Co-ordinator Helvetas until 2007; attached to Helvetas projects since 1970

What is it that made a little mountainous country in the European Alps and another little mountainous country in the heart of the Himalayas in Asia click as sustainable development partners? In my analysis, there are several factors that contributed to this situation.
Firstly, it is the human dimension – the quest to know the unknown and to reach out to the world. It is the personal friendship between the daughter of a Swiss industrialist and a future queen of Bhutan that sparked off the relationship between their two countries. Secondly, it is the geo-political similarities that the two countries share which very much placed Switzerland in an advantageous position to guide Bhutan's development. Both countries are landlocked and situated between big neighbours – Switzerland is bordered by Germany, France, Italy and Austria; Bhutan by China and India. Therefore, their people share a natural instinct for survival and a distinct fear of domination by other nations and consequently a loss of national identity and sovereignty.
Historically, Switzerland shared a similar system, whereby local warlords and church leaders dominated the people and property in their jurisdictions prior to the establishment of the Swiss Confederation in the nineteenth century. Up until 1907, when monarchy was established, Bhutan had a similar feudal system whereby provincial and local nobilities and clergy ruled their turfs with a nominal central government run by a 'Deb' (temporal ruler) elected from their members.
Ecologically, both countries share similar climate and terrain although the range of variation in climate and vegetation is much wider in Bhutan. Traditionally, both countries have very limited natural resources with glacier fed waters, pastures and forests being the primary natural resources on which people are dependent for a living. Both countries have four distinct seasons. While snow with the ski industry is Switzerland's white

12

13 Physical map of Bhutan

gold, river water is Bhutan's white gold with the revenue it earns from hydropower. In terms of language and ethnic distribution, again both share similar patterns. While Switzerland has German, French, Italian and Romanch speaking peoples in the north, west, south and east respectively, Bhutan has Ngalong, Tshanglong, Bumthap and Lhotshampa as its four main linguistic groups. Similarly, Bhutan shares the kind of love-hate relationship with Tibetans to the north and Indians to the South, from where it has drawn its religion and cultural traditions just as the Swiss share them with the Germans and French.

People and culture

Switzerland has a population of 7,556,900 million people as of 2006, of which more than 20% are foreigners. It has four major ethnic groups based on languages: German (63.7%), French (20.4%), Italian (6.5%), Romanch (0.5%) and others (9.0%). The majority of the people are Christians with Roman Catholics (41.8%) and Protestants (35.3%). Moslems make up 4.3% of the population and others account for 3.2%. There is a significant proportion of people (11.1%) with no religion.

The population of Bhutan according to the Census 2006 was 672,425 people with the largest concentration in Thimphu, the capital city. There are 19 different languages spoken in Bhutan (Pommaret 1997). The official language is Dzongkha "the language of the Fortresses." English is used as the standard medium of instruction in schools and in official correspondences. The other main languages are Sharchopkha, Lhotshamkha and Bumthangkha.

14 Physical map of Switzerland

- Jura (10%), average altitude 700 meters (2297 ft) above sea level
- Plateau (30%), average altitude 580 meters (1902 ft) above sea level
- Alps (60%), average altitude 1700 meters (5577 ft) above sea level

15

Governance and Administration

The Swiss Confederation was founded in 1291 and has been a Federal Republic since 1848. It is made up of 26 Cantons. The government, or Federal Council, is a collegial board consisting of seven members. The parliament consists of two chambers with equal rights: the Council of States (cantonal representation) with 46 members and National Council (representation body of the people) with 200 members. The 200 members of the National Council and the 46 of the Council of States are elected by the citizens on the basis of the various political parties.

Bhutan has been a hereditary monarchy since 1907. The present King Jigme Khesar Namgyel Wangchuck ascended the throne in 2006, after his father the Fifth King abdicated unexpectedly at the young age of 51.

The National Assembly was dissolved in 2007 after its 87th session to give way to the new form of governance, i.e. an elected government according to the Constitution. As of 2008 it will comprise 47 members in the Lower House, representing the 47 newly delineated constituencies, and 25 National Council members (Upper House) representing the 20 districts and 5 eminent personalities nominated by the king. The party with the majority seats will form the government and the other will provide the opposition. The king will be a constitutional head of state and will not have any direct role in governance.

16 Political map of Bhutan

Geography

Switzerland has a total area of 41,285 sq.km, of which 74.5% are productive (30.8% forests, 36.9% arable land and 6.8% residential areas) and 25.5% are covered by water, unproductive land or barren land. The highest elevation is the Dufour Peak of the Monte Rosa at 4,634 m above sea level and the lowest point is the shore of the Lago Maggiore at 193 m above sea level. As it stands today Switzerland got its final boundaries in 1815, when Valais, Neuchâtel and Geneva joined the Swiss Confederation.

Bhutan borders the Tibet Autonomous Region of China to the north and the Indian states of Assam and West Bengal to the south, Arunachal Pradesh to the east and Sikkim to the west. The country spans about 300 km from east to west and 170 km from north to south. The latest revised land area following demarcation with China and India is 38,396 sq.km, of which

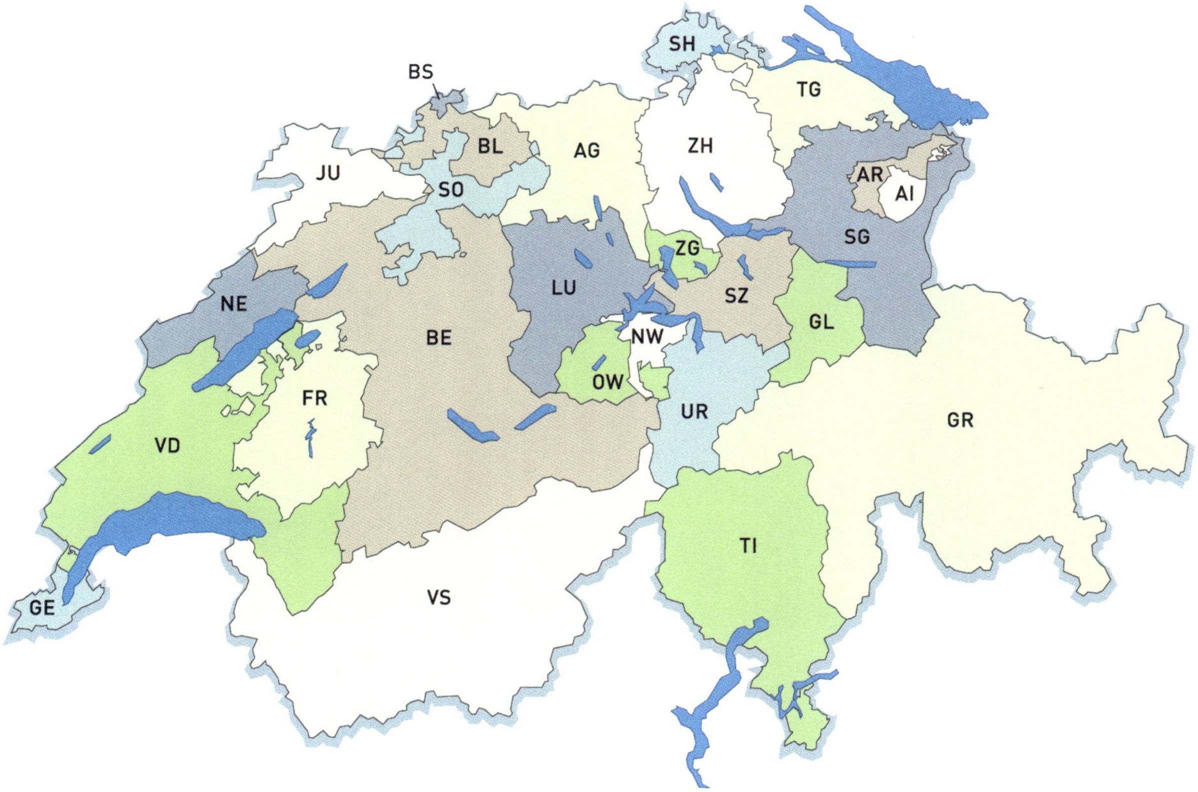

17 Political map of Switzerland

less than 8% is arable and more than 70% are under forest cover of some sort. The rest is under water and consists of barren lands, including permanent snow cover. Elevation ranges from less than 100 m above sea level at the border with India to over 7500 m at the highest point on the border with Tibet.

Bhutan can be divided into three distinct physiographic regions on the basis of altitude and corresponding rainfall and temperature. The southern foothills range in altitude from less than 100 m to about 2000 m.a.s.l and comprise the Siwalik Hills together with a narrow strip of flat plains along the Indian border. The Inner Himalayas make up the main river valleys and steep hills and rise in elevation from about 2000 m to over 4000 m. The Great Himalayas to the north along the Tibetan border consist of snow-capped peaks and alpine lands varying in altitude from around 4000 m to over 7500 m.

In Kürze

So beginnen Märchen: 1948 begegnen sich zwei Prinzessinnen in London - Ashi Kesang Choden Dorji und Lisina, Tochter aus der Industriellenfamilie von Schulthess. Die Freundschaft der jungen Frauen verbindet bald auch ihre Familien. Die Heirat von Ashi Kesang mit dem Kronprinzen Dasho Jigme Dorji Wangchuck im Jahre 1952 begründet eine tiefe Freundschaft der Königsfamilie Wangchuck mit der Familie von Schulthess – bis auf den heutigen Tag.
Weit weg und doch so nah: Bhutan und die Schweiz haben vieles gemeinsam. Kleines, gebirgiges Land, mit schöner, aber rauer Natur. Eingeklemmt zwischen mächtigen Nachbarn, in ständigem Abwehrkampf um die nationale Identität und Souveränität. Wasser und Holz als einziger Reichtum; grosse sprachliche Vielfalt. Historisch gesehen lebten beide Länder in einem feudalen System, beherrscht von regionalen Kriegsherren und Kirchenfürsten.

En bref

Ainsi commencent les contes de fées : en 1948, deux princesses se rencontrent à Londres. Ashi Kesang Choden Dorji et Lisina, fille de l'industriel suisse Fritz von Schulthess. L'amitié entre les deux jeunes femmes réunit bientôt leurs familles. Le mariage d'Ashi Kesang avec le prince héritier Dasho Jigme Dorji Wangchuck en 1952 scelle une profonde amitié entre la famille royale Wangchuck et les descendants de la famille von Schulthess, une amitié aujourd'hui encore vivante.
Très éloignés et pourtant si proches : le Bhoutan et la Suisse ont de nombreux points communs : de petits territoires montagneux, et une nature d'une beauté sauvage. Coincé entre des voisins puissants, le Bhoutan est en lutte constante pour défendre l'identité et la souveraineté nationale. L'eau et le bois comme seules ressources énergétiques et une grande diversité linguistique le caractérisent. Historiquement, les deux pays ont vécu sous un régime féodal, dominé par des chefs de guerre régionaux et des pontifes.

Key indicators

by Dr. Pema Gyamtsho, Minister for Agriculture, former Dy-Resident Co-ordinator Helvetas until 2007; attached to Helvetas projects since 1970

Agro-ecological zones/Types of vegetation	
Common name	Scientific name
Wet Subtropical	
Sisso	Dalbergia sissoo
Khair	Acacia catechu
Sal	Shorea robusta
Sua grass	Pollinia ciliate
Humid Subtropical	
Alnus	Alnus nepalens
Walnut	Juglans regia
Magnolia	Magnolia campbellii
Maple	Acer cappadocicum
Rhododendron	Rhodendron arboretum
Warm Temperate	
Oaks	Quercus semicarpifolia
Blue pine	Pinus wallichiana
Spruce	Picea spinulosa
Bamboo	Bambusa arundiacia
Rhododendron	Rhododendron arboretum
Cool Temperate	
Fir	Abies densa
Juniper	Juniperus recurva
Hemlock	Tsuga dumosa
Larch	Larix griffithiana
Birch	Betula utilis, B. alnoides
Alpine	
Dwarf rhododendron	Rhododendron leonopodium
Juniper	Juniperus recurva

18

19

Climate

Switzerland's climate varies from almost continental, with low temperatures and precipitation in the east, to Mediterranean in the south with significantly higher temperatures and level of precipitation. The temperatures depend primarily on the elevation while precipitation is influenced by the winds from the Atlantic ocean.

In Bhutan too, there is a large variation in climate influenced primarily by the variation in altitude. The climatic conditions range from hot and humid subtropical conditions in the lowlands lying south, to tundra with perpetual snow and ice conditions in the great Himalayan zone in the north. The southwest monsoon lasting from mid-June to September is a dominant factor influencing the climate and accounts for 60-90% of the annual precipitation. The annual precipitation varies around 300 mm in the north to around 1000 mm in the temperate zone to over 5000 mm in the southern foothills.

Agro-ecological zones

Switzerland is broadly divided into three geographical zones that also largely determine the agro-ecological conditions. These zones are alpine (60%), middle land called plateau (30%) and Jura (10%). The alpine zone is covered by snow and alpine meadows that serve as summer pastures for cattle. Most of the agricultural lands are located in the middle lands, while the Jura consists of mountain forests and pastures.

Bhutan is commonly classified into six agro-ecological zones based mainly on altitude and precipitation. These zones are used to define the country's eco-floristic zones and agricultural ecosystems with each zone having more or less a distinct vegetation cover and agricultural practices. They are alpine (above 3600 m with rainfall <650 mm), cool temperate (2600-3600 with rainfall between 650 – 850 mm), warm temperate (1800 – 2600 m with rainfall between 850-1200 mm), dry subtropical (1200-1800 m with rainfall 850-1200 mm), humid subtropical (600-1200 m with rainfall 1200-2500 mm) and wet subtropical (150-600 m and rainfall >2500 mm).

Vegetation

Due to the variation in altitude from 195 m to over 4,000 m above sea level, Switzerland displays a vertical zonation of plant species.

As in Switzerland, the wide variations in macro and micro-climatic conditions in Bhutan have resulted in the distribution of a great diversity of vegetation within a limited geographical area. The southern foothills are mostly covered by dense forest of deciduous trees while many different varieties of plants, flowers and trees cover the inner regions.

Major crops grown in Bhutan		
Crop	**Area in acres**	**Production in mt**
Paddy	47,306	68,573
Maize	76,941	77,298
Wheat	11,583	4,352
Barley	3,701	1,735
Millet	15,238	3,793
Buckwheat	8,720	2,887
Potato	7,715	35,340
Chilli	2,315	2,849
Apple	368,413 trees	5,113
Orange	1,761,030 trees	29,616
Others	472,501 trees	4,319

Livestock type and numbers in Bhutan		
Type	**Population**	**% of households owning**
Cattle	320,510	78
Yak	34,936	2
Equine	27,882	24
Sheep	22,879	6
Goats	31,328	16
Pigs	41,404	38
Poultry		66

20

Land use

In Switzerland, 74.5% of the land area is productive (30.8% forests, 36.9% arable land and 6.8% residential areas) and 25.5% are covered by water, unproductive land or barren land. It has in comparison to Bhutan, more favourable terrain for agriculture and infrastructure development. Its gentle slopes and undulating landscape is conducive to intensive farming using modern machinery and equipment. The country's own agricultural production meets about 60% of its food requirements. Swiss agricultural policy, however, is highly regulated with fixed prices and quota restrictions maintained on several products. Domestic production is protected through imposition of restrictions on imports as well as customs and duties on imported goods.

A detailed survey carried out by the Ministry of Agriculture in 1995 showed that about 72% of Bhutan's total land area was forested, of which around 8% was scrub vegetation; the actual tree covered area was about 64%. Much of Bhutan's forests are found on steep mountain slopes where they are relatively inaccessible for commercial exploitation and where there is a high risk for environmental damage if exploited. Arable agriculture land accounts for only about 8% of the total land area and this number is probably close to the maximum area suitable for cultivation. Only about 4% of the land is under natural pastures which however, does not reflect the actual area used for grazing as forest, scrub forests and agricultural fallows are also used for grazing at one time or other. The remaining 16% includes permanent snow-covered areas, marshland and water bodies, rocky outcrops, barren lands and human settlements.

The agricultural land mainly consists of chushing (irrigated cropland), kamshing (dryland), orchard and tseri (tree fallows). Paddy is the main crop grown on chushing which extends above 2500 m and maize is the dominant staple crop grown on kamshing.

The average land holding size varies from district to district with Bumthang in central Bhutan having the highest land holding per household. There around 37 percent of all households own more than 10 acres of land, whereas in Trashi Yangtse in eastern Bhutan only 1 percent owns more than 10 acres and close to 70% own less than 3 acres.

Bhutan has a policy of achieving 70% self-sufficiency in food grains and currently imports well over 30% of its requirements (largely rice) from India to meet its annual needs. Domestic production of cereals and cash crops are supported through subsidies on seeds and fertilizers, purchase of farm machinery and equipment and development of farm infrastructures. Bhutan is still in the process of accessing WTO membership and there is a degree of apprehension on the benefits of a free market economy especially in the agricultural sector.

Whereas, in Switzerland most farms are commercially operated and specialized in certain crops or livestock, the Bhutanese farming system is still dominated by subsistence farming characterized by a mix of several practices involving use of crops, livestock and forest resources. Livestock is an integral part of the Bhutanese farming system. The value of keeping livestock extends beyond the production of milk, meat and fibre production. In many areas, the primary purpose of keeping livestock is to provide draught power and manure to support crop production. In addition, livestock also serves as a security asset for rural farmers in times of crop failure as they can be readily exchanged for cash or food grain. The main types of livestock owned by farmers are cattle, yak, buffaloes, equine (horse, mules, donkeys), sheep goats, pigs and poultry. Open grazing in forests, pastures and agricultural fallows continue to be main practice for the ruminants.

The development of the livestock industry is in many parts of the country hampered by religious sentiments, which prevents the killing of unproductive animals, and thereby reduces the viability of livestock based enterprises.

Forest and biodiversity

Forests cover some 31% of Swiss territory. Most of the forest areas in Switzerland are directly managed by communes or by private owners and timber is commercially exploited.

Bhutan has a rich forest cover of over 72% of the total land area including scrub forest cover of around 8%. The forest and biodiversity in the country are influenced by altitude and rainfall.

Both Switzerland and Bhutan boast very high floral and faunal biodiversity. It is estimated that Switzerland is home to over 50,000 species of plants and animals. However, only 83 of the animal species are mammals and most are bats and small animals with over 30,000 insect species. Bhutan is included along with the rest of the eastern Himalayas as one of the ten global 'hotspots' of biodiversity. Within its small geographical area, it contains a recorded number of over 5,500 species of vascular plants, more than 770 species of birds and 165 species of mammals with several species being endemic to Bhutan. This rich species diversity indicates an equally rich genetic diversity. In recognition of its unique conservation opportunity, the country has dedicated over 26% of its territory to parks and protected areas with an additional 9% demarcated as biological corridors linking the protected areas. As a result, more than 35 percent of the country's area is under some form of conservation management. The country has presently 9 national parks and wildlife sanctuaries.

Source: Biodiversity Action Plan for Bhutan 2002, Ministry of Agriculture, RGOB, Keen Publishing (Thailand) Co. Ltd.

21 Rare mammal: musk deer

Forest type and distribution in Bhutan

Forest type (Altitude range masl)	Main species	Area (in ha)
Fir forest (2700 – 3800)	Fir, Hemlock, Birch, Larch, Rhododendron, Juniper	345,302
Mixed conifer forest (2000 – 2700)	Spruce, Hemlock, Larch, Birch	486,827
Blue pine forest (1800 – 3000)	Blue pine, Oak, Rhododendron	128,593
Chir pine forest (900 – 1300)	Chir pine, Lemon grass	100,899
Broadleaf mixed with conifer (900 – 3000)	Oak, Blue pine, Spruce, Hemlock	135,789
Upland hardwood forest (2000 – 2900)	Oak, Maple, Castonopsis	450,000
Lowland hardwood forest (150 – 700)	Sal, Sisso, Teak	440,000

Water

Switzerland and Bhutan have both very good fresh water resources in the form of numerous springs, stream, ponds, rivers and glacial lakes. In Bhutan, every year these water bodies are replenished by the monsoon rains in summer and by snow in winter. On a global scale, Bhutan has one of the highest per capita availability of water (58,000 m^3). The table below shows the comparison of water availability and usage between Bhutan and Switzerland

Water offers the most economically and environmentally promising sector for economic development of Bhutan. The country has an estimated hydropower generation potential of 30,000 MW and as of 2007, the total installed capacity was 1464 MW representing a little over 3% of the total potential. Source: www.bhutannewsonline.com, www.bea.gov.bt

Water availability and usage

(m^3, a.pers)	Bhutan	Switzerland	World
Availability	58,000	5,000	7,000
Consumption	13	363	664
Domestic (%)	36	42	6
Industry (%)	10	57	21
Irrigation (%)	54	1	73

Source: Zurcher and Choden (2003).Bhutan: Land of Spirituality and Modernisation, Role of Water in Daily Life, New Delhi

Hydropower development status in Bhutan

Power Plant	Capacity	Status / Assistance
Chukha	330	Operational 1977 / India
Kurichu	60	Operational 2002 / India
Basochu	64	Operational 2001 / Austria
Tala	1,020	Operational 2006 / India
Punatsangchu	1,095	Under construction / India
Dagachu	114	Under construction / Austria
Mangdechu	670	Planned / India
Kellungchu	200	Operational 2001 / NL
Sankosh	4,060	Planned / India
Total	7,613	

22

Economy

Switzerland's rapid economic progress took place only after World War II and is based on a highly qualified labour force. The key economic sectors include many domains, such as mechanical and electrical engineering, pharmaceuticals, watches, banking, tourism, insurance, human resources, shipping and logistics.

The World Bank, in its country policy and institutional assessment report, rated Bhutan's macro-economic performance to be the best in the region in 2005 with a score of 5.2 (scale 1 to 6) and assessed its policies and institutions to be among the top three in the region with a score of 3.8. Over the last two decades, economic growth has averaged over 7%, being very capital intensive and fuelled primarily by the rapid expansion of the hydro-power and construction sectors. The fast growth in these sectors has altered the structure of the economy with the share of the agriculture sector (including forestry and livestock) declining from some 40% in 1992 to 21.8% in 2005. However, agriculture still remains the single largest contributor to the national economy and remains critically important as most Bhutanese depend on it for their livelihood.

The high growth rates of the economy have been underpinned by very high rates of savings and investment. Over the last 15 years from 1991 to 2005, investments have been growing at around 13% a year, nearly twice as fast as the real GDP growth of 6.6% over the same period. The high rate of investment has been sustained on account of the high domestic savings and net capital inflows largely on account of Official Development Assistance (ODA) from the country's development partners including Switzerland. In 2005, the net capital inflow was around 21% of GDP. Foreign Direct investment (FDI) still remains nominal and comprised a little over a percent of GDP. Tourism continues to be a major foreign exchange earner with gross receipts of US$ 20 million in 2006. The total revenue earned in 2005-06 financial year was Nu 6,902 million, the growth rate over the last five years averaging 7.86%.

From an annual total development expenditure of Nu 1,814 million in 1990/91, expenditures have grown to Nu 17,775 million in 2005/06. The budget approved by the National Assembly for 2006/07 was Nu 18,300 million. Capital expenditures did comprise around 52% of the total expenditures in the last fifteen years and have grown at an average annual rate of 19%. Current expenditures on the other hand have grown at about 14% a year on average and comprised around 45% of the total development expenditure over the same period. Debt servicing has generally accounted for around 3% of the budget expenditure.

The social sector has been given the highest priority and accounts for 30% of the development budget for the year 2005/06. General public services accounted for another 24% and around 12% were spent on the agriculture sector. The Roads, Energy, Human Settlements and the Communication sectors respectively received around 10%, 6%, 6% and 3% of the total development expenditures.

As a result of the sustained strong growth in development expenditures, both capital and current, the fiscal deficit has been growing since 2000. On average the fiscal deficit has constituted over 6.5% of GDP between 2002 and 2006 and has been financed through a mix of domestic and external borrowings.

Domestic revenue

Domestic revenues between 2000 and 2005 have grown at an average of 8% a year from Nu 4,671 million in 2000/01 to Nu 6,903 million in 2005/06. This is expected to increase drastically with further hydro-power plants commissioned. Revenues comprised around 23% of GDP in 2005/06. Since 2000, tax revenues have contributed substantially and are now around 54% of the total revenue. Excise duty and sales tax were the major contributors and accounted for around 19%, 12% and 9% of total revenues. Personal income tax introduced in 2001 has been rising marginally and on average contributed 1.8% of the total revenue. Non-tax revenues were derived mainly from dividends/transfer of profit from government investments, which alone accounted for 29% of total domestic revenues and about 63% of the total non-tax revenues.

External Resources

The country has relied heavily on Official Development Assistance (ODA) from development partners to finance virtually all of its capital development expenditures so far and has been a major factor in the development success that the country has enjoyed. In the last decade, ODA disbursements to the country averaged USD 114 million annually with around 80% of this constituting grant assistance, the balance being soft loans. In 2006, ODA disbursements amounted to USD 153.5 million which comprised 14% of GDP, around three fourths of which were from bilateral sources.

1 Euro equivalent Nu 61.80 (April 2008)

In Kürze

Hier steht ein Nebeneinander volkswirtschaftlicher Kennzahlen, die auf Ähnlichkeiten und Unterschiede zwischen Bhutan und der Schweiz hinweisen: Beim Klima, der Vegetation, der Pflanzen- und Artenvielfalt, usw. Beide Länder können sich nicht selbst versorgen mit Agrarprodukten. Beider Landwirtschaften sind auch in hohem Masse subventioniert, und die Bauern beider Staaten sind äusserst skeptisch in bezug auf die Öffnung ihres jeweiligen Agrarmarktes.
Bhutan ist wie die Schweiz ein enormes Wasserschloss: Den 700'000 Bhutanern stehen pro Jahr und Kopf 58'000m^3 Wasser zur Verfügung, den 7,5 Mio. Schweizern 5'000m^3. Wasser wird denn auch in Form von Hydropower Geld in die Staatskassen spülen, sobald die vielen Kraftwerkprojekte einmal fertig gebaut sind und Strom nach Indien liefern.

En bref

Différents indicateurs économiques montrent des points communs ainsi que des différences entre le Bhoutan et la Suisse : similarités en ce qui concerne le climat, la végétation, la diversité des plantes et des espèces, etc. Aucun des deux pays n'est en mesure d'assurer son approvisionnement en produits agricoles, les agricultures des deux pays sont largement subventionnées, et les agriculteurs des deux pays sont particulièrement sceptiques quant à l'ouverture de leurs marchés agricoles respectifs.
Tout comme la Suisse, le Bhoutan est un gigantesque château d'eau: chacun des 700'000 bhoutanais dispose de 58'000m^3 d'eau par an, alors que les 7.5 millions de suisses en ont 5'000m^3. L'eau est convertie en argent par l'intermédiaire de centrales hydroélectriques, cet argent alimente les caisses de l'Etat bhoutanais maintenant que de nombreux barrages sont achevés et que l'électricité peut être livrée à l'Inde.

23 Sunday market in Thimphu

Bhutan – where women (almost) always have their say

Fragments from a conversation between Dorje Dölma, a farmer lady from central Bhutan and Martin Brauen, Lecturer at Ethnographic Museum, University of Zurich, 1994

"Two female farmers, one from Bhutan, the other from Switzerland are trading places – as if by magic. That's the fantasy. The Bhutanese woman Dorje Dolma would suddenly be living in, let's say, Schuders/Prättigau in the Canton Grison, up near the forest line, and the Swiss woman-farmer Tina in Bumthang..."
Sense and nonsense of an exchange of women-farmers, from a letter by Peter Leisinger (MD, ex Bumthang) to Martin Brauen

Doubts

One day Dorje Dukpa came by and told me he had received a letter from Sahib (Martin Brauen), asking whether I wanted to visit Switzerland. I said, "That can't be right, did it really have my name in the letter?" When Dorje Dukpa confirmed my name in the letter, I still didn't quite believe it and told him I couldn't just agree to the offer and that I would like to ask my son for advice. When I told this to the people in my village, they all told me I should think over the matter very deeply because Switzerland is far away, I could get sick or perhaps even die there and then my son would suffer a great deal because of that. So, I had a two-day ceremony carried out and I asked a nun what I should do. "Actually", she said, "it would be a good thing if you would go, because you will experience new things", she said to me. "On the other hand the trip will certainly be stressful." Then I went to see Dorje Dukpa and told him that I couldn't travel, because I could not leave my aunt alone, she is sick and she doesn't look too well anymore. But Dorje Dukpa's wife told me I should reconsider my position. She said that my aunt wasn't really that ill and moreover, she was not really all alone and besides, her husband would accompany me on the trip to Switzerland. So my son and I decided to have another ceremony carried out. During the ceremony Dorje Dukpa wanted to have my answer right then and there. Because I still wasn't certain, my son decided to go immediately to the hermit at the Lugra monastery and ask him for advice. He made 'mo', a divination, which turned out positively. I could readily go on the trip. It will turn out well, he said. So I decided I would accept the invitation. But I told no one in my village about my decision except my brother and sister-in-law.
Suddenly I was told I had to be ready to travel within three days. The passport would have to be issued. I was very excited because I had gotten neither my two fields nor my rooms ready. So I decided to go to the hermit on my own. When I arrived, I was entirely nervous. "What's the matter this time?" asked the monk. I told him everything and asked him, what I should do. The hermit calmed me: "It is totally without danger, if you go. Your 'mo' is favourable. You are very fortunate to be able to travel to Switzerland. It says in my book, happy is the one who can enter the land that the ocean cannot reach. Whoever visits such a country will have a long life." Now that I know Switzerland a little, I also think that that country is like a 'sbas yul', a hidden country (an earthly paradise). I told no one except my close relatives, the astrologer and some monks that I would travel to New Delhi and then on to Switzerland. The astrologer knew it because I wanted to find out, whether the actual day of travel would be favourable. He found the day to be very favourable. I insisted that he also check his book about that and so he did and it turned out that the date was indeed auspicious and so I decided that I would travel on that day.

Impressions

In Paro I was greatly impressed when I saw the airplane. My son said to me: "Mother, you are going to fly in this airplane up there" and pointed into the sky where I saw a small airplane. "Ooh", I thought, "how can all the people who wait here, fit into that plane?" I had imagined that the airplane would be maximally as big as a large bus. But when I stood very close to the actual airplane, I realized its tremendous size. "Oh dear, I've got to go inside there and travel, I'll sure get dizzy", I thought. When I was inside, it began to move, so I bent my head down toward my lap and didn't look out the window anymore. When the airplane first moved, I had a little anxiety. "Hopefully all goes well", I thought, but when we were fully airborne the plane didn't shake as much any longer. First I closed my eyes, but after that I got accustomed to flying. In New Delhi, the airplane I entered was even more gigantic. In that airplane they even brought us a meal, but I didn't feel like eating anything. But it was astonishing; they brought a meal for everyone, just like that.

The airport in Zurich was even larger, even more gigantic. I saw there stairways that turned, doors that opened by themselves, and I stood on a self-moving stairway and nearly fell over had not someone supported me. I saw a large lake after my arrival in Zurich, for the very first time! It looked as large as if it would cover the area of my village and its surrounding fields twice or thrice over. Also I saw ships on the lake. I never had seen that before. "If the train could somehow stop or slow down a bit", I thought, "then I could observe all the many things going by", but the train moved so quickly, I nearly got dizzy, and I nearly vomited again. "If the train were to stop", I thought to myself, "I would like to look more closely at the people on the ship, what kind of people they are, what they look like, how they travel, etc., then I could tell the people in my village at home about it all". But the train sped on, I could make out things only briefly and I cannot really tell a lot about it all.

Comparisons

In my country we don't raise animals for slaughter. At Tina's place I saw that they raise pigs and rabbits and later they kill them for food. That's totally different from where I come from. We don't kill animals because of our religion. If they die on their own, maybe because they fall off the side of a cliff, then we eat it. We do not breed animals for killing, that is against our religion.

At Tina's, I also observed the milking of cows. I found it so astonishingly that one doesn't have to milk the cows by hand, but rather the machine does it all. I looked in front and back of the cow, then at the cow first from one side and then the other, but I still couldn't quite figure out exactly how it happens. I saw simply that the udders got smaller and smaller, that the milk gets sucked into the metallic nipples. And all the milk they feed the calves, they drink it all very quickly and it's gone. At home, in my country, if we waste a drop of milk, we regret the loss and here they give so much milk to the calves. That's really astonishing.

Religion

As far as religion is concerned, I really didn't experience any in Tina's family. I found, religion plays no role at all. In my place at home, I have a small altar; I didn't see anything like that in Tina's home. But she was so very kind and put a prayer drum in my bedroom and said: "Please feel totally at home here, you can use this prayer drum." Because she had seen that I have a prayer drum at home in Bhutan.
Once I went with Tina and her children to church. There, everyone sat on benches. Sometimes the minister spoke, sometimes

everyone sang. I did not understand, what the minister said. But I think he talked about religion. That's the same at home, there the monks speak and teach you. If I could understand it, it would be the same, only the language is different. I thought to myself: "The minister must speak for such a long time, he must certainly have a dry mouth and he doesn't get to drink tea even once. At home, everyone would get something to drink. The village people would offer some kind of food and a drink. Here in the church, everyone seems so desiccated, so dried out." At the end, there was wine in a chalice. They said that it means blood, but it was really wine. Each person took a small swallow from the cup. Some even took two or three swallows; those must have been people who were really thirsty. I thought: "If I should be asked to drink, I must say no; I cannot drink from a cup out of which others have drunk too." I really watched very carefully and I thought, "The people must be really thirsty if they were not allowed to drink during the entire ceremony." The chalice came closer, it was my translator's turn, but he did not take a drink. Tina also didn't drink; neither did the people from the television, so, neither did I.

In Paradise?

Here, in Switzerland, all the houses have electric light and water, they have everything. It's not like at home where I have to go and get water and firewood from outside. Here you can cook with electricity and there's no smoke. At home in my place I have to burn wood to make a fire, there's smoke and it burns your eyes. The houses here are stable, gigantic, and it is beautiful, almost like in paradise. When I saw all this, I remembered that our high monks always preached, we should pray every day for a good heart towards other people, and then we would get to paradise. They describe paradise as a place where there are many yellow, red and blue flowers, really magnificent flowers. If one gets to paradise, there are totally different kinds of food to be had, whatever your heart desires. There you have no more sorrow or cares. When I arrived in Switzerland, I had really the impression that I had arrived in our place called paradise. Everything is here what one needs. Everything is simple. I can hardly believe it.

But, there are also some more negative things: I'm concerned the way the old people are treated here. You raise the children for a long time, show them love and in the end they go their own ways. The sons marry and form their own households, the daughters also, and then the older people are alone at home. Certainly, there is money available, I heard they have social security pensions, health insurance, all that I am told exists and is no problem. The problem I believe exists therein that the older people can no longer walk on their own and they must go shopping for their groceries and that they can only accomplish with great effort and pain. I saw older people carrying heavy grocery bags all alone in the streets. Then I thought: "It is sad if the children are not there and nobody is there to help." In my country the children help their elders. The children say: "Just sit over there in your corner and pray, and we do everything else." The meals are cooked and brought to them. Also their daughters and sons-in-law look after them. If they did not, the entire village would speak badly about them. In this way, the old people are well taken care of, in their hearts and minds too. There's always someone nearby and around them.

People from the television company asked me how I felt in Switzerland, what I think. "It all looks really good", I said. "In Switzerland, everyone can read. In church I saw how everybody held up a book and read in it." In Switzerland, the children are sent to the school from an early age on; in my country, only certain people can send their children to school because the others must help out at home with work. It is wonderful that here everyone can read and write. But the worst thing I find is that the children simply go away later and leave the parents alone by themselves. I find that very sad.

When we see tourists in Bhutan we think that they are all quite rich because they are dressed beautifully and carry with them so many things. They must be enormously wealthy, we think, they don't need to work hard; as if money fell from heaven. Now I have seen that people have to work quite hard here and that nobody really has time.

Machines

At Tina's I saw they have a machine for milking cows, and one for drying grass. That was very impressive. At home I have to work for weeks on end and here the same amount of work is done in three days. Of course, it makes a lot of noise but it is easier on the body; you don't need to work as hard.
Before, when Sonam and Martin came to visit us from Switzerland, I said I would like to have a threshing machine. After that I always thought how wonderful it would be if they sent me a machine like that and I would no longer have to thresh by hand. But now at Tina's I saw that it really is not as simple as all that. Such machines are so large and expensive, and moreover one cannot send it to such a far place and finally, if the machine has a defect, then someone has to be able to repair it, but we are not able to do that. When I considered all that, I saw that in having such a machine it would be connected with quite a few other large problems. Simply to have a machine, is not the end of it.

In Bhutan, in my neighbouring village, they purchased a mechanical thresher. If we want, we can thresh with it our grain too. But for each hour of use, we must pay because the people who purchased the machine paid an exorbitant amount of money for it. The machine also makes a hell of a lot of noise, stinks of gasoline and you get sick if you stand too near it. So I never make any use of it in order to thresh my grain. I have also the feeling that the flour tastes differently after threshing it with this machine.

Was it worth it?

I am happy that I was able to travel to Switzerland. It was a great joy to visit all my friends and acquaintances in Berne. I was so happy to see the shrine room in the home of the mother of Sonam Dölma, who is a nun and prays a lot, and I was able to join her in prayer. I was able to have many talks as well with her family and was able to drink much salted tea, I really felt at home there. That's why I liked it there. Had I not known Sonam Dölma and her husband, surely, I wouldn't have come. But I couldn't stay here forever. I would like to go back to my village.

Source: Martin Brauen, Irgendwo in Bhutan – Wo die Frauen (fast) immer das Sagen haben, 1994

25

In Kürze

Dorje Dolma, eine Bäuerin aus dem Bumthang Tal soll die Schweiz besuchen. Sie zögert, bespricht sich mit Familie und Nachbarn, fragt Mönche um ihren Rat, opfert den Göttern, konsultiert den Astrologen.
Schliesslich willigt sie ein und erlebt ihren Kulturschock. Die Zustände in der Schweiz sind paradiesisch, aber es gibt auch Dinge, die ihr missfallen: Milch wird verschwendet um Kälber zu mästen, Tiere werden geschlachtet ihres Fleisches wegen. Im Haus ihrer Gastfamilie gibt es keinen Altar – Religion hat offenbar keinen Platz im Alltag. Am traurigsten aber findet sie, dass Söhne und Töchter aus dem Elternhaus wegziehen, selber einen Haushalt gründen, und die Eltern aufs Alter sich selbst überlassen.
Gestaunt hat sie über den Maschinenpark der Bauern: Maschinen zum Melken der Kühe, zum Schneiden und Trocknen des Grases, zum Dreschen des Korns. Aber wie sollte sie die Maschinen nach Bhutan bringen? Wer sollte die Maschinen reparieren? So praktisch sie sein mögen, sie würden andere, grössere Probleme mit sich bringen.

En bref

Dorje Dolma, une paysanne de la vallée de Bumthang, est censée visiter la Suisse. Elle hésite, se concerte avec sa famille et ses voisins, demande conseil aux moines, fait des offrandes aux déités et consulte l'astrologue.
Finalement, elle est d'avis d'y aller, et elle va vivre son choc culturel. Le contexte de la Suisse est paradisiaque, mais il y a des choses dont elle désapprouve: le lait est gaspillé pour nourrir les veaux, des animaux sont abattus à cause de leur viande. Dans la maison de ses hôtes, il n'y a pas d'autel, la religion n'a manifestement pas de place dans la vie de tous les jours. Ce qui l'attriste le plus est le départ des enfants de la maison parentale pour fonder leurs propres foyers, laissant ainsi les parents seuls pendant leur vieillesse.
Le parc des machines l'a bien étonné: des machines à traire les vaches, d'autres pour couper et sécher l'herbe et pour battre le grain. Mais comment faire pour transporter ces machines au Bhoutan? Qui sera prévu pour les réparer? Aussi pratiques qu'elles apparaissaient, ces machines apporteraient leur lot de problèmes autres et plus grands.

Strategic lines in development

26

Development philosophy of Bhutan

by Dr. Pema Gyamtsho, Minister for Agriculture, former Dy-Resident Co-ordinator Helvetas until 2007; attached to Helvetas projects since 1970

27

Philosophy

The overriding development philosophy meticulously adhered to, is to pursue a cautious approach absorbing the best that modern science and technology have on offer and blend it with the best of the country's tradition. For example, all buildings in Bhutan are required by law to use traditional architecture while adopting modern technologies and using materials like cement and steel. Another unique feature of the development approach was the attention given to protecting the country's fragile environment by according high priority to the conservation of forests and biodiversity. It is due to this concern that sectors with high economic potentials like mining, logging and mass tourism are not exploited. Even in sectors like agriculture, a deliberate attempt was made to limit the use of chemical fertilizers and pesticides to reduce the impact on the environment. According to the UN's latest Human Development Report 2006, Bhutan's human development index is ranked at 135 out of 177 countries listed with a value of 0.538 in the medium human development category.

Instruments

Bhutan follows a five-year development planning cycle called the Five-Year Plans (FYP). They provide the development policy and strategic and fiscal framework for a given five-year period. Currently, the country has concluded 9 FYPs.

Over the last three plan periods, the broad priorities and objectives of development have been to maintain a broad based growth, improve self-reliance and sufficiency in food, achieve sustainable and balanced development, enhance quality of life in rural areas, support decentralization and peoples' participation in governance and development, private sector development and conservation of both cultural and natural resource endowments.

Planned socio-economic development only began in 1961 with the launch of the First Five-Year Plan (1961-66). This plan was almost exclusively funded by India and was focused on building the road from the border town of Phuntsholing to Thimphu as well as establishing basic education, health, agriculture and animal husbandry facilities. Other bilateral donors including Switzerland and multilateral agencies like the United Nations Development Programme (UNDP), started playing an important role in the country's development from the 4th Five Year Plan onwards (1977-1981). In 2007, the country completed the 9th Five-Year Plan, by which time, it has made tremendous all-round progress.

FYP	Period	Main development focus	Budget allocations (Nu. Millions)
1	61-66	Road construction, social service	174.70
2	66-71	Road construction, health and education, agriculture	221.40
3	71-76	Road construction, hydropower, education, health, forestry	355.00
4	76-81	Education, agriculture, hydropower, tourism	778.00
5	81-86	Decentralisation, health, education, agriculture	4,338.00
6	87-92	Decentralisation, hydropower, security	9,559.24
7	92-97	Security, hydrowpower	15,590.70
8	97-02	Security, governance	35,169.28
9	02-08	Democratisation, ICT	70,000.00
10	07-12	Poverty reduction, good governance	

1 Euro equivalent Nu 61.80 (April 2008)

Milestones

1. Life expectancy increased from 44 years in 1972 to 66 in 2005
2. Per capita income increased from a meager US$ 150 per capita in 1970 to US$ 1200 by 2006
3. One university with 10 affiliated colleges in education, natural resources, engineering, science and humanities
4. Adult literacy rate of 53% as opposed to less than 5% in 1970
5. Primary net enrollment rate of 77% in 2005
6. Infant (under five) mortality rate per 1000 live birth reduced to 61.5 by 2005
7. 84% and 89% of population have access to safe drinking water and sanitation
8. 57% of population have access to grid electricity
9. Revenues from sales of hydropower reached Nu. 1,059 million in 2006
10. Tourism industry has developed steadily with a total earning of USD 18.55 million in 2005.
11. Road network of 4500 km connects nearly all major settlements in the country

In Kürze

Die strategische Planung der sozio-ökonomischen Entwicklung Bhutans begann 1961 mit dem ersten Fünfjahresplan. Wie die Tabellen belegen hat das Land seither enorme Fortschritte gemacht. Peinlich genau achten die Behörden darauf, dass moderne Technologie sich mit traditionellen Methoden verträgt, und dass die Umwelt nicht strapaziert wird. So müssen alle Neubauten in der architektonischen Tradition des Landes gebaut werden. Wirtschaftssektoren mit grossem Potential, wie Bergbau, Tourismus und Holzschlag werden zurückhaltend entwickelt. In der Landwirtschaft wurde die Anwendung von Düngemitteln und Pestiziden gezielt verringert.

En bref

La planification stratégique du développement socio-économique du Bhoutan a débuté en 1961 avec le premier plan quinquennal. Comme le montrent les statistiques, le pays a fait d'énormes progrès depuis cette époque. Les autorités sont très attentives au fait que les nouvelles technologies soient compatibles avec les méthodes traditionnelles et que l'environnement ne subisse pas de pressions excessives. Ainsi toute nouvelle construction doit être construite selon les traditions architecturales du pays. Les secteurs économiques qui ont un grand potentiel, comme les mines, le tourisme et l'exploitation du bois, sont développés avec retenue. Dans l'agriculture, l'application d'engrais et de pesticides a été intentionnellement réduite.

From Switzerland to Druk Yul via Nepal

by E. Werner Külling, former Secretary-General Helvetas Zurich / Switzerland; Resident Coordinator Helvetas / SDC 2006-2008, Thimphu, Bhutan

The Five Helvetas Working Principles

- Basis
- Self-help
- Justice
- Self-reliance
- Partnership

The Working Principles are in large measure in agreement with the political development ideas of the King and the government of Bhutan. They represent a meaningful supplement to their own Buddhist development philosophy known as "Gross National Happiness".

The four Helvetas Working Areas

- Infrastructure in rural areas
- Sustainable management of natural resources
- Education and culture
- Civil Society and the State

The working areas correspond to the primary needs of Bhutan.

The five Helvetas Working Approaches

- Learning through dialogue between cultures
- Protecting the environment
- Striving for equality between man and women
- Acting with economic and social responsibility
- Preventing crisis – building peace

helvetas

Toward the middle of the 1970's, Fritz von Schulthess, Chairman of the Swiss "Foundation pro Bhutan" recognized that the Bhutan Program needed better professional guidance and should be given a secure long-term financial foundation. This, especially in view of the technical limits of his company 'DESCO von Schulthess' and his increasing age. He turned for advice and support to the Swiss Federal 'Service for Technical Cooperation' (DftZ), today known as the 'Swiss Agency for Development and Cooperation', (SDC), a unit of the Swiss Ministry of Foreign Affairs. There, his request was viewed favorably although no direct engagement in Bhutan was planned. Instead, it was proposed that he seek a collaborative agreement with Helvetas, Switzerland's private, oldest, politically and religiously neutral development organization. Helvetas had been engaged since 1956 in similarly situated rural development programs in neighbouring Nepal. The Nepalese cooperative model was to be put into operation and lessons learned there were to be optimally applied and put to use in Bhutan.

At first, Fritz von Schulthess, was not too enthusiastic about this proposal. He feared that a private organization might be, as far as finances were concerned, on insecure grounds. Such fears were, however, quickly dispelled. The collaboration proved successful and the Swiss federal government through DftZ/SDC guaranteed the Helvetas funding. As of July 1st, 1975, the "Foundation pro Bhutan" concluded an implementation contract with Helvetas. Legally, however, the Foundation remained the responsible project authority. Fritz von Schulthess took a seat on the Board of Directors of Helvetas, till some years later, when the by then quite extensive Bhutan Program had been fully integrated into the overall organization of Helvetas and the Foundation was dissolved. Looking back it is clear that the association with Helvetas as a Non Governmental Organization (NGO) – given its working style and policies - certainly was and is the ideal development partner for the small kingdom in the Himalayas. And of course, the reverse is valid as well.

Since the start of the collaboration with Bhutan from the 1960's till 2008, the 'Foundation pro Bhutan', Helvetas and Swiss Development Cooperation have spent approximately 150 million Swiss Francs for development programs in Druk Yul. This per-capita development contribution is actually very high, especially when you compare it to figures from other development countries in the South. But this is no accident. In Bhutan one can get an essential understanding and overview of the small country, a very good condition which Bhutan can offer to a partner country such as Switzerland. As a consequence, the collaboration with the government is relatively efficient, simple and uncomplicated.

New challenges for 2008

Bhutan's visionary 4th Dragon King, H.M. Jigme Singye Wangchuck (1972 – 2006) is a statesman and leader of an extraordinary format. He has introduced changes which will have long-term consequences: Beginning in spring 2008, Bhutan will become a) a constitutional monarchy and parliamentary democracy, b) promulgate its new (and first) constitution, and c) have both a government and an opposition political party. The king does not doubt that his people are supportive and mature enough to accept such incisive changes for both State and society. He considers the present moment auspicious. And just so that his surprised and astounded people would really trust his intentions, the 51-year old King stepped down after 34 years of being regent and installed his oldest son, Crown Prince Jigme Khesar Namgyel Wangchuck, 28, as the new 5th Druk Gyalpo. Everyone is convinced that the challenge of democracy must be a full success and serve as a model for the countries of the region. And indeed, there are reasons for optimism.

Of course, such far-reaching reforms also affect the various organizations of the international donor community, including Helvetas. Many of them plan to become strongly engaged in the areas of Good (Local) Governance. They wish to support the efforts of the government at decentralization and promote civil society developments through NGO's and economic activities by the private sector.

In view of the new challenges beginning in 2008, Helvetas and SDC have begun to take into consideration a continuing cooperative development perspective reaching to 2012. As before, the engagement in rural development will continue as a priority. The currently running programs will continue and will take especially into account the requirements posed by the framework of "Local Governance and Decentralization". As before, improvement of economic and social conditions in rural areas of

28 Werner Külling and HM Jigme Singye Wangchuck

29 Werner Külling and Pema Gyamtsho

Bhutan is of the highest priority. After all, two-thirds of the population live primarily through agricultural activities. The increasing migration of young persons into the capital Thimphu and the few other rising cities need to be slowed down; this too remains an important policy postulate of Helvetas.

Personal views based on my experiences

I have spent many years of my professional career with Helvetas. Especially, the three decades, since the middle of 1975, serving as the Secretary General at the head office in Zurich gave me the opportunity to formulate, shape and accompany the cooperative development activities with Bhutan, the country and its people. I visited the country for the first time in January 1979 and subsequently about ten times. This has allowed me to experience first hand its rapid developments, not all of them, necessarily and understandably, always positive. Since the very beginning, Bhutan has impressed me always in a special way. Next to their superior culture, visible through its majestic Dzongs, the Buddhist everyday life, the religious festivals in their monasteries, and life in the rough and fascinating mountain panorama, it is Bhutan's people, these unusually friendly, intelligent, sensitive, peace-loving and circumspect-reserved women and men who capture spirit and soul and make it so difficult to ever let go. As a consequence, a Westerner often needs to step back again and again, to regain his critical senses rather than be taken in fully. In my time as Secretary General, I had ample opportunities to become acquainted with most partner countries of Helvetas in Asia, Africa and Latin America, and to strive for comparisons, regardless of how problematic such comparisons might be. Within the framework of a 'domestic political perspective' transposed into global dimensions, the need for an equalizing cooperative development effort is uncontested. Of course, this is often known to be a complex, difficult, frustrating and controversial "industry" and a challenging task. But this is true for all large and important global projects, especially when these concern life and the survival of humanity itself. And yet, there are pleasant and encouraging experiences. We do see examples of meaningful exchange. There is mutual learning and respectful intercourse of peoples and cultures, success stories, regardless of how we interpret what such 'success' ultimately might mean.

No doubt: Bhutan, which has often been designated as 'a special case', can rightfully take its place internationally as one of the more "shining examples". "Gross National Happiness!" Why is that the case? That question is often asked. But I believe, one has to supply the answer oneself. And in addition, it probably helps if you have lived and worked for some time in this country and it has grown on you and you have grown fond of it. Otherwise you can't understand it. I am grateful that at the end of my professional career with Helvetas, I was given the chance to experience Bhutan close at hand as the resident coordinator. For me it is a fortunate closure and it strengthens my conviction that the Bhutan-Switzerland friendship and partnership must continue to live on, whatever form this might take.

In Kürze

Seit dem Beginn der Zusammenarbeit mit Bhutan haben die Stiftung für Bhutan, Helvetas und die Schweizerische Entwicklungshilfe gut 150 Mio. Franken investiert. Werner Külling, Generalsekretär von Helvetas, hat drei Jahrzehnte lang die vielen Projekte geprägt und koordiniert. Seit 2006 ist er als Koordinator in Thimphu, von wo er Rückschau hält. Er hat die Entwicklung in Bhutan aus nächster Nähe mit verfolgt. Er ist über die Jahre mit den meisten Partnerländer von Helvetas in Asien, Afrika und Lateinamerika vertraut geworden. Er kann Vergleiche ziehen. Es gibt für ihn keine Zweifel: Bhutan, oft als Spezialfall bezeichnet, kann für sich zurecht in Anspruch nehmen, ein herausragendes Beispiel erfolgreicher Entwicklungszusammenarbeit zu sein.

En bref

Depuis le début de la coopération avec le Bhoutan, la Fondation pro Bhoutan, Helvetas et la coopération suisse ont investi plus de 150 millions de francs suisses. Werner Külling, secrétaire général d'Helvetas jusqu'en 2005, a marqué de son empreinte et coordonné les nombreux projets pendant plus de trois décennies. Depuis 2006, il est à Thimphu en tant que chef de délégation, ce qui lui permet de porter un regard sur le passé. Il a suivi de très près le développement du Bhoutan. Au cours des années, il a appris à connaître la plupart des pays dans lesquels Helvetas est active en Asie, en Afrique et en Amérique latine. Cela lui permet de faire des comparaisons. Pour lui il n'y a aucun doute: le Bhoutan, souvent cité comme un cas particulier, peut se targuer d'être un exemple de réussite de la coopération au développement.

Aid policy – from sectors and agents

by Dr. Saamdu Chetri, Dy-Resident Co-ordinator Helvetas / SDC, 1988-2006

Half a century ago, the Cooperation between Bhutan and Switzerland began starting at a personal level in 1958. Since then, Switzerland has contributed about 150 million Swiss Francs. Switzerland has unconditionally received the friendship from the throne and the people of Bhutan and became one of the highly preferred development partners in Bhutan. For the last 20 years, the Swiss cooperation set the need and request of the royal government of Bhutan mainly in the three sectors Education Youth and Culture, Renewable Natural Resources (RNR), and Rural Infrastructure. The following graphs give the readers the pattern of support in the last four country programmes.

The operational cost of Bhutan Programme Coordination Office remained at 4% of the entire portfolio, the lowest of 22 countries where Helvetas was present. The graph indicates consultancy costs steadily going up, corresponding to the reduction of expatriates from the projects. The peak with 20 expatriates was reached 1992. With increasing impacts of the human resource development efforts the country office began handing over the programmes/projects to competent Bhutanese personnel, with back-up services through missions or short-term consultancies.

The share of multilateral projects varied largely, many of them were later taken over by bilateral programme, easing the management. The fifth country programme 2008-12 takes all the elements of the three sectors but with a strong rural and regional focus. Thus, the policy is swinging back from a national and sector orientation. It is believed that everything must return to its source ultimately. This gives a good feeling that the country's socio-economic growth has been substantial, surpassing anyone's imagination.

1984, ten years after Helvetas had taken over the Foundation Pro Bhutan, a review was made in the valley of Bumthang. Apart from the impacts of the projects, many social changes have taken place, largely due to institutional changes and the decentralisation policies and infrastructure improvement in the country.

The people in Bumthang felt the assistance being spread unevenly. They felt those who had access or were near the projects/programme benefited the most. They said there was no balanced spread in distribution of development wealth. Many felt that the change was positive while a few felt otherwise and stated "father taught the son but now son teaches the father," and another one said that development has made them lazy, they depend on gazettes for their day-to-day work; the watch tells them when to wake and go to sleep, radio tells them when to start planting the kind of crop. A country woman said, "I have seen many Swiss people in Bumthang but I don't know for what purpose they are here and what they are doing"

Public information has been weak in the process of development and is still so. There may be enough information everywhere but delivery and feed-back channels are very weak, even to this day. The survey indicated that Renewable Natural Resource (RNR) was felt a priority with animal husbandry topping the preference list in the 1980's, followed by agriculture. Industrial development, followed by forestry, was not rated as a priority. Health was given undisputed priority among all the Swiss programmes until the 1980's.

Helvetas has given the highest priority to Human Resource Development (HRD) right from the beginning through building technical and management capacities in the various projects. Many of these trained persons held high positions in the ad-

Swiss assistance by sectors

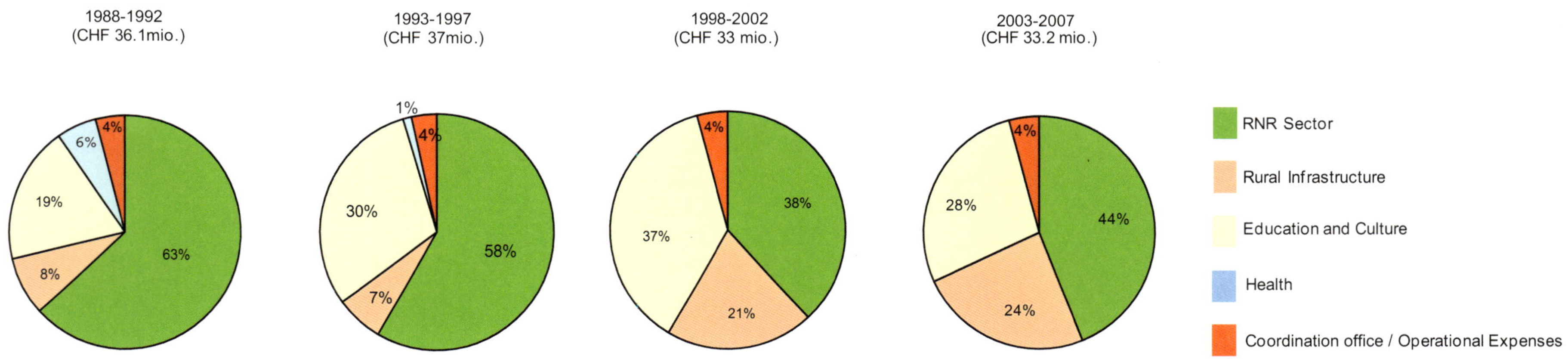

Technical Assistance				
Expatriates	40%	39%	17%	12%
Consultancies	5%	7%	11%	9%

ministration, such as members of parliament, royal advisors, chief of planning staff etc.

In general, external assistance does bring high expectations at all levels and lets the partner often lean back with the attitude that the donor will do everything. From a donor perspective, the limited absorption capacity of the government, due to its limited size, difficult donors' coordination due to donor competition, and unbalanced regional growth due to concentration of activities in the west for many years, are some of the impediments to a regionally balanced development in Bhutan. The highly scattered settlement structure in rough terrain, on the other hand, poses severe difficulties in providing public services (schools, health, water, roads and electricity) at reasonable cost.
Bhutan enters into a new era with democratic governance. It is more than likely that the Swiss cooperation will have an even bigger role to play to support strengthening of governance aspects at the rural level, one of the focal points of Swiss assistance. Even though Swiss cooperation through Helvetas might be limited to two intertwined aspects, alleviation of poverty and good governance.

Swiss bilateral and multilateral assistance (CHF mio)

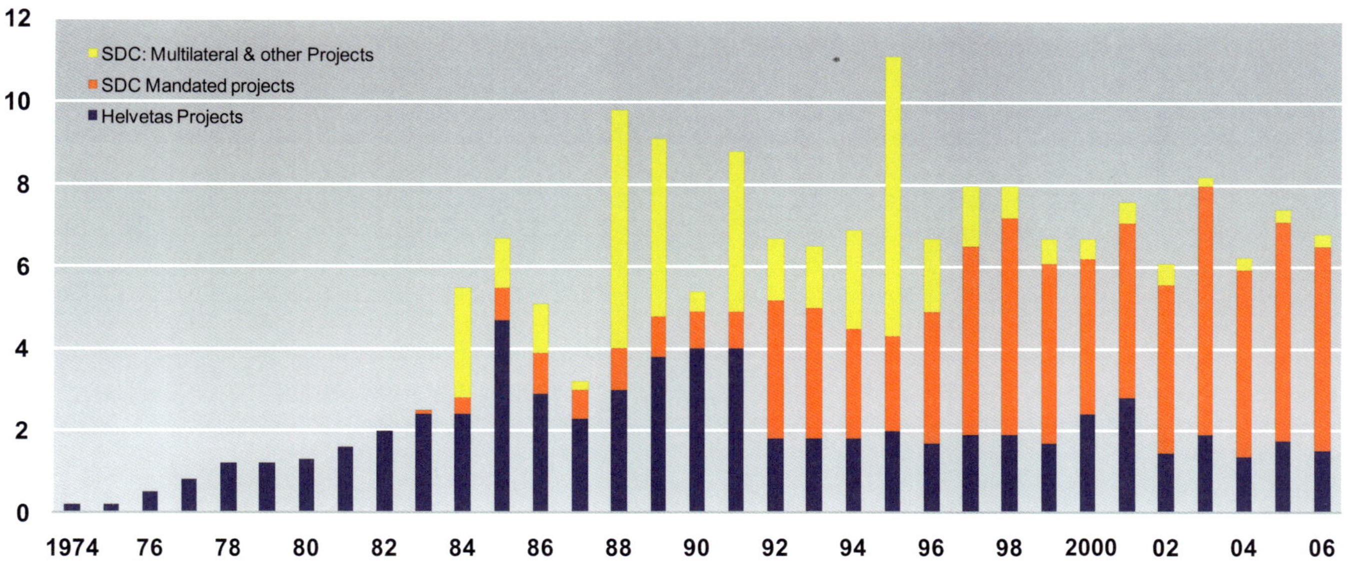

In Kürze

Ausbildung und Kultur, erneuerbare Ressourcen und ländliche Infrastruktur waren die Felder, auf die sich die Zusammenarbeit der Schweiz mit Bhutan konzentrierte. Die Grafiken veranschaulichen die prozentuale Verteilung der eingesetzten Mittel. Von Beginn weg legte Helvetas grossen Wert auf die Aus- und Weiterbildung der Bhutanesen. So konnten im Laufe der Zeit immer mehr Projekte in die Verantwortung der Einheimischen gegeben werden. Die Reaktionen in Bhumtang sind unterschiedlich, einige haben das Gefühl von der Entwicklung übergangen worden zu sein. Hilfe von aussen weckt hohe Erwartungen, kann die Empfänger träge machen in der Meinung, die fremde Hilfe werde die Probleme schon lösen. Das aktuelle Programm, das bis 2012 laufen soll, legt den Schwerpunkt auf ländliche und regionale Entwicklung. Jetzt, wo das Land eine demokratischere Regierungsform erhält, gilt es die lokalen Strukturen zu entwickeln und die neuen politischen Führungskräfte zu stärken.

En bref

La formation et la culture, les ressources naturelles et l'infrastructure rurale ont été les domaines sur lesquels la coopération suisse avec le Bhoutan s'est concentrée. Les graphiques montrent la répartition en pour-cent des moyens engagés. Dès le début, Helvetas a accordé une grande importance à la formation des Bhoutanais. Ainsi, au cours du temps, la responsabilité d'un nombre croissant de projets a pu être remise à des personnes locales. Les réactions à Bumthang sont diverses, d'aucuns pensent que le développement a été trop rapide. L'aide extérieure suscite de grande attentes, elle peut aussi démobiliser les bénéficiaires de l'aide, amenant ceux-ci à penser que l'aide extérieure résoudra leurs problèmes. Le programme actuel, qui doit s'étendre jusqu'en 2012, met l'accent sur le développement rural et régional. Alors que le pays s'est doté d'une forme de gouvernement démocratique, il convient de développer les structures locales et de renforcer les nouveaux dirigeants politiques.

Why Swiss Assistance took roots in Bumthang

by Dr. Saamdu Chetri, Dy-Resident Co-ordinator Helvetas / SDC, 1988-2006

The development cooperation between the land of Guru Rimpoche on a flying tigress and the land of Heidi, the Alpine Swiss girl, would capture much media attention nowadays. But this friendship-inspired cooperation between the two countries, one highly developed and the other least developed, took roots quietly way back in 1973 in Bumthang.

The compelling circumstances that forged this relationship need some explanation for people to understand why the seed of this cooperation was sown in Bumthang of all the places in Bhutan. Bumthang (valley meaning the holy water bowl) looks like the Swiss alpine landscapes and the Swiss developed an instant liking for the valley. In addition, not so long ago, Bumthang was the seat of the central government and the Wangchuck Dynasty ruled the country from here. In terms of religion, the valley is a holy place in Bhutan, being blessed by Guru Rimpoche. The famous Kurjey Lhakhang houses the impressions made by the 8th century teacher while meditating seated against a rock. These common landscapes and inspiring religious beliefs may have played a role for this cooperation to start from Bumthang.

The other important driving force was the real need for Bhutan to explore for more sustainable livelihood opportunities for the Bumthaps. Bumthang, being a high altitude valley was unproductive due to its harsh climate setting. The Bumthaps mainly depended on livestock for their livelihoods. And those days, Bumthaps used to migrate with their livestock to warmer pastures for about three months in a year. These warmer pastures were located in Lhuentse, Mongar, Trongsa and Zhemgang. Every year, the local residents fretted when the Bumthaps came back with their herds to graze in their pastures. This migration with large herds of cattle created social tension and disputes due to grazing and land ownership rights. The migrating cattle overgrazed the land and brought diseases. However, the local people had to live with this practice since it was a time-honoured tradition. But, late His Majesty, King Jigme Dorji Wangchuck, being visionary leader, knew that such a system of unbalanced interdependence would eventually bring disharmony in the Bhutanese society. And he was determined to address this issue. Therefore, His Majesty searched for donor cooperation to make the Bumthaps self-reliant. Being on top of his development agenda, the third King must have instructed his brother, His Royal Highness, Prince Namgyel Wangchuck, the then Minister for Trade, Industry and Forest on the urgent need to set up a project in Bumthang. In upholding the last royal wish, the first Swiss assistance through a foundation known as Pro Bhutan started in July 1973.

This humble beginning of a friendship-inspired cooperation has stood the test of time. The Bhutan-Swiss cooperation stands as solid as the Alps and the Himalayas. At present, the area of cooperation has diversified and matured. Bhutan and Switzerland share tremendous good will and friendship and stand as equal partners in the community of nations. Let this be our humble tribute to the visionary leaders, late Majesty, King Jigme Dorji Wangchuck and late Fritz von Schulthess, the architects who shaped Bhutan-Swiss cooperation.

In Kürze

Warum ausgerechnet Bumthang? Die Region hat Ähnlichkeiten mit alpinen Landschaften in der Schweiz. Die Schweizer schlossen die schönen Täler schnell ins Herz. Bumthang ist religiöses Zentrum, war lange Zeit Regierungssitz der Wangchucks. Vor allem aber wollte der König etwas für die Bauern tun, die in dem rauen Klima ein karges Leben führten. Jedes Jahr zogen sie mit ihren Herden für mehrere Monate in tiefer gelegene Gegenden. Sehr zum Ärger der dortigen Bauern, weil die fremden Kühe alles Gras wegfrassen. Das führte zu sozialen Spannungen. Der König suchte nach Möglichkeiten, der Landwirtschaft in Bumthang eine nachhaltigere und produktivere Entwicklung zu geben. Im Juli 1973 startete die Schweizer Stiftung "Pro Bhutan" ihr erstes Projekt.

En bref

Pourquoi précisément à Bumthang? La région a certaines similitudes avec des paysages alpins helvétiques, si bien que les Suisses se sont vite sentis chez eux dans cette belle vallée. Bumthang est le centre religieux du pays et a été pendant de longues années le siège du gouvernement des Wangchucks. Toutefois, ce que le roi voulait avant tout, c'était de faire quelque chose en faveur des paysans de cette région dont les conditions de vie difficiles étaient liées au climat rude. Chaque année ces paysans devaient migrer pour plusieurs mois dans des régions plus clémentes, avec leurs troupeaux, ce qui créait des tensions avec les agriculteurs résidant dans ces régions : en effet, les vaches transhumantes broutaient l'herbe des pâturages. Le roi cherchait des solutions pour rendre l'agriculture de Bumthang plus durable et plus productive. En juillet 1973, la Fondation suisse "Pro Bhutan" démarrait son premier projet.

30 Jakar Dzong and Wangdichoelling Palace, Bumthang

Dangbo, Dingbo Bumthang o

by Françoise Pommaret (Tashi Om) Tibetologist, Researcher at CNRS, France who has worked and lived in Bhutan on and off since 1981

The Bumthang expression Dangbo, Dingbo means roughly "Once upon a time" and was popularised by Kunzang Choden in her book FolkTales of Bhutan, White Lotus, 1993.

The Mahindra jeep was sliding backwards. The night was falling, the rain was coming hard on the canvas top of the car. Jakar was still 10 kms away, on the other side of the murderous red mud of Kikila pass (3000m). We were in July of the year 1981 and it was our third day on the road from Thimphu to Bumthang. From Trongsa in the morning we had been battling with the road, but the Kikila climbing was the last straw.

In 2007, we drive in comfortable cars and reach Bumthang in 8 hours from Thimphu. The Kikila is black topped and does not even look like a pass any more.

It was another time, which will soon fade in the memory but for me it is still vivid and forever associated with my Swiss friends from Bumthang. In "those days", the road going through Bhutan was still a dirt road, Bumthang had hardly any electricity, no telephone, no hotels, and no shops to speak of. The only real building in the town of Chamkhar below Jakar dzong was the Bank of Bhutan. No vegetable market either. Radishes, turnips, chilis and spinachs made the daily diet with buckwheat pancakes and noodles. Everybody was almost living in autarchy and rice was kept for special occasions. The potato cultivation had started under a Swiss programme in these high valleys where rice did not grow. However many Bhutanese were hesitant to eat them, accusing them of all sorts of ills, echoing the problems that Parmentier faced when he introduced potatoes in Europe in the 18th century. Goiter was still prevalent because of the lack of iodine in the diet. The "Swiss guest-house" was an old place with an outhouse under an apple tree which, in autumn, was the favourite haunt of bears at night. The Swiss workshop was heaven sent, the only place to repair a car for 350 kms.

All these memories are telescoping in my mind but the names of my Swiss friends are fresh, Lisette and René, Fritz, Walter, Anne-Marie and Dominique, Christoph and Marie-Noelle. They were tough like the people in Bumthang. They accepted a rough and uncomfortable life in exchange for fascinating pioneering work and friendships sealed over cups of ara or schnaps, and many long drives in battered cars to Thimphu.

They were strong-headed, stubborn foresters and agriculturalists from rural Swiss 'cantons', not very incline to analyze with an anthropological mind the Bhutanese culture. Nevertheless, they got along just fine with the Bumthang people because on both sides, there was respect for sincerity, hard work, desire to improve the land, and to get out of poverty. Of course, there were quarrels and misunderstandings as in any partnership but a frank discussion, as diplomats say, usually solved the problems.

As an outsider to both parties, I never had anything to do with Helvetas in Bhutan, and I certainly cannot comment on the various programmes, which were implemented all these years. However when I go to Bumthang now, I stand witness of the incredible changes and living standards improvement that a good partnership between dedicated peoples of different cultures, strongly supported by their governments, can bring.

In Kürze

Es war einmal: 2007 fährt die Tibetologin und intime Kennerin von Land und Leuten in einem komfortablen Wagen in acht Stunden von Thimphu ins Bumthang Tal. Da kommen Erinnerungen hoch: Im Juli 1981 hatte die Fahrt im harten Jeep auf schlammigen Naturstrassen drei Tage gedauert. In Bumthang gab es kaum Elektrizität, kein Telefon, keine Hotels, keine Läden. Alle lebten praktisch autark von Rüben, Chilis und Buchweizen. Reis gab es nur aus speziellem Anlass. Die Schweizer bauten Kartoffeln an, die von den Einheimischen nur zögerlich angenommen wurden; sie machten die Knolle für alle möglichen Leiden verantwortlich. Die Reisende denkt an ihre Schweizer Freunde, diese starrköpfigen und zähen Förster und Agronomen. Und sie staunt, was eine engagierte Partnerschaft von Menschen aus unterschiedlichen Kulturen erzielen kann.

En bref

Il était une fois: en 2007, une tibétologue connaissant très bien le pays et ses habitants se rend dans un véhicule confortable de Thimphu à Bumthang, en huit heures. Et elle se souvient: en juillet 1981, le même trajet effectué dans une jeep cahotante avait pris trois jours sur des pistes boueuses. A Bumthang il n'y avait pour ainsi dire pas d'électricité, pas de téléphone, pas d'hôtels, pas de magasins. Tous les habitants vivaient en quasi autarcie, de raves, de piments et de sarrasin. Le riz n'était servi qu'à des occasions spéciales. Les Suisses ont cultivé des pommes de terre, que les habitants de Bumthang ont mis du temps à accepter; les tubercules étaient accusés de tous les maux. La voyageuse pense à ses amis suisses, ces forestiers et agronomes à la tête dure. Et elle s'étonne à la vue de ce qu'un partenariat engagé entre personnes de cultures différentes peut générer.

31 Farmhouse kitchen in Khertso, Bumthang

Transitions in Cooperation

32

Friendship from the beginning

by Dr. Saamdu Chetri, Dy-Resident Co-ordinator Helvetas / SDC, 1988-2006

33 HM Queen Mother, Ashi Kesang Choden Wangchuck (1960)

34 Lisina von Schulthess (1955)

1948

Two gracious ladies met during their studies at the house of citizenship in London in 1948 and became very close friends; Ashi Kesang Choden Dorji daughter of Raja S. T. Dorji and Rani Chöni Dorji and Lisina von Schulthess, daughter of Fritz von Schulthess and Monica von Schulthess, Swiss Industrialists. In November 1949, Mr. and Mrs. von Schulthess visited the Dorji family in Bhutan House, Kalimpong on their invitation. It was the beginning of a long lasting friendship between the two families and the two mountainous countries Switzerland and Bhutan, which are similar in size, locked in between giants, and share challenging topographical settings. Ashi Kesang Choden's family, since the beginning of the Wangchuck dynasty, had very close relation with the throne and had served as Deb Zimpons and chieftains of Haa since 1907.

When, in 1952, Ashi Kesang Choden tied the royal matrimonial knot with the Crown Prince, Dasho Jigme Dorji Wangchuck, the legacy of friendship with the von Schulthess family expanded to the throne of Bhutan. Thereafter, a very strong personal friendship developed between the King, Jigme Dorji Wangchuck and Fritz von Schulthess, who called him Pön.

1952

In April 1952, on invitation of Dorji family, the Schulthess family (Fritz von Schulthess, Monica von Schulthess, their daughters Adrienne Schulthess and Cornelia Schulthess) for the first time entered Bhutan via Haa, escorted by Ashi Tesla Dorji from Samtse. They drove from Kalimpong Bhutan House to Chamurchi, an Indian border town close to Samtse followed by a hard six days' ascent to Haa on foot, mules and ponies. They were the guests of the Dorji family in Haa.

After a few days of their arrival, His Majesty Jigme Dorji Wangchuck invited them to visit Paro where they lived for six nights as royal guests. Fritz von Schulthess was impressed with the striking resemblance Bhutan had with Switzerland in terms of landscape and forest. Bhutan became very close to his heart and between 1950 and 1972 for over two decades several close interactions took place between the throne and Fritz von Schulthess, but all at the personal level; operation of Jigme Palden Dorji in 1950 at Zurich, the royal entourage visited Switzerland in 1953 to give birth to Ashi Sonam Choden Wangchuck at a Zurich hospital.

During this period, His Majesty had interesting visits to Cham, Lugano and other places, experiencing the different kinds of life and culture of ethnically diverse Switzerland.

1955

In September 1955, they again visited Bhutan. This time it was via Phuentsholing to Thimphu and then to Paro where they had an audience with His Majesty, the King of Bhutan.

Both the early visits to Bhutan House, Kalimpong and Bhutan took place during turbulent times; in 1949 Indian Independence and separation of Pakistan, and annexation of Tibet by China where thousands of Tibetan had fled to India and Bhutan. After 1955, their visits to Bhutan were rather frequent. They constantly kept in contact despite a messy postal system. Fritz von Schulthess was invited in 1958, which coincided with the visit of Dr. Jawarlal Nehru and Indira Gandhi to Bhutan. Nehru, during his visit promised bilateral development assistance to Bhutan through a five-year plan mechanism. All these years, the only external assistance the country had received was on a private basis from the Swiss Industrialist, Fritz von Schulthess.

Druk Yi-sing Wangyel for Fritz von Schulthess

1961

In 1961, the year India began its first five-year assistance, the Schulthess family had travelled to Thimphu through a very rough trail, driving on a jeep with a load of seven people and rations. They visited Thimphu again a year later. This time the trip was extended to Gasa, Lingshi, Punakha and Wangdue. The Schulthess family was accompanied by Mr. and Mrs. Gugelmann, also Swiss entrepreneurs.

1965

In 1965, they made another visit to Bhutan. It was one of the turbulent times in Bhutan. This time they were accompanied by Nari Rustomji, Bhutan's Prime Minister Jigme Palden Dorji's friend, as the advisor to the Sikkim throne who from time to time was also providing advice to the throne of Bhutan through an Indian advisor, Prithivi Bakshi. They had flown close to Samtse and travelled as far as Bumthang on helicopter and their journey took them to Trashigang, where they had met Fathers Mackey and Kafey, and Brother Quinn, who were early foreign volunteers in the field of education in Bhutan.

The group exited out to Samdrup Jonkhar and flew back from Gauhati. May be their exploration in Bhutan ended during the following visit in 1967, which took them from Thimphu to Punakha, Gasa, and to Lunana. They were accompanied by Professor Augusto Gansser, and Dr. Blanche Olschak from Switzerland. It may be the first time that some studies on glaciers of Bhutan were done during this trip by Professor Gansser who was a geologist from the Swiss Federal Institute of Technology (ETHZ) in Zurich.

1967

The year 1967 was a special year in the life of Schulthess family. They not only had the opportunity to meet with Karmapa, head of Drukpa Kajugpa sect, but His Majesty the king of Bhutan, Jigme Dorji Wangchuck conferred to Fritz von Schulthess the Nation's first award of "Druk Yi-sing Wangyel" in appreciation of his support to Bhutan. It may be very appropriate to put the abstract of the translation citation for the award conferred:

"The beautiful and fascinating country of Switzerland is my second country and Fritz von Schulthess of Cham is like my second father.

Apart from the very intimate friendship between us, he has always been a great help and source of inspiration to me and to the people of Bhutan.

He is as Bhutanese more than a Bhutanese and he always did his very best to help the people of Bhutan and contributed tremendously towards the prosperity and progress of Bhutan.

In recognition of his invaluable services and love to the people and country, I, Druk Gyalpo Jigme Dorji Wangchuck, am pleased to confer on Mr. Schulthess the Nation's first award of Druk Yi-sing Wangyel."

In Kürze

Im April 1952 besuchten Fritz von Schulthess und seine Frau Monica Bhutan zum erstenmal. Die Reise von Indien war anstrengend: sechs Tage lang zu Fuss, oder auf dem Rücken von Maultieren. Beide waren tief beeindruckt von der Schönheit des Landes. In Paro genossen sie die Gastfreundschaft des Königs Jigme Dorji Wangchuck. Fritz von Schulthess nannte ihn kurz und bündig Pön. Während der nächsten 20 Jahre reiste Fritz von Schulthess immer wieder nach Bhutan, zweimal war die Königsfamilie auch zu Gast in der Schweiz.
1967 verlieh der König seinem Schweizer Freund die höchste Auszeichnung des Königreichs: Druk Yi-sing Wangyel – in Anerkennung der Unterstützung durch die Familie von Schulthess. "Fritz von Schulthess von Cham ist wie ein zweiter Vater zu mir", schrieb der König in die Urkunde.

En bref

En avril 1952, Fritz von Schulthess et sa femme Monica visitèrent le Bhoutan pour la première fois. Le voyage à partir de l'Inde était pénible: 6 jours à pied ou à dos de mulet en longeant la rivière. Tous deux furent émerveillés par la beauté du pays. À Paro, ils apprécièrent l'hospitalité du roi Jigme Dorji Wangchuck. Fritz von Schulthess l'appelait simplement Pön. Pendant les 20 années suivantes, Fritz von Schulthess s'est rendu régulièrement au Bhoutan, et à deux occasions, la famille royale fut accueillie en Suisse. En 1967, le roi décerna la plus haute distinction du royaume à son ami suisse: Druk Yi-sing Wangyel, en reconnaissance du soutien de la famille von Schulthess. "Fritz von Schulthess de Cham est comme un deuxième père pour moi" écrivait le roi dans l'acte joint à la distinction.

Our contribution to the development of Bhutan

by Fritz von Schulthess, Entrepreneur, in: Souvenirs from Monica and myself. Journal for his grandchildren, Easter 1982

35 Monica and Fritz von Schulthess

36 Fritz von Schulthess, HM Ashi Kesang Choden Wangchuck, HM Jigme Dorji Wangchuck

In return for the largess and extremely generous hospitality, which the king of Bhutan had extended to us, we tried to give Bhutan something in return.

Stoves and chimneys

First, we sent Franz Bruderer, an expert furnace and chimney craftsman from the town of Schöftland in the Canton Aargau, Switzerland to Bhutan. At the beginning we had noticed that the kitchens in Bhutanese houses used an earthen 'chulo', an open hearth for cooking. There was no chimney for the smoke to escape out of the house. As a result, people sat permanently in thick smoke in their kitchens. The kitchens and everything in them turned pitch black from soot and, of course, the consumption of firewood was disproportionately large. So we thought that a Swiss expert could show them, how, when you build a new house and/or a kitchen, you can equip it with a chimney or a flue. Also, we thought, our expert could show them how, by using a fireplace (cheminées) in winter, rooms could be kept warm. Naturally, all this was meant only for the royal family. Our man remained in Bhutan for three months and taught young Bhutanese how to build chimneys and fireplaces. The king did not want to hear about the smoke reducing flues. This probably would have changed the old habits too much.

Radio connections

In 1964 the king asked me about a Swiss radio expert. For the control of the borders, mainly against China in the mostly uninhabited and wild mountain areas, he had installed small border posts. The messages brought through runners to Thimphu took several days and the orders back to the posts took again the same amount of time. A radio connection was very valuable for the king. The Indian government would have liked to install such a connection but the Pön (King) wanted to receive information without any possible Indian 'adaptation' or interference.

We sought therefore a radio technician, who in addition should also be a practical man, and found Arthur (Turi) Christen [Tenzing Dorji]. Until his documents and papers were ready for his mission, quite a few months elapsed. Finally, at the end of April 1965, he could finally enter Bhutan. He proved to be a very versatile and practically talented man. He built the desired radio stations and quick radio connections and links were achieved. Unfortunately, he had to work with obsolete equipment. The receivers and transmitters consisted of old US army equipment from the Second World War. Since Bhutan had practically no foreign exchange reserves (tourism hadn't started yet) new material had to be procured through the Indians and for obvious reasons they refused such requests.

Turi Christen suffered from the fact that there was no bread to be found in all of Bhutan. He asked us, therefore, to send him some yeast but that was difficult at that time, because yeast didn't come packaged in tins. Well, we finally managed to send him some. Now, Turi built a baking oven out of an old gasoline barrel and started to bake his own bread. Soon his bread was in demand from many sides. So he set up a real bakery for which we had to send all kinds of equipment from Switzerland. Next to its radio activity he now ran a bakery with an adjoining tearoom. That business quickly prospered, earning a good reputation under the name of "Swiss Bakery".

In addition to this, all the clocks and watches of the entire royal family as well as cars were sent to him for repair.

While Turi worked at the expense of the government of Bhutan, we – over the years – sent different experts at our expense. But unfortunately, they could not really prevail in their set duties and tasks. First we sent a second radioman as Turi's assistant, then an auto mechanic for whom it was planned that he teach young Bhutanese how to look after automobiles and perform small repairs. He was able to do nothing else but repair the cars of the Royal family at no expense to them, which is not something that can be called development assistance. So in due time we sent him back to Switzerland.

Haflinger Horses

The king had also the wish to try out Haflinger horses in Bhutan. We bought in Innsbruck, Austria at the expense of the king a stallion and five mares. Accompanied by the 18-year old son of the seller, by the name of Schweisgut, the animals travelled to the port of Bremen in Germany to be shipped by an East German ship to Calcutta. Because the Suez Canal was closed at that time, the poor horses had to cross the equator twice, and had to go around the Cape of Good Hope to get to India. In Bombay, the young assistant bought Indian hay so that the animals could get used to the new fodder. After nine months of travel in great heat on the ship they arrived in Calcutta. There, the dockworkers refused to unload the East-German ship, so that the poor animals had to wait another 40 days in enormous heat outside the port of Calcutta, before the strike was finally ended. I was at that time in Bhutan and was able to arrange that these horses were to be transported on trucks only as far as Phunthsoling. From there they would go on foot to Thimphu. In that way the horses could get used to walking again and also adjust to the great differences in climate and elevation. The Haflinger breed turned out to be ideal for Bhutan. They bred well and were crossed successfully with domestic horses. Later, the Austrian government provided for fresh blood by sending another group of horses as a gift to Bhutan. The Haflinger horses were used in Gogona and later in Bumthang in some of our projects.

Erosion control

In 1968, we were again on a short visit in Bhutan. For two weeks prior to our arrival it had rained incessantly. The rivers had risen and, here and there, landslides had obstructed the rivers and temporarily dammed them up. Because it kept raining, the creeks and rivers swelled to new heights and broke through the emerging barricades and obstructions. The waters tore trees from their roots and large rocks came rushing down, crashing what was in the way of the torrents of water. Many bridges were destroyed, including the charming bridges in Paro, Thimphu and Wangdiphodrang, but also the chain bridge above the confluence of rivers in Thamchogang. Only in the year 1980 were the chains found again. More than 70 houses were destroyed at that time.
The rains and floods in the Indian plain, especially in Jalpaiguri, caused an even greater disaster. These events strengthened me in the view that Bhutan had to have greatly improved agriculture and forestry development, serving primarily the forests, so that erosion does not get the upper hand. These hundred-year old bridges would not have been destroyed if the depletion of forests had not gone on unchecked.
Thus, our Dairy-and-Forest-project has the goal of showing the Bhutanese how they can get a better return from their agriculture while simultaneously preserving and using the forests by sustainable harvesting.

37 The Royal Family

Cheese production

At the beginning our project had no clear purposes. I knew that they produced cheese in Nepal. Swiss churchmen (Swiss Fathers) in Kalimpong also produced cheese, which was in high demand. So, I thought, let's get going! In Switzerland in 1967 I hired a cheese expert, by the name of Josef Dubach, in Switzerland and sent him to Bhutan to start cheese production. He travelled to Bhutan and once there was sent near the vicinity of the Black Mountain area: At an elevation of 4000 meters he started to build his dairy. When it was all beautifully finished and the building had been furnished with real copper kettles and the like, Dubach realized that there was not enough milk. The cows only produced one to two litres of milk a day. That wasn't even enough to raise the calves. Dubach gave notice and we sent a second cheese-maker, Fritz Maurer, who quickly changed gears. He realized that he first had to go in for real dairy farming. The breed of cows in Bhutan was very resistant to the harsh weather and in good health, but it produces little milk and yields hardly any meat to speak of. Thus, he had to get cows which gave much milk and whose meat was also to be put to good use. From an Indo-Swiss-farm in Kerala, India, Fritz Maurer was able to buy a number of Swiss brown cows and breeding bulls. The transport of these animals from far away India to Gogona in Bhutan, where Fritz Maurer had decided to build his dairy farm, was beset by much bureaucratic obstructions, because at the various border posts overzealous officials did not want to let the animals pass, because they were afraid of diseases and of the risk of infection. Finally, the transport reached Gogona where it was snowing and the animals could recover from the heat of India. Now the necessary fodder had to be procured. All kinds of seed were sent from Switzerland, clover, cabbage and grass. But the yields differed widely. The first hay was produced and other products landed in the silos. During summer, the cows were out on the meadows, during the night they could go to the newly built stable, so that soon a pile of manure was available for increasing the yields. The Bhutanese were in the habit of cultivating their land for one year and thereafter letting it rest for two years. We were able to show the local population that if you fertilize the land with manure there would be a yield each year.

38 HM Jigme Dorji Wangchuck and Fritz von Schulthess (1955)

How to get on with setbacks

But there were also setbacks. For example in the first year, the cabbage seeds from Switzerland brought a great yield for silage. In the second year however the cabbage butterfly had developed and devoured the entire harvest.
And our brown cattle had difficulty in adapting to the other foodstuffs. Then ticks developed, against which the local cattle was immune, but they invested by the thousands the bellies of our good brown cows until they were nearly or entirely dead. In the whole of Bhutan no means against this tick was to be found. Finally, after long months we got a remedy from Switzerland. It turned out that we had to crossbreed local and Swiss cows in order to get the most favourable animal for successfully inhabiting this country. The exact ratio of crossbreeding, which is best for Bhutan, whether 50/50, 75/25 or 25/75%, can only be determined locally by rather long-time trials.
In the mountain valleys around Gogona (about 3000 meters above sea level) the local population is very conservative. They viewed our development efforts rather sceptically. Because Fritz Maurer was the only foreigner in Gogona and the local people only spoke the Bhutanese language, he had to quickly learn the local language. As soon as he could make himself understood, he was able to explain his ideas to the people. Then slowly the ice melted, reticence and restraint disappeared. The local people noticed soon that more cows grazed now on their pastures than before when the cows were out day and night, summer and winter. They also noticed that fertilizers allowed them to cultivate their fields not only every third year but each year and gave a higher yield than before. The good looks and the yield of the cows, which had been crossed, with the Swiss cows also made an impression.

How to celebrate a birthday

Fritz Maurer took up residence in the Gömpa (monastry). This Gömpa is a cult site and inhabited by many lamas. But most of the lamas don't live there but on their farms with their wifes and children.
In 1972 when I celebrated my 70th birthday in Gogona, we paid the main lama a visit in his beautiful house. He treated us royally with buttered tea, Chang and Arrack which was served in big water glasses. Because it was only 11 in the morning we didn't drink too much of it. Then in the evening there was a large birthday party in the Gömpa. The people naturally came to the party in droves, because we served some treats. It was thinned rum, rice and vegetables. The main lama with his wife was also there. She must have drunk the rest of the Arrack after we had left her house. In any case, one glass of the drink sufficed to get her so inebriated that she sat for hours as stiff as a broomstick in a remote corner of the holy place. This was however an isolated case. When I was in western Bhutan, I didn't see any alcohol abuse to speak of.

Better use of the woods

Next to cattle raising, we also promoted the care and maintenance of the forests. We sent Swiss forestry engineers and foresters to Gogona. As the general population gradually came to realize that they could get a higher yield from the land under cultivation, they also realized that it was wrong to cut down the forests simply to get more land for herding the cows as they had done in the past. We also had to make clear to the people that it was wrong to cut only the trees at the forest edge and not look after the rest of the forest. In this way they reduced the available forest but in the deeper parts of the forest, the trees suffered from overaging and huge half rotten trees took away so much light that hardly any new young trees managed to grow. So we built small forest trails and/or built small gravity cable-cranes in order to get into the interior parts of the forests and care for the trees there. Clear cutting was avoided whenever possible. This way the population still got their firewood for their kitchen but also for building their houses, etc. We also introduced other ways to make better use of the wood. For example, the Bhutanese didn't know the saw. With the hatchet they cut a single wooden board out of a whole tree. We introduced the wood saw and showed them how, depending on the diameter, it was possible to cut four or more boards out of one log. In this manner we brought many other good practices from Switzerland to Bhutan.
But our efforts in cattle-raising and forest management were no instant success. It needed many years of sustained efforts to show good results and speak of success. This led us to look for ways of reaching our goals more quickly.

Growing other products than rice

Although the Bhutanese subsist mainly on rice, they were quite interested in growing other products, especially if they were able to sell them quickly, as for example, the potatoes. All of their potatoes were susceptible to potato blight. We were in a position to import disease resistant seeds from Switzerland and other countries, for example Mexico. Already in the first year the harvesting success was great and after two, three years, the "Swiss potatoes" were renowned in all of Bhutan and this mainly because the yield was a multiple of the previous potato harvest. But the successfully saturated market became a problem. So the government stepped in, bought the potatoes at harvest time, developed proper means of storage and sold their potato reserves gradually in the country as well as to export markets.
Another problem was the marketing of apples. In 1952, the year of our first trip to Bhutan, we hardly saw any apple orchards. The government started to promote apple production by giving away young trees to their farmers. Beginning in the seventies, there was a great overproduction of apples. They were the kind of apples, which did not keep for very long. Fritz Maurer decided to buy two large cider presses in Switzerland. This permits us now to pick the apples immediately. For the cider, a good market exists in Bhutan and India.

39 Opening of the Aum Monica Project, Bumthang, 1976

Project handing-over

In 1967 our project began with the efforts of Josef Dubach to make cheese in Maneting; it was continued as an agricultural and forestry enterprise by Fritz Maurer in Gogona in 1969. We were able to hand over this project to the local people while a Swiss agriculturalist stood by to give advice or lend a helping hand if need be. In the same year the' Rural Development Project' was started in Bumthang that has since developed admirably. In Bumthang a hospital under the direction of a Swiss physician was affiliated with the agriculture and forestry project.

"Aum Monica Project"

While my wife Monika and I alone originally led the entire project which we financed with the help of friends, in 1971 the Swiss Government began to support us financially after the Foundation 'Stiftung Pro Bhutan' was set up. As the load of administrative work became increasingly heavier and I could no longer execute it correctly, I turned over the administrative and financial direction in 1974 to HELVETAS, the Swiss Development Organisation for assistance to developing countries, headquartered in Zurich. This organisation continues to lead the project to the highest standards, whereby the mission tasks are always increasing. Unfortunately our work in Bhutan was also beset by grave accidents. One of our young Bhutanese counterparts was murdered in the vicinity of Gogona by a group of thieves, another died in a car accident and our excellent colleague and expert in all matters of cattle-raising, Ernst Meister, perished while on a boat trip in Charmarchu.

We thank all our Swiss and Bhutanese colleagues for their efforts and we are saddened that the work is also connected with large risks.

On the occasion of our visit in 1976, the project was opened officially by Monica in the presence of Tenge Lyonpo. It was baptized the "Aum Monica Project", which name was later abandoned by HELVETAS. Monica spoke some suitable words and cut the silk ribbon. On this occasion I would like to sincerely thank Tengye Lyonpo, HRH Prince Namgyel Wangchuck for his efforts and assistance for making the project a success.

In Kürze

Mit Schreibmaschine geschrieben und mit Originalphotos illustriert, so hat Fritz von Schulthess seinen Enkeln die abenteuerlichen Erlebnisse in Bhutan weitergegeben. Er erzählt, wie er als erstes den Ofenbauer Franz Bruderer aus Schöftland nach Bhutan schickte, damit er dem königlichen Haushalt anständige Öfen baue. Als nächstes kam ein Radioexperte, weil der König eine Funkverbindung zur Grenze mit China wünschte. Turi Christen war der Mann, der nicht nur sämtliche Uhren reparierte, sondern später auch noch die "Swiss Bakery" in Thimphu begründete. 1967 wurden Josef Dubach und Fritz Maurer ins Drachenland geschickt, um Milchwirtschaft und Käseproduktion zu entwickeln. Forstwirtschaft war ein weiterer Schwerpunkt. Wenn die Bhutaner ein Brett brauchten, fällten sie einen Baum und schlugen mit Äxten ein Brett zurecht. Die Schweizer lehrten sie, dass man mit einer Säge aus einem Stamm mehrere Bretter schneiden kann. All diese Projekte und viele mehr, finanzierte die Familie von Schulthess aus eigener Tasche, oder mit Hilfe von Freunden. 1971 wurde die Stiftung pro Bhutan gegründet, 1974 übergab Fritz von Schulthess die Projekte an Helvetas.

En bref

C'est au moyen de rapports dactylographiés agrémentés de photos originales que Fritz von Schulthess a transmis ses impressions du Bhoutan à ses petits-enfants. Il raconte qu'en tout premier, il avait envoyé le constructeur de poêles Franz Bruderer de Schöftland au Bhoutan afin qu'il construise des fourneaux "convenables" pour la famille royale. Ensuite il envoya un expert en communication radio car le roi voulait disposer d'une liaison radio avec la frontière chinoise. Cet expert était Turi Christen, qui ne se contenta pas de réparer toutes les montres et horloges, mais qui ouvrit également la « Swiss Bakery » à Thimphu. En 1967, Joseph Dubach et Fritz Maurer se rendirent dans le "Royaume du Dragon" pour y développer la production laitière et fromagère. La foresterie était un autre point fort. Lorsque les Bhoutanais avaient besoin d'une planche, ils abattaient un arbre et façonnaient une planche à la hache. Les Suisses leur ont appris à scier les troncs pour en tirer plusieurs planches. Ces projets et beaucoup d'autres ont été financés par la famille von Schultess, ou avec le soutien d'amis. En 1971 fut créée la Fondation Pro Bhutan, et en 1974 Fritz von Schulthess remettait les projets à Helvetas.

Swiss Kids: We got two Bhutanese elephants!

About 1.000.000 persons a year are visiting the Zoo of Zurich, half of them are kids. The two elephants Druk and Chhukha have lived there for 40 years. Thus, more than twenty million kids have enjoyed seeing the Bhutanese elephants – a present of the 3rd King of Bhutan. Twenty million words of thanks are going to Bhutan.

20 million words of thanks sent to Bhutan

Swiss newspapers informed in 1968 in detail:
Accompanied by loud and repeated flourishes, little Chhukha welcomed the visitors of the zoo. However, only protest due to hunger could have been the reason for this powerful music. As fast as lightning, she lowered her trunk into the bucket of milk, guiding it into her mouth and back. The director of the zoo explained that Chhukha is just outgrowing infancy and she still has a problem with ingesting liquid food the way older elephants do. The full-grown elephant does not absorb the water through the trunk; he just fills it and then leads it to his mouth in order to quench thirst.

One of the biggest problems was the transport of the two elephants from Bhutan. Finally, an airplane was organised with a rear to be flapped sideways, thus allowing for an entrance broad enough for the elephants to be pushed through. The keeper, Ruedi Tanner, accompanied the two little elephants on their journey around the world. The initiator was Fritz von Schulthess in 1968.

Unfortunately, Chhukha died in 2006. During those 40 years of her life she was a tremendous eater and grew over time from a little girl-elephant of 220 kg to a lady-elephant of 4500 kg. Druk, the other elephant, still lives in the zoo and now enjoys respect and consideration.

In Kürze
Der König war dankbar und revanchierte sich: Mit zwei Elefanten für den Zürcher Zoo. 1978 kamen die Elefantenbabys "Druk" und "Chhukha" mit dem Flugzeug in die Schweiz. Der Zootierpfleger Ruedi Tanner begleitete die Dickhäuter auf ihrer langen Reise.

En bref
Le roi, reconnaissant, offrit en contrepartie deux éléphants au zoo de Zurich. En 1978, les éléphanteaux "Druk" et "Chhukha" arrivèrent en Suisse par avion, accompagnés pendant ce long voyage par le gardien de zoo Ruedi Tanner.

40 Young elephants in the Zoo of Zurich

41

42

A wonderful present of the King of Bhutan

43 Old Lady Chhukha dancing (2006)

The Foundation Pro-Bhutan

by Dr. Saamdu Chetri, Dy-Resident Co-ordinator Helvetas / SDC, 1988-2006

Dairy and Forestry Project in Bumthang

In 1971 the people of Bumthang asked His Royal Highness (HRH), Prince Namgyel Wangchuck, for a dairy farm in Bumthang. In those days, Bumthang was considered one of the poorest districts in the country. It was also the wish of His Majesty to begin development work in Bumthang. During the same year, Fritz von Schulthess decided to start the so-called Foundation Pro-Bhutan to give the assistance a broader and secured base. Peter A. Wiesmann visited Bhutan as the first Swiss government official on the request of the Foundation to support the Dairy and Forestry Project in Bumthang. Based on his advice, the Foundation later sought assistance from Helvetas, a Swiss Non-Governmental Organisation formed in 1955 in Switzerland. The success of dairy development and the early base of Swiss Assistance to Bhutan are due to the committed patronage of HRH Prince Namgyel Wangchuck (brother of the 3rd King), the Tengyel Lyonpo (Minister for Trade, Industry and Forests).

Under the Foundation Pro-Bhutan, the Dairy and Forestry Project (DFP) was created in Bumthang in 1972-73. DFP was governed by a board of directors chaired by HRH, the Tengyel Lyonpo. For the office's infrastructural set-up land was selected at Bapalythang and at Kharsumpe; a historical building along with an old apple orchard became part of the project area. Due to the fodder shortage at Gogona, six purebred brown Swiss cows were sent to Bumthang. Ernst Meister, a competent cattle breeder, arrived at Gogona and later moved to Bumthang, where he unfortunately drowned kayaking in the Chamkhar River. During this time, the important decision was taken that cows should not be purebred, as they were not strong enough in the harsh environment of Bumthang.

In 1973 a preparatory mission was set up by the Foundation Pro Bhutan, consisting of Prof. F. Fischer, forestry expert, Dr. R. Schatz, economist, and Dr. M. Menzi, agronomist. During this visit the Dairy and Forestry Project was shaped into a full programme and a full-fledged cattle breeding programme was started. The forestry programme on the other hand could not be defined as concretely as the animal husbandry wing. Although the project was still to be signed, the work in Bumthang had already started.

A value chain for potatoes

Within a short period of his posting, Walter Roder – the fodder expert – shifted his base in February 1974 from Gogona to Bumthang. During the same year, four young boys who were trained for some years received Nu 10,000 each to begin their own farming at Phobjikha. Tragically, bandits, later on, killed one of them. A very positive aspect of these trial farmers was the spread of potato seed growing. Later the valley became the major potato seed-growing place in the country. A first review in Bumthang was made on the progress of potato farming, after having distributed seeds in 1970 (400 kilograms wart resistant potatoes imported in 1970, the two varieties "Swiss red" (also called "Desiree") and "Maritta" were distributed by Dasho Nishioka to people in most valleys including Paro . Before, farmers had stopped the production of potatoes, lacking a market. With the support of the project, where Fritz Maurer was again instrumental, farmers were promised an outlet for their produce and were asked to go ahead and produce lots of potatoes. He linked the potato producers with the Food Corporation of Bhutan, as an outlet for potato marketing. In the first year, producers made cash sales of 40 metric tons of potatoes. This boosted the production and potatoes subsequently became the major cash crop. In ten years the production figures had multiplied by a factor of 50, bringing cash income to a large part of the country's population.

Medical clinic

Even though on a small scale, in 1974 a medical mobile clinic was established, covering the central region of Bhutan where the projects were taking shape. A certain amount of curative medical support to health around Sha Gogona, on a voluntary basis, had already begun in 1972 through two trained nurses, namely the wives of Ernst Meister and Hans Jutzi. The work of the two ladies did not only include the provision of basic medicine, but their voluntary assistance helped in creating trust for the project in the area. However, as the entire central part was suffering from little or no medical support, Dr. F. Töndury and Miss Cadalbert built up a mobile clinic in Bumthang, which was a welcome relief. The mobile clinic did not succeed, however, and Dr. Marcel Brüderlin established a permanent clinic at Wangdicholing. Dr. Richard Frey, followed by Dr. J. Ruckstuhl in 1975 succeeded him; thus, four doctors followed one another within two years. Between 1974 and 1994, there were 11 medical Swiss doctors who worked for the health programme in Bumthang.

44

Pioneers

Leo Caminada, a forest engineer, began his duty at Bumthang. As was the case with most Swiss, his first job was building the infrastructure before concentrating on forestry work. The major forestry work began with the repair and renovation of Lamegompa, an old Dzong, which was the summer residence of the first King. It was handed over to the Dairy and Forestry Programme as forestry centre by HRH, the Tengyel Lyonpo. The building was renovated and the training centre was established along with divisional and other forestry administrative offices. The forestry activities did not seem to be as well planned and targeted as the Dairy Division. This possibly was due to the lack of basic information and data on the forestry side. To begin the forest activities more consistently, a second Swiss forest engineer, Christof Frei joined the division.

With the increasing number of expatriates, the vehicle park also grew and there was a need to establish a vehicle workshop. The first mechanic, R. Schmidhalter, was posted and in 1974 the infrastructure for repair work and maintenance began. As development work expanded, other service units were required. In order to meet the demand for seasoned sawn timber in the market and for the project, a sawmill with intermediate technology, running on water-turbine, was built.

In the same year Peter Maurer made a study to link the three isolated valleys of Khotokha, Gogona and Phobjikha to the national highway by a ropeway, as it was not possible to build a road on this terrain. For various reasons the ropeway project was delayed by almost ten years. Nevertheless, under the patronage of HRH, the Tengyel Lyonpo, and according to the plan of Prof. Fischer, the 5.2 kilometres ropeway was established between Chuzomsa, resting at an altitude of 1500 meters above sea level (masl), to 2800 masl at Khotokha. This ropeway was used largely to exploit the forestry and agriculture products from Khotokha valley.

Handing over

The year 1974 ended with a good note by the handing over of the Dairy Farm at Sha-Gogona to the lama-community (gomchens). It was the first kind of income generating venture being handed over to private initiative. They took it willingly, because they did not have any property of their own. For a smooth transfer, a project agreement was drawn. The dairy farm was priced at Nu 100,000, which was treated as a loan to be repaid over a period of ten years. An important clause of the agreement was that the gomchens would start cultivation and totally stop the shifting cultivation, which was a great achievement.

The year brought an important landmark in the history of Swiss assistance. His Majesty visited Bumthang for the third Five Year Plan discussion and during this visit he commended that the project should be integrated into the government system and no longer stay as an independent project. This was considered a prerequisite for an integrated development.

45 The Swiss team at Bumthang, ca. 1974

In Kürze

1971 begann die Stiftung Pro Bhutan mit aktiver Unterstützung durch das DEZA mit ihrem Programm für Milch- und Forstwirtschaft in Bumthang. Sechs Stück Braunvieh wurden importiert, junge Bhutaner wurden zu Bauern ausgebildet. Resistentere Kartoffelsorten liessen die Produktion rasch wachsen. Eine mobile medizinische Klinik wurde installiert. Krankenschwestern und Ärzte begannen mit der medizinischen Versorgung der Bevölkerung. Die Zahl der Schweizer nahm ständig zu, was nach entsprechender Infrastruktur wie Reparaturwerkstätten für den wachsenden Wagen- und Maschinenpark rief.

En bref

En 1971, la Fondation Pro Bhutan démarrait son programme de production laitière et forestière à Bumthang avec le soutien actif de la DDC. Six vaches de la race brune étaient importées, alors que de jeunes Bhoutanais étaient formés comme agriculteurs. Des variétés de pommes de terre résistantes permirent une forte augmentation de la production. Une clinique médicale mobile était installée. Des infirmières et des médecins commencèrent à fournir des soins médicaux à la population. Avec un nombre de Suisses résidants en constante augmentation est apparue la nécessité de disposer d'ateliers de réparation pour assurer l'entretien du parc de véhicules et de machines.

Fighting the yak disease

by Fritz von Schulthess, in: Souvenirs from Monica and myself. Journal for his grandchildren, Easter 1982

47 Dogs, the carriers of the tapeworm

Pön (King) once told me in Switzerland that in certain areas of Bhutan there is a great amount of yaks that die due to a strange disease. The sick animal spins round for a couple of days and finally dies. The reason for it is not clear. From staff members of the veterinary hospital in Zurich, we learnt that we probably are confronted with a tapeworm, which develops in the yak body and causes a bubble in the animal's brain, which then leads to its death. The course of disease is described as follows: The shepherd's dog feeds from the perished yak and therewith ingests this bubble. The bubble contains the tapeworm, which develops in the dog's stomach and produces eggs that are digested together with the dog's excrement. The yak feeds from the grass where such eggs are dropped and the tapeworm develops in the yak body. The director of the veterinary hospital in Zurich was not entirely sure about the diagnosis and therefore asked me to bring along an affected brain after my next travel to Bhutan. Thus, Monika and I brought along a large yak brain in a big bottle. The first diagnosis has been confirmed.

3000 pills for healthy dogs?!

As a first donation to the development aid in Bhutan, the Swiss offered 3000 pills against this disease. The Bhutanese yakherders, however, had troubles to understand that they had to give the pills to their dogs in order to save the yaks from further affection. After many explanations the yakherders were finally convinced. Today, as far as I know, the disease has almost entirely disappeared.

In Kürze

Pön erzählte seinem Schweizer Freund von Yaks, die an einer sonderbaren Krankheit verendeten: Tagelang drehten sie sich im Kreise, um dann plötzlich zusammenzubrechen. Fritz von Schulthess erzählte die Geschichte dem Direktor des Tierspital Zürich, der ihm riet, bei der nächsten Reise ein Yak-Hirn mitzubringen. Ursache sei wohl ein Bandwurm, der das Gehirn der Yaks befalle. Und siehe, es war der Bandwurm, übertragen durch den Kot der Hirtenhunde. Die Schweiz schickte 3000 Pillen nach Bhutan – der erste Akt eidgenössischer Entwicklungshilfe.

En bref

Pön racontait à son ami suisse que des yaks mouraient d'une maladie particulière : pendant des jours entiers, ces animaux tournaient en rond avant de s'effondrer. La cause probable était un ténia s'attaquant au cerveau des yaks. Fritz von Schulthess rapporta cette histoire au directeur de l'hôpital vétérinaire de Zurich qui lui conseilla de ramener un cerveau de yak lors de son prochain voyage. Le diagnostic du ténia fut confirmé, ce parasite étant transmis par les crottes des chiens de bergers. La Suisse envoya 3000 pilules au Bhoutan, ce fut le premier acte de la coopération suisse.

Change of Guard to Helvetas

by Dr. Saamdu Chetri, Dy-Resident Co-ordinator Helvetas / SDC, 1988-2006

The visit of Professor Dr. Martin Menzi, a founding member of Helvetas, in 1973 was already an indication that Helvetas was going to take over the Foundation Pro-Bhutan. Together with Professor Fischer he had planned the Dairy and Forestry Programme. The programme was rapidly growing and thus becoming too large for the Foundation. Therefore, on the request of Fritz von Schulthess, the programme was taken over by Helvetas in Bhutan on July 1, 1975.

Landless farmers

During the process of shifting the programme from Gogona to Bumthang, it was realized that land was in the hands of a few and there were many landless families. With Fritz Maurer's initiative, the project managers proposed to grant loans to the farmers for buying land. As HRH Tengyel Lyonpo was the patron of the Dairy and Forestry Programme (DFP), the scheme was approved and the project managers became responsible for handling the scheme.

The first steps that had to be taken by Helvetas were to dissolve the board and to align the management with the official structure under the concerned departments. The year 1975 saw the construction of infrastructure. A carpentry workshop was developed for catering to the project needs and the people of Bumthang. 11 brown Swiss bulls were imported from the Indo-Swiss project in Patiala, India. They became the backbone of the breeding programme until artificial insemination was practised.

All agriculture and animal husbandry programmes were taken over by the Swiss Project. In April 1977, Fritz Maurer was appointed as the District Agriculture and Animal Husbandry Officer. This was an important step towards decentralisation, which helped the effective local decision-making when there were no modern communications means. During the same year, a mechanical technical adviser arrived, who was instrumental in tuning the future of the vehicle workshop towards privatisation. The first successful experiments on manufacturing apple juice were done and a food-processing unit was developed. The last Swiss expert stationed at Gogona was attacked by a bear and returned to Switzerland. The government took over the extension services, while Helvetas only backstopped it until coming back with a bigger programme, the Bhutan National Potato Programme.

Dasho Tshering Wangda, probably the first Bhutanese youth trained by the Swiss Cooperation in export and import trades, stayed in Switzerland for more than five months in 1975/6. On his way back home he carried a few kilograms of different kinds of fodder seed for pasture development in Bhutan.

Reorganisation

The DFP was renamed Rural Development Project (RDP) in 1978, the horse breeding programme took shape and discussions on a new programme on potato production began. The road construction to Phobjikha began with the technical support provided by Helvetas, executed by the Public Works Department. It was a first step towards opening the three valleys of Phobjikha, Gogona and Khotokha. The Bumthang forest range and four other district departments came under the direct control of the RDP. The duty of a zonal medical officer was also assigned to the Swiss and a logging centre and a sawmill were set up at Domkhar in Bumthang .

With the expansion of the programme there was a growing need for a permanent coordination office. The government accepted the proposal made in 1981 and two years later the office was set up in Thimphu. The year is marked with big changes in the management of Helvetas. During his visit to the district for finalisation of the 5th Five Year Plan (FYP), His Majesty the Druk Gyalpo ordered to dissolve the Board of Directors which oversaw the management of the programme. This allowed Helvetas to work directly with the agencies of the government. A Bhutanese delegation led by the Deputy Minister of the Planning Commission visited Switzerland to frame the future programme. The Forestry Training Centre at Lamegompa was set up in 1983 and the forestry programme began to grow on more solid grounds.

In 1982, a delegation from Switzerland led by Ernst Werner Külling, Secretary General of Helvetas, prepared a detailed study on possible areas of intervention. In April 1983, Ernst Reinhardt joined Helvetas Bhutan as the first Resident Coordinator and set up the Coordination Office in Thimphu, supported by his very dynamic wife Annegret. The major task of the Coordination Office between 1983 and 1985 was to consolidate ongoing projects, to prepare the handing-over of various projects and functions of expatriates to local personnel, and to develop mid-term planning covering the 6th FYP. This included outlining avenues for multilateral projects as well as co-ordination with the local donor community.

During 1986, the Swiss Agency for Development Cooperation signed an agreement with Helvetas mandating the organisation to coordinate and implement all bilateral and multilateral aid programmes in Bhutan. The Swiss assistance broadened its base with the agreement of a country programme between 1987 and 1992 with 35 million Swiss Francs. A new vast project that has links up to the present day under the extension programme, the High Altitude Area Development Project (with the Integrated Livestock and Fodder Development Programme), corresponding to the country programme was launched. It covered the temperate zone of Bhutan from east to west. A 40-bedded hospital was designed. The agreement to support the Suspension Bridge Programme was signed, funded through United Nations Capital Development Fund (UNCDF). An intensive discussion began to establish a National Agriculture Institute at Wangdue. Interestingly enough, town planning was initiated by Helvetas – then an important developer – an area of intervention that was shelved for unknown reasons after preparing a few town plans of Punakha, Bumthang, Pemagathsel, Damphu/Tsirang, Deothang/Samdrup Jongkhar, and having trained a town planner. A Kheng area development programme was investigated. Other projects were a small business development programme, Primary Education, Forestry II, Liquid Nitrogen Plant.

The decade of 1980's can be concluded with the remarks of Ernst Reinhardt, the first Resident Coordinator to Bhutan: "Despite early confusion created with the launching of decentralisation process, especially in decision and power delegation matters, the government recognized the need to make the system efficient and effective with productive administration, an approach to 'management by objectives'."

In Kürze

Das Programm wuchs schnell und brachte die Pro-Bhutan-Stiftung an die Grenzen ihrer Möglichkeiten. Auf Ersuchen von Fritz von Schulthess übernahm Helvetas am 1. Juli 1975 die Verantwortung für die Zusammenarbeit mit Bhutan. Die Verantwortlichen von Helvetas verlangten nach einer besseren Koordination. Der König löste das Direktorium auf, welches bisher die einzelnen Projekte überwacht hatte. 1983 wurde der Helvetas-Stützpunkt Bhutan in der Hauptstadt Thimphu begründet; Ernst Reinhardt war der erste ortsansässige Koordinator, tatkräftig unterstützt von seiner Frau Annegret. Seine Hauptaufgabe: die über weite Teile Bhutans verstreuten Projekte zu konsolidieren, und diese soweit voranzubringen, dass sie in die Verantwortung der Einheimischen übergeben werden konnten. Weiter galt es Perspektiven für den 6. Fünfjahresplan zu entwerfen, unter welchem die Schweiz zwischen 1987 und 1992 35 Millionen Franken investierte. Ernst Reinhardt sagt über seine Erfahrungen in diesen Jahren: "Trotz anfänglicher Konfusion durch den Prozess der Dezentralisierung, erkannte die Regierung die Notwendigkeit das ganze System effizient und effektiv zu machen mittels einer guten Administration und durch Führen mit Zielvorgaben."

En bref

Avec la croissance rapide du programme, la Fondation Pro Bhoutan touchait à ses limites. À la demande de Fritz von Schulthess, la responsabilité de la coopération avec le Bhoutan fut transmise à Helvetas le 1er juillet 1975. Les responsables d'Helvetas exigèrent une meilleure coordination. Le roi releva de ses fonctions le directoire chargé jusque là de surveiller les projets. En 1983, Helvetas installait son siège bhoutanais dans la capitale Thimphu, avec Ernst Reinhardt comme premier coordinateur résidant, épaulé par sa femme Annegret. Ses tâches principales consistaient à consolider les projets éparpillés sur une grande partie du territoire bhoutanais, et de faire en sorte que la responsabilité de ces projets puisse être transférée à des personnes locales. Il s'agissait également de planifier le 6ème plan quinquennal dans lequel la Suisse a investi 35 millions de francs entre 1987 et 1992. Ernst Reinhardt racontait à propos de ses expériences au cours de ces années: "Malgré une certaine confusion initiale liée au processus de décentralisation, le gouvernement a reconnu la nécessité de rendre le système dans son ensemble plus efficace et plus efficient au moyen d'une bonne administration et par la définition d'objectifs."

48 Building identity

Development Programmes. Essentials

Renewable Natural Resources Development

49

Integrated natural resources management

by Prof. Dr. Martin Menzi, Co-Founder of Helvetas, Senior Advisor to the RNR-sector from1976-2006, Co-Director NRTI 1992-1994

In the course of the continuous process of decentralisation and devolution of powers and responsibilities to the local authorities, the order of the day seems to be the establishment of "Integrated Gewog Centres", from where all the Government agencies involved and active at Gewog level will offer their services to the local communities. In the 'Green Sector' the Ministry of Agriculture started to take an integrated approach almost 20 years ago: "Integration" was the basic philosophy when the "Natural Resources Training Institute" (NRTI, now 'College of Natural Resources' under the Royal University of Bhutan) was conceived. Housing under one roof the training and education of professionals in forestry, agriculture and animal husbandry should not emphasize only the many common components of the respective disciplines, but also bring together from the very beginning of their professional carrier the future extension agents who later on will have to coordinate their efforts (and not to compete) in serving the farmers and rural communities.

Farmers as the stewards of diverse natural resources are forced to follow an integrated and multidimensional strategy - why not should those who serve them as advisors apply the same optic? The sustainable management of natural resources calls for a holistic and systemic approach, not only at the level of the individual farmer or the traditional village community, but even more so at the national level. The same philosophy of integration and mutual interaction was the guiding principle when the national Renewable Natural Resources (RNR) Research programme was conceived and launched more than ten years ago. A 4x4 matrix structure consisting of four national programmes (agriculture, forestry, livestock and horticulture) as one dimension and four regional zones from West to East as the other. Bhutan is ruled by many other people who still are so captive of outdated departmental thinking and structures that they cannot pioneer an integrated approach in natural resources management.

In more than 12 years, NRTI – the first integrated 'green sector' institution and a landmark of bilateral development cooperation between Bhutan and Switzerland - has brought out almost one thousand RNR diploma graduates. It is most rewarding to meet them all across the country in different functions and positions, be it in RNR extension, RNR research or other services, and it is encouraging indeed to see how well they collaborate and coordinate their activities in the interest of their clients – the multidisciplinary farmers and village communities. Even if some conservative forces may try to re-establish the 'good old order', they will not succeed in turning back the wheel of progress and development. A new 'integrated generation' of well trained, experienced and committed professionals will take the lead and head for new promising horizons.

The Renewable Natural Resources (RNR) sector, where about 80 percent of the Bhutanese population still live in rural settings, has received the highest assistance from Helvetas and still is the most important sector. Swiss assistance in RNR has continued for about 50 years, and has included livestock, forestry and agriculture projects. Metaphorically, we still see 41 percent of the rural population below the poverty line defined at Nu 748 per capita per month. On the whole, every one of three Bhutanese is still poor according to the Household Income Expenditure Survey 2000. Helvetas commitment in the livestock/ fodder sector was progressively reduced and phased out during the late 1990's.
An expatriate, who had returned home after completion of his assignment as an extension expert attached to East Central Research Systems, Jakar, wrote in his report, "there is big satisfaction while working in Bumthang today as Helvetas Advisor. We can really see the impact of the past projects in this valley and generally the people are very pleased and grateful for it." He notes that all eight programmes in RNR, health and private sector still functioned well.

In Kürze

80 Prozent der Bevölkerung leben in ländlichen Gegenden. Seit 50 Jahren konzentriert sich die Schweizer Hilfe in Bhutan darum auf die Entwicklung erneuerbarer natürlicher Ressourcen: Viehzucht, Forstwirtschaft und Landwirtschaft. Seit 20 Jahren verfolgt das Agrarministerium einen integrierten Ansatz. Ausdruck davon ist das Institut für Natürliche Ressourcen der Universität Bhutan, in welchem alle Spezialisten ausgebildet werden, die später die Bauern und die Gemeinden beraten. Über tausend Studentinnen und Studenten haben bereits ein Diplom absolviert. Martin Menzi erwähnt konservative Kräfte, welche die gute alte Ordnung vermissen. Sie werden das Rad aber nicht zurückdrehen können. Eine neue Generation mit integrierten Managementmethoden hat längst die Führung übernommen.

En bref

80 pour-cent de la population bhoutanaise vit en milieu rural. C'est pourquoi la coopération suisse au Bhoutan s'est concentrée depuis 50 ans sur le développement des ressources naturelles renouvelables : élevage, foresterie et agriculture. Depuis 20 ans, le ministère de l'agriculture applique une approche intégrée. L'institut des ressources naturelles de l'université du Bhoutan, dans lequel tous les spécialistes appelés à conseiller les agriculteurs et les communes sont formés, en est une expression. Plus de 1'000 étudiantes et étudiants ont déjà obtenu un diplôme en agriculture, foresterie ou dans un autre domaine spécialisé. Martin Menzi rappelle que malgré certaines forces conservatrices qui regrettent le nouvel ordre établi, cette évolution est irréversible. Une nouvelle génération de dirigeants, qui ont intégré les méthodes modernes de management, a pris les commandes.

50

51

52

Agriculture – life vein of the country

by Prof. Dr. Martin Menzi, Co-Founder of Helvetas, Senior Advisor to the RNR-sector from1976-2006, Co-Director NRTI 1992-1994

53 Buckwheat

54 Barley

55 Paddy

Essential features

In relative terms the contribution of agriculture to Gross Domestic Product (GDP) is steadily declining. Other sectors, like hydropower, tourism etc. are gaining ground more and more. Still, within the rather complex development process, agriculture, forestry, animal husbandry, handicrafts, local trade and services remain vital components of the national economy. Even more so, they are essential features of a national identity and their contribution to Gross National Happiness (GNH) is probably more important than their share in GDP. Farmers and village communities are the custodians of natural resources, of cultural values and traditions and of a unique biodiversity in a pristine environment.

Lasting impacts

Since the very beginning of Bhutan-Swiss development cooperation, Helvetas/SDC have always given special emphasis and high priority to the promotion of rural development projects, be it for the efficient management and use of natural resources, for the development of human capacities or for establishing rural infrastructure. Lasting impacts of successful joint efforts are many: From cattle breeding and dairy development to sustainable forest management and wood processing, from countrywide potato production to comprehensive area development programmes, from integrated training of professionals to a national RNR research system, and last but not least from training of farmers and village leaders in various skills to the promotion and support of community-based development initiatives and local governance.

Challenges

Bhutan's rural sector in general has gone a long way – and again, particularly agriculture is facing tremendous new challenges:

On one hand

- it will be livelihood for a majority of Bhutan's population for quite some more time to come,
- it is expected to contribute to 'national food security' by producing at least 70% of the total food grain requirements and
- it has to preserve the natural environment also in the interest of other, fast growing sectors of the economy (hydro power, tourism etc.),

and on the other it is supposed

- to open up to a partly liberalised global market (WTO),
- to compete with freely imported commodities on the local market and
- to be subjected to stringent internationally valid sanitary regulations and quality standards.

56 Potato

57 Chili

Threats

For natural and socio-economic reasons (topography, communication network, climate, availability of land and size of holdings etc.) chances for a further intensification and for increasing the efficiency of agricultural operations are limited. Bhutanese farmers will hardly be in a position to compete with (distorted) world market conditions in the production of staple commodities. Regional specialities and seasonal advantages may offer certain chances, but to survive on niche products and exclusive comparative advantages alone will hardly be a realistic option for the whole of Bhutan's farmer community, nor can it provide a sound base for assuring national food security and independence.

Post globalisation

It has to be acknowledged that agriculture is a multi-functional component of the national economy. Farmers and rural communities are not only producing food and other daily requirements; they are also the guardians of the natural environment and an important part of national identity. These vital contributions to GNH are worth not only due recognition, but also monetary compensation – complementary to or in lieu of global trade regulations. It is to be hoped that Bhutan will find ways and means to keep the agriculture and rural sector alive and fit also for a post globalisation era inspired by diversified federative structures and economic concepts.

In Kürze

Landwirtschaft ist die Lebensader für Bhutan – weit über ihre volkswirtschaftliche Bedeutung hinaus. Bauern und Dorfgemeinschaften sind die Hüter des natürlichen Reichtums, der kulturellen Werte und Traditionen. Ihr Beitrag zu Gross National Happiness ist wichtiger als ihr Anteil am Sozialprodukt. Die Landwirtschaft wird unter Druck kommen, muss sich den globalisierten Märkten öffnen, und internationaler Konkurrenz stellen. Die strukturellen Bedingungen (Topografie, Klima, usw.) erlauben keine grosse Produktions- und Effizienzsteigerung mehr. Das Land wird also Wege suchen und finden müssen, wie es seine Bauern und den Agrarsektor schützen und bewahren kann.

En bref

L'agriculture est un secteur vital pour le Bhoutan – bien au-delà de son importance économique. Les paysans et les communautés villageoises sont les gardiens des richesses naturelles, des valeurs culturelles et des traditions. Leur contribution au bonheur national brut est plus grande que leur apport au produit intérieur brut. Aujourd'hui, l'agriculture est sous pression, car elle doit s'ouvrir à des marchés globalisés et à la concurrence internationale. Les conditions structurelles (topographie, climat, etc.) ne laissent pas entrevoir une forte progression de la production et de la productivité. Le pays sera par conséquent contraint de trouver des options lui permettant de protéger ses paysans et son secteur agricole.

Brief account on agriculture and livestock development

by Dr. Saamdu Chetri, Dy-Resident Co-ordinator Helvetas / SDC, 1988-2006

Agriculture: During the 1980's there was considerable decrease of buckwheat cultivation, a moderate reduction in wheat and barley cultivation, while a very heavy increase of potato production. Buckwheat, until recently, was the staple food of Bumthang and everybody cultivated it. Slowly the potato overtook and now there are intensive trials in rice cultivation. Potatoes have been the major cash crop and Bumthang flourished with it due to climatical conditions and improved techniques. Changes in food habits are apparent, potatoes now forming a good part of the meal. It was once believed to cause stomach pain and was not fit to offer to guests. However, Bhutanese still prefer rice to any other kind of food, partly due to the fact that rice was abundantly available through Food Corporation Bhutan (FCB).

Lack of manpower has been one of the reasons for the reduction of staple food production of buckwheat, wheat and barely. Partly, the lack of manpower has also helped in reducing the shifting cultivation, which was further discouraged by the government. Migration of people with their herds of animals to the much poorer South has almost stopped with development at large, pasture management and food supplies from the Food Corporation of Bhutan.

Extension Programme

East Central Region - Agriculture Development Programme (ECR-ADP):

This programme began in 2002 as a continuation of the earlier Renewable Natural Resources Extension Programme Bumthang and Trongsa with extended mandates to four Dzongkhags, instead of just two.

Of the several components in Human Resource Development/training, communication and dissemination of information, technical assistance, local development initiatives (LDI), the last one has the most direct approach in contributing to poverty alleviation at the rural settings. The concept of LDI is initiating community groups to venture into income generating activities, such as poultry, fishery farming, piggery, vegetable farming, dairy production, etc. Groups are formed considering several criteria and financed on contributory mechanisms depending on the group's financial strength.

As of 2006 the project supported 43 LDI consisting of 534 members in the region. The outcome of these groups in terms of earnings is tangible indeed. Some of the selected activities achieved under the project are: 50 kilometres of farm-road, 16 kilometres of irrigation channels, market sheds, depots for orange collections, construction and improvement of several RNR centres, promotion of different agriculture and livestock programmes, farmers training and study tour programmes in different fields, institutional setup and mobility, and extension kits to extension staff.

Fodder seed production has received over 20 years of assistance from the Swiss cooperation. Today, Bhutan does not import grass-seeds anymore, which it did for a long time. Selected farmers have begun to grow seeds to supply them to the centre at a good price, which in turn sells to the farmers for their pasture development. Today there is wide agreement that, in terms of success of the livestock, this is mainly due to fodder management.

Cross breeding programme with the Brown Swiss began in the early 1970's, first confined to Wangdi and Bumthang, later under the High Altitude Programme Development in Tongsa. Ultimately, it was extended across the temperate zone of the country. To fit the Bhutanese environment best, the exotic inheritance should be between 50 and 75 percent of the bloodline. Import of frozen semen from Switzerland was reduced with the establishment of a local semen collection centre and the set-up of Liquid Nitrogen Plant with the assistance of the Swiss. The choice of breed is now left to the farmers in Bhutan; many still use Brown Swiss, especially in Bumthang. Others buy from the contract bull breeders who have formed an association under which the first seed money is provided by Helvetas.

The story of the Haflinger horses breeding programme did not last long. His Majesty the late third King imported the first Haflinger horses in 1968. The formal programme started in 1987, its aim was to prevent inbreeding and improve the genetic make-up of the indigenous horse population by crossbreeding up to an exotic inheritance level of 25 to 50 percent. After 20 years of breeding, doubts sprang up on the sustainability of the programme and the choice of breed. Furthermore, the farmers often preferred the surefooted mules. Thus, Helvetas backed out from the horse-breeding programme in 1996.

Recovering loans – a success story

During the mid 1970's, Helvetas through the initiative of Fritz Maurer had started an agriculture loan scheme. Loans provided to the landless people put them in a position to buy land for agriculture activities such as potato plantation or pasture development to rear animals. Terms and conditions of lending were very simple and without interest rates. The Swiss have pioneered the agriculture loan system in Bhutan. They had understood that as there was no development bank, revolving fund mechanisms were very important to boost the agriculture and livestock sector in the country. Therefore, with increasing programmes and changes, several such funds were instituted for different purposes, such as fodder programme, mobility programme, and small business programme or agriculture loan schemes.

An interesting story on this scheme goes like this: It happened that a woman who took a loan to buy land could not repay it. Despite several reminders and follow-ups the loan was going bad. In order not to let the borrower down and not to have a bad loan, the Swiss took the decision to marry her and pay the loan on her behalf. Thus, Fritz Maurer became a true Bhutanese.

In Kürze

Hier wird Rechenschaft abgelegt über Erfolg und Misserfolg einzelner Projekte. Die Kartoffelsorten "Désirée" und "Maritta" sind ein durchschlagender Erfolg, genauso wie die Produktion von Grassamen. Gelungen ist auch die Kreuzung von Schweizer Braunvieh mit einheimischen Kühen. Ein Flop war dagegen das Zuchtprogramm von Haflinger Pferden. Die Bauern vertrauten lieber ihren trittsicheren Maultieren.
Ein Erfolg ganz anderer Art war die Einführung von zinslosen Darlehen für Landlose. Fritz Maurer hat damit angefangen. Dazu gibt es eine hübsche Anekdote: Eine Frau konnte auch nach wiederholter Abmahnung das Darlehen nicht zurückzahlen. Damit er keinen Verlust abschreiben musste, und um die Schuldnerin nicht im Stich zu lassen, heiratete er die Frau, zahlte das Darlehen zurück und wurde so zu einem waschechten Bhutaner.

En bref

Voici un compte rendu du succès et de l'échec de quelques projets. Les variétés de pommes de terre "Désirée" et "Maritta" importées de Suisse ont connu un très grand succès, de même que les semences fourragères importées. Un autre succès est le croisement des vaches brunes avec les vaches locales. Par contre, l'importation de chevaux de race Haflinger a été un échec. Les paysans leur préfèrent les mulets dont l'agilité sur les sentiers escarpés est inégalée.
Un succès d'une toute autre nature a été l'introduction de prêts sans intérêt pour des sans-terre. Fritz Maurer (que nous connaissons déjà) en a été l'initiateur. À ce sujet, il y a une jolie anecdote : malgré des efforts répétés, une femme ne parvenait pas à rembourser son crédit. Pour éviter de devoir amortir cette dette, et aussi pour ne pas laisser cette débitrice sur le carreau, il l'épousa, paya lui-même la dette et devint par la même occasion un véritable Bhoutanais.

58

College of Natural Resources, Lobesa / Wangdue

by Dr. Saamdu Chetri, Dy-Resident Co-ordinator Helvetas / SDC, 1988-2006

Message from HRH Ashi S.C Wangchuck, Representative of His Majesty in the Ministry of Agriculture

I am pleased that the Natural Resources Training Institute (NRTI) is being formally inaugurated this year. This is truely a milestone in the history of Bhutan's institutional development. We can henceforth look forward to a steady flow of qualified technicians from NRTI. NRTI graduates will be in the fore-front of rural development initiatives. They will be the most critical link in the chain of implementing development activities at the dzongkhag, gewog and village levels.

I am most confident that the graduates from NRTI will perform their tasks with dedication, integrity and skills. The integrated nature of their courses should enable them to be sensitive to the complex farming systems that prevail In Bhutan. They should be of immense benefit to the farmers who need assistance, guidance and information.

Without the generous assistance of Helvetas and SDC, NRTI would not exist today. I am pleased to acknowledge the invaluable assistance that the Swiss have provided, and are still providing, to develop our critical human resources in the rural sector. I would also like to pay a special tribute to Dr. Martin Menzi and his wife, Kungold Menzi, who contributed selflessly to the establishment of the NRTI.

I wish all the staff and students of NRTI well in their present and future endeavours.

(S.C. Wangchuck)
REPRESENTATIVE OF HIS MAJESTY

Natural Resources Training Institute (NRTI), renamed as College of Natural Resources (CNR) in 2003, was built to house the training for RNR extension agents hand in hand in a co-ordinated and integrated approach in agriculture, animal husbandry and forestry. This new approach, in line with the needs of an equally integrated agriculture, was not well received in all quarters. Yet, the government was committed to begin the approach that was fully supported by the Swiss Cooperation in Bhutan. Efficiently, a number of educated and committed persons were selected and intensively trained in Europe in methodology and curriculum development. The team led by Prof. Dr. Martin Menzi began the curriculum development in 1989. The first batch of extension training programme began in July 1992 in Thimphu and was later shifted to Lobesa, where the main complex was still under construction. The first batch of 65 students finished their studies in July 1995. The complex was officially handed over to the government on 11 November 1995. The complex can house two batches (150 students), while the third batch is at the last stage taking apprenticeship training of six month in the field for practical exercises. So far the institute has trained more than 900 extension agents in three areas of RNR. They are posted in each of the 205 Gewogs (commune) in three fields; livestock, agriculture, and forestry.

CNR was one of the first institutions in the country with a good proportion of professional faculty members. Because of this fact the diversification of activities could took place. In 1999, they began the professional services in research, facilitation and training under the renewable natural resources sector. Simultaneously, it became very essential to upgrade the knowledge and skills of extension staff through in-service trainings, due to the changing needs and improving farming technologies through research and modernisation. In the third area, they were requested by Helvetas to provide Farm Business Training to farming youth wishing to take up on - and off -farm business in poultry, vegetable growing, mushroom farming, piggery etc. The Swiss assistance envisaged different institutions at a later stage to provide training to young Bhutanese who were interested to go back to farming.

Today the CNR is well equipped institutionally, with knowledge management assisted by library systems, computer laboratory, internet and local area networking facilities, with research collaboration and external networking with other institutions and with renewable natural resources sectors.

With the changing education system and raising the basic education level to class ten, it became essential to raise the level of entry to extension diploma to class 12. As a result, the duration of diploma training was reduced from three years to two years. It is not sure whether reduction of field attachment from ten to two months would benefit the long-term sustainability of the diploma system at all. However, with changing times and increasing demands, the diversification of the Natural Resources College mandate is inevitable.

In many ways, the RNR concept in Bhutan is unique in the world with renewable natural resources institute and now college, matrix research system centres, Gewog extension centres, etc. and thus it becomes very important to have a comprehensive in-country training strategy for RNR staff. This is very crucial in future. Prof. Dr. Martin Menzi writes in his final report in 1994, "the stage is set for making a relevant and lasting contribution to sustainable rural development – but the high objectives and expectations remain a permanent challenge! Form, content and variety of training programme have to be improved, adapted and up-dated continuously. The concept of professional, dynamic and effective training and service institution calls for a high level of efficiency, flexibility and motivation. It implies organisational structures and administrative mechanisms which can be attained only under a management with high degree of autonomy, professional competence and distinguished sense of commitment and responsibility."

NRTI winning an award EXPO 2000 Hannover

The Natural Resources Training Institute (NRTI), now College of Natural Resources at Lobesa, has been selected as a special project in the fields "Natural Resources, Knowledge, Information and Communication" by EXPO 2000 Hannover in Germany.

59

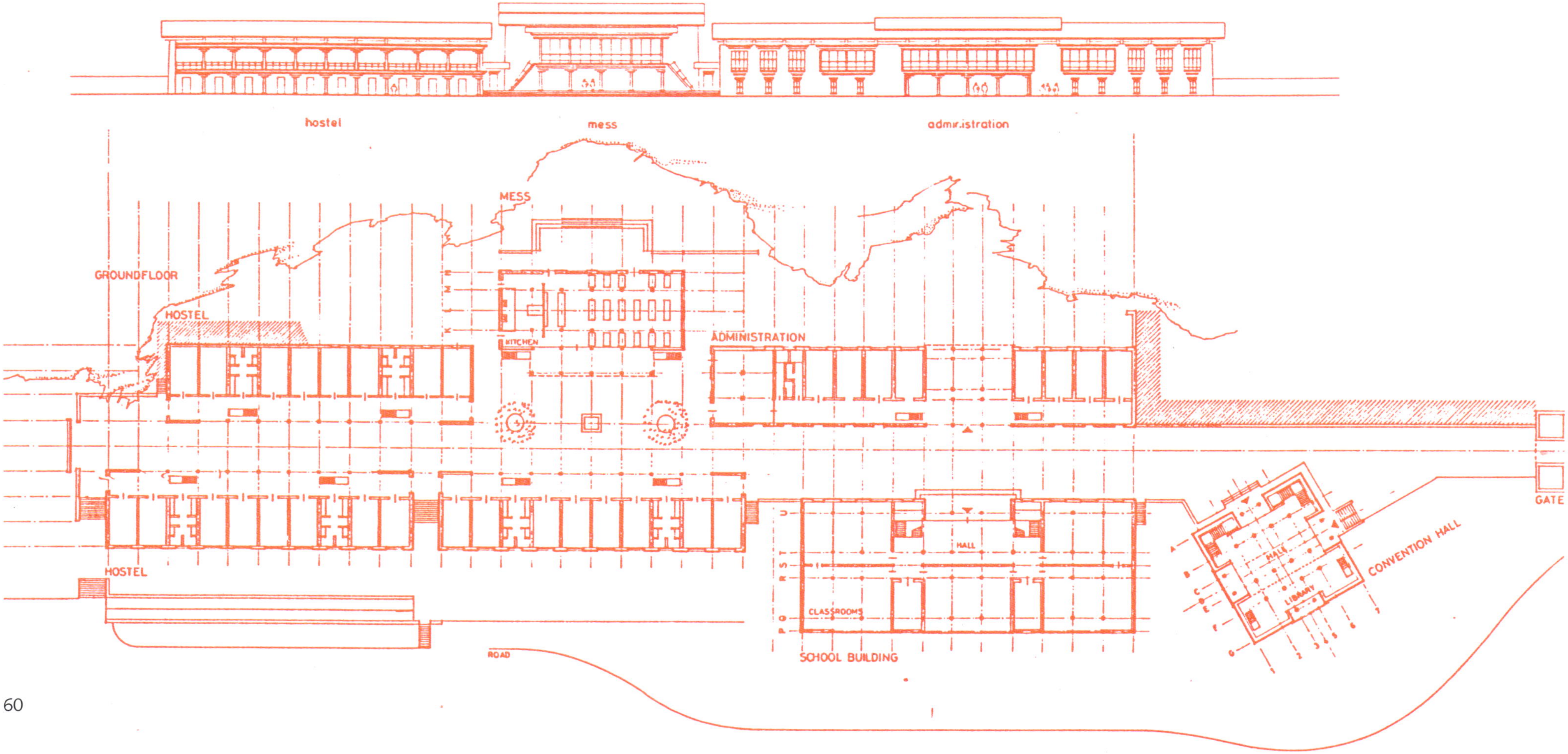
hostel
mess
administration
GROUNDFLOOR
MESS
HOSTEL
KITCHEN
ADMINISTRATION
HOSTEL
GATE
CONVENTION HALL
HALL
LIBRARY
CLASSROOMS
SCHOOL BUILDING
ROAD

60

61

The architectural project planning was a massive task, undertaken by the Swiss architects Felix Sigrist, Ueli Ruegg and Daniel Schwitter within a few months only. Some experience gained from the Bumthang hospital construction was very useful in terms of management and contractors.

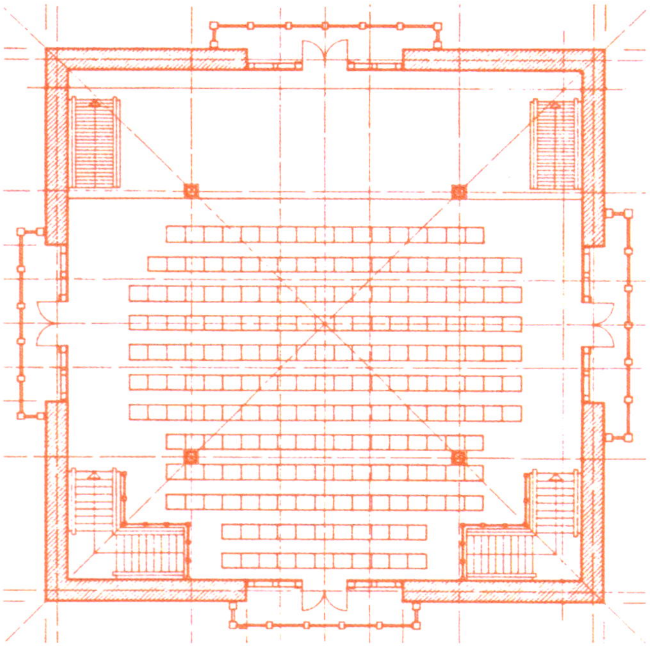

62 Convention hall

63

Cubes, inside and outside spaces

The special feature of the entire construction is the concise organization of different buildings and outdoor spaces. Ancient Dzongs are not only models for construction, materials and colours, their quality lies especially in the use of space. The various buildings surrounding courtyards in the monasteries of Thimphu, Tongsa, Paro or Punakka are no doubt of unique quality. The discussion of open spaces developed into the central theme of the NRTI project. The central passage connects the different buildings. Several entryways to hostels, student's dining hall, administrative and school buildings are oriented on this axis. At various points, spaces between buildings allow for glimpses of the valley. A central square in front of the students' dining hall resulted by moving it back from the axis. The tower with its convention hall has become the trademark of the school because of its position by the gate, as well as by diagonal arrangement. The construction follows the slope and, with its elongated form, it interacts with the broad valley.

The project was mandated to Helvetas on a turnkey base, the Swiss being fully responsible (project management Daniel Rothacher). Throughout the construction, they kept high vigilance in traditional designs, installation techniques and cost controls. The project provided on-the-job training and capacity development of all staff, technicians, craftsmen, semi-skilled labourers, and maintenance staff. One of the major efforts of the Swiss was to include the concept of maintenance already at the design stage, in particular for the critical sewage, water, electrical systems and water facilities.

64

In Kürze

Im Institut für Natürliche Ressourcen werden Berater in Landwirtschaft, Viehzucht und Forstwirtschaft integral ausgebildet, um dann ihre Landsleute in den Dörfern zu beraten. Seit 2003 gilt dieser integrierte Ansatz, der zu Beginn nicht überall gut aufgenommen wurde. Helvetas unterstützte den Ansatz von Anbeginn, holte motivierte Bhutaner nach Europa zur Ausbildung als Instruktoren. Ein Team unter Martin Menzi begann 1989 mit der Entwicklung der Lehrpläne. 1995 verliessen die ersten 65 Studenten die Ausbildung. Im gleichen Jahr wurde der Neubau an die Regierung übergeben. Bis heute hat das Institut über 900 Berater ausgebildet, Daneben gibt es auch Lehrgänge für junge Leute, die nur im Nebenjob einen Bauernhof betreiben, oder für jene, die nach der Schulzeit wieder zurück in die Landwirtschaft möchten.

En bref

Des agents de vulgarisation en agriculture, élevage et foresterie sont formés à l'institut des ressources naturelles. Ils ont ensuite pour fonction de conseiller leurs compatriotes dans les villages. Cette approche intégrée, en vigueur depuis 2003, n'a pas fait l'unanimité lors de son introduction. Helvetas a soutenu cette approche depuis le début et a sélectionné des Bhoutanais motivés afin qu'ils soient formés en Europe, pour devenir des instructeurs. Une équipe d'entre eux, sous la conduite de Martin Menzi, a démarré l'élaboration de plans d'études en 1989. En 1995, les 65 premiers étudiants ont terminé leurs études. La même année, les bâtiments neufs de l'institut ont été remis au gouvernement. A ce jour, l'institut a formé quelques 900 agents de vulgarisation. Il y a par ailleurs des formations destinées à des jeunes souhaitant être agriculteurs à temps par-

About respecting Bhutanese architecture

by Daniel Schwitter, Architect, Project Manager Bumthang hospital and NRTI construction

65

66

67

68

69

70

The most important buildings that Helvetas initiated in Bhutan date back to the years between 1987 (Bumthang Hospital) and 2000 (Paro Teacher Training Center). Thanks to the technical know-how of the local small trade, the high level of Bhutanese building culture, and the people's strong feelings with respect to tradition in general, it was possible to construct all these buildings in the traditional Bhutanese style. Its two most salient characteristics are „timelessness" and „spirituality". This archaic style has been reigning in Bhutan for the past 1500 years. It has steadily adapted, in a very smart manner, to the given basic facts such as materials, climate, technology, and social behaviour. In spite of this, or perhaps thanks to this strategy, this very particular style has lost nothing of its unique appeal. As a matter of fact, neither the style itself nor the technology have changed during all these centuries, they were simply optimized on a continuous basis (the importance of this fact may be fully understood when comparing the situation in Central Europe where a number of very different styles alternated in the course of the past 1500 years). A strong affinity to religion has an influence on each young Bhutanese's life and therefore also on the building culture. Individual aesthetic preferences follow behind the much more important values, which are expression, didactical value, and traditional craft. Real masters try to imitate in the best possible way. Craftsmen aim to have each detail correlated to a symbolic and ritual background. My frequently asked question:" Why all this?" has never been answered to my satisfaction. Buildings are built like this, because it has always been done so since time immemorial, and because experience has proven positive.

The term "architect" does not exist in the traditional Bhutanese building culture. A carpenter from within the family or the neighbourhood does the work of individual house building. He is the construction manager. The term „master builder" is used with secular and public buildings, quite similar to ancient times in Europe. These master builders are responsible for everything that is necessary to construct a building. There are no experts for design, static works, construction, management, etc. The architects of Helvetas had to take over such tasks, at least at the beginning when the first big constructions were realized. Due to poor communication, it was not possible to obtain good advice by experts within a reasonable lapse of time. Therefore, the Helvetas architect in-charge had to take over the interesting but demanding role of "master-builder".

It was a real challenge to the many Swiss architects who had been working in Bhutan, to satisfy the needs of modern times such as hygiene, comfort, space, and light, etc. on the one hand, and to respect at the same time traditional values like spirituality, ambiance, and specific technology of the traditional Bhutanese building style, on the other. They risked drifting either into "adapted Kitsch" or „rational modernity", thus failing to produce a balanced solution. The "Swiss Dzongs" in Bumthang, Lobesa, Paro, etc, as the locals call them, are the result of a successful merger of both the traditional and the modern styles. They can be taken as an example for sustainable development that combines excellent Swiss quality and western technology with the charming traditional Bhutanese handicraft.

In Kürze

Der archaische Baustil ist seit 1500 Jahren der gleiche geblieben. Es gibt in Bhutan keine Architekten, der Zimmermann ist der Baumeister. Es war eine grosse Herausforderung für die Architekten von Helvetas bei ihren grösseren Bauten die Anforderungen an Hygiene, Platz und Licht mit den traditionellen Ansprüchen an Atmosphäre und Spiritualität zu verbinden. Die Akzeptanz der Bauten bei der Bevölkerung ist der Beweis dafür, dass der Spagat zwischen Tradition und Moderne gelungen ist.

En bref

Le style de construction archaïque est resté inchangé depuis 1500. Au Bhoutan, il n'y a pas d'architectes, le charpentier est le maître d'ouvrage. Pour les architectes d'Helvetas, la prise en compte des critères modernes en matière d'hygiène, de place et de lumière tout en respectant les exigences traditionnelles d'ambiance et de spiritualité, ont constitué un grand défi. Le fait que ces constructions nouvelles sont bien acceptées par la population démontre que le grand écart entre tradition et modernité a été un succès.

RNR research systems

by Dr. Saamdu Chetri, Dy-Resident Co-ordinator Helvetas / SDC, 1988-2006

Research in Bhutan was not structured, but was applied at different times for different reasons. In the mid 1990', the necessity for an organised RNR Research System was felt. A planning team led by Prof. Dr. Martin Menzi came up with the concept of RNR matrix for research strategy (subject matter X regional needs). In order to diversify agricultural production, enhance productivity and improve household economy on a sustainable basis, four research centres, each with different national and regional mandates, have been established in Bhutan. All the centres contribute to the national food security.

Adaptive research

In order to undertake adaptive research, identify and package relevant technologies and to generate information, all four centres bank on: a) intensification, diversification and increasing the production and productivity of the farm, b) increasing the role of livestock in the household economy, nutrition and farm productivity, c) enhance the productive and regenerative capacity of the forest resources, d) investigate on the social, economic and institutional factors that are basic to and impede the development of the RNR sector for ensuring the sustainable production and income generating activities, e) adapt the process and methodologies for community based natural resources management, fostering participator approaches in development, and f) provide technical support to the Dzongkhags' RNR sector and other related programmes.

With the achievement of a substantial investment in capacity building through HRD and training, it is expected that the research qualities of the four centres will be further improved. The expertise achieved will allow specialised research in relevant areas. There is now more confidence in the staff, which will further enhance the research quality on a regional level.
Helvetas/SDC supported two of the four research centres: Jakar east central region (Bumthang, Trongsa, Zhemgang, and Sarpang) with the national livestock research mandate starting in 1995 and Yusipang western region (Thimphu, Paro, Haa, Chukha, and Samtse) with the national forestry research mandate starting in 1996. The support was extended in the late 1990's to the other two research centres as well, Bajo west central region (Gasa, Punakha, Wangdi, Tsirang, and Dagana) with national field crop mandate and Wengkhor eastern region (Monggar, Lhuntse, Trashigang, Tashiyangtse, Pemagatsel, Samdrup Jongkhar) with national horticulture mandate.
For almost a decade only Swiss assistance was visible in the RNR sector. It might be reasonable to note the achievement of each centre in the last decade here.

Research Centre Yusipang

The western region with the forestry research as national mandate, has the objective to contribute to enhancing productive and regenerative capacity of the forest resources safeguarding against any degradation of forest and water resources and most importantly the loss of biodiversity. Ensuring environmental sustainability is a Millenium Development Goal, which has a high priority in Bhutan, being one of the ten hotspots in the world.
Forestry research did not always follow a stringent plan, but was often tempted to incorporate new ideas of donor-driven programmes, oblivious to whatever had already been established. Often, old long-term activities were sacrificed to new ones, which undermined the success of any programme. To strengthen the research in forestry, a sub station was built at Dala and became functional in 2002 to address the research needs and capacities in the broadleaf forests.

Research Centre Bajo

The west central region with a national mandate of research in field crops, is foreseen to co-ordinate the research on rice, maize, wheat, other minor cereals, oilseeds and grain legumes. The research thrust on field crops are: to continue to introduce, identify and breed for better crop varieties resistant to major diseases and pests; to contribute to develop improved production management practices through weed, nutrition and water management; to continue to collect and maintain local germplasm for future use and to maintain and adequately supply the breeder seeds to growers.

Research Centre Jakar

Research Centre Jakar caters for the research needs of east central region. Its national mandate is to coordinate the livestock research and development with the main objective to improve the household economy and the nutrition of rural and urban population. This mainly by increasing the farm productivity, lessening the grazing pressure on forests through improved livestock breed, feed and fodder availability, and maintenance of livestock health. The centre started as the first one offering research planning workshops, both focussing on its national mandate and on regional review and planning.

Research Centre Whengkhor

Research Centre Whengkhor, covering the eastern region, has the horticulture national mandate. The centre's objective is to contribute to agricultural and horticultural diversification, so that household food security, income and employment potential of small farm agriculture is enhanced through sound conservation and development of economically and ecologically sustainable farming practices. Its regional mandate is to act as a focal centre and test locations for the six eastern Dzongkhags for various commodities and disciplines that actually fall under its jurisdiction and actively collaborate with other regional research centres. Apart from its national mandate it is also the focal point for maize and legumes, pig and poultry research, non-timber forest product and water management research.

In Kürze

Bhutan hat eine weitgehend intakte Umwelt. Wälder bedecken zu 70 Prozent die Landfläche. Die Verfassung schreibt vor, dass der Anteil nicht unter 60 Prozent fallen darf. Zum Schutz dieses natürlichen Reichtums hat ein Team unter der Leitung von Martin Menzi in den 90-er Jahren ein strukturiertes Forschungsprojekt für eine nachhaltige Nutzung der natürlichen Ressourcen ins Leben gerufen. Ziel war und ist eine vielfältigere landwirtschaftliche Produktion, eine Steigerung der Erträge und damit verbunden eine Zunahme der Haushaltseinkommen. Und das alles bei möglichst schonendem Umgang mit der Natur.

En bref

L'environnement du Bhoutan est encore intact. Les forêts couvrent 70 pour-cent du territoire. La Constitution prescrit que la part des forêts ne doit pas être inférieure à 60 pour-cent. Pour protéger ces richesses, une équipe de chercheurs, sous la conduite de Martin Menzi, a réalisé un projet de recherche sur la gestion durable des ressources naturelles dans les années 90. L'objectif consistait à développer une agriculture diversifiée, productive et durable permettant aux ménages ruraux d'en tirer un revenu croissant tout en préservant les ressources naturelles.

71 Cattle show

RNR Research Centre, Jakar

by Dr. Saamdu Chetri, Dy-Resident Co-ordinator Helvetas / SDC, 1988-2006

72 Perspectives

The Renewable Natural Resources Research Centre (RNR-RC) in the east central region rests on a spur that has a commanding view over the Bumthang valley.

During the planning and execution of these buildings, several considerations were kept in mind: respect for the Bhutanese architecture as being the main tradition; site with low utility for agriculture; use of local materials and skills; including modern planning and construction technology for utility; quality; and solidity. The traditional buildings concept included functional modern amenities (including the heating system) that can be easily maintained with special attention to the design and installation of electricity and sanitary. The construction cost stood at about Nu 60 millions.
In 1996, a historic regional agriculture centre at Bhur, Gelephu, was taken up as the RNR-Research sub-station. Offices, laboratories, stores, machinery sheds, staff quarters, fencing, irrigation facilities, roads and a lot of other infrastructure were built.

Special reporting on Jakar Research Centre:
A usual dome structure was discovered during the excavation of the foundation, 1.5 meters deep. After consultation with the National Commission for Cultural Affairs, the site was protected. An archaeological team from Swiss-Liechtenstein Foundation for Archaeological Research was invited to investigate the structures. The carbon dating on the implementations indicated late 8th century habitation. There was yet another site that had been built during the second half of the 16th century. On the royal command the latter was abandoned and the site was used for construction, while the former site has been preserved. The objects recovered were fragmented millstone, wood/shingle, metaphoric rocks, oxidised pottery in red-orange colour, oxidised iron pieces, vegetal string fragments, and mineral fragments.

Yusipang, about 10 kilometres from Thimphu to the east, is the RNR-RC for the western region. It has a long history of affiliation with the Swiss cooperation. In 1983, when the potato programme was to begin, this place was chosen as the site of the office of the Bhutan National Potato Programme and a few small offices, research laboratories and few staff quarters had been built. The place had served as the tissue culture centre for the potato research programme. In 1996, Yusipang became the research centre for the western region for forestry and the co-ordination body at the national level. This centre has also been declared as the centre for organic produce outlet. The Swiss agreed to build two buildings for administration with 14 rooms, staff quarters for 40 people, and research with 7 rooms. The construction of buildings and roads and an expansion renovation of the centre were done at a cost of Nu 2 million. The centre covers and area of 120 acres. As every centre was required to have a sub-station, the western region identified Dala as its centre for a broad leaf forest research.

The RNR-RC eastern region, situated in Whengkhor, Mongar, was appointed as the horticulture research station. It was ultimately built with funds from Japan and the International Fund for Agriculture Development, which both contributed over Nu 110 million. The Swiss, at the same time, built the staff quarters.

In Kürze

Der Fokus der schweizerischen Zusammenarbeit mit Bhutan war immer auf die Entwicklung der Landwirtschaft und der Forstwirtschaft gerichtet. Dazu gehörte auch die nötige Infrastruktur: Mit Schul- und Verwaltungsbauten, mit Forschungseinrichtungen im Bumthang Tal wie auch im Westen und im Osten des Landes. Die Projekte waren darauf ausgerichtet, einen möglichst direkten Nutzen für die Bevölkerung abzuwerfen. In Zhemgang zum Beispiel wurde eine Markthalle errichtet, in der die Bauern aus den umliegenden Tälern ihre Produkte verkaufen können. So haben die Bauern ein Einkommen, und die Versorgung der Stadt mit Frischprodukten, die zuvor im Argen lag, hat sich stark verbessert.

En bref

La coopération suisse avec le Bhoutan s'est toujours concentrée sur le développement de l'agriculture et de la foresterie, ainsi que l'infrastructure liée à ces secteurs : écoles et bâtiments administratifs, installations de recherche à Bumthang, ainsi qu'à l'Est et à l'Ouest du pays. Les projets étaient conçus de telle sorte que la population puisse si possible en tirer un bénéfice direct. À Zhemgang, par exemple, une halle de marché a été construite. Dans cette halle, les paysans des vallées avoisinantes peuvent vendre leurs produits. Ainsi les paysans peuvent améliorer leur revenu tout en assurant un meilleur approvisionnement de la ville en produits frais.

Rural Development Training Centre, Zhemgang

by Dr. Saamdu Chetri, Dy-Resident Co-ordinator Helvetas / SDC, 1988-2006

The Rural Development Training Centre in Zhemgang caters to the needs of the decentralised trainings in farming business and creates rural opportunities for income generation and employment. The project office has been built overlooking the Zhemgang Dzong. The complex is developed over an area of 65,000 square feet, the centre covers 16 acres. The infrastructure building included roads, administrative and school buildings, and the poultry, piggery and machinery workshop. Not to forget the hostel complex for trainees and staff.

The East Central Region-Agriculture Development Project has provided different infrastructures to the region. Today, a market shed constructed in Zhemgang facilitates access to market. Farmers can thus sell their agricultural produce, boosting not only their agricultural production but also cash income of the rural households. It has helped in overcoming the shortages of vegetables in the town. Another achievement is the construction of over 50 kilometres of farm road under different gewogs in the east central regions; it is expected to contribute substantially to the rural farmers in terms of their accessibility, production and access to markets.

73

Swiss Potato and its impact on poverty alleviation

by Dr. Saamdu Chetri, Dy-Resident Co-ordinator Helvetas / SDC, 1988-2006

74

Potato first came to Bhutan in the 17th century when George Bogle, the team leader of the British Mission, brought it with him. It is believed that during his travel from present day Pasakha to Thimphu, he gave a handful of potato seeds to the farmers of Chapcha, the first high altitude area appropriate for potato cultivation on his route of travel. This is the first written account of introduction of potato to Bhutan and the historical perspective on how the potato came to Bhutan from Europe. Obviously, potato did not become a household name at that time, as there is no written information.

However, another introduction of potato in Bhutan started some three hundred years later, in the 1970's. A handful of potato seeds was sent by Fritz von Schulthess through a traveller to grow in Bhutan. His guess that those potatoes would do well in the alpine conditions of Bhutan proved correct. This prompted Fritz Maurer to bring 400 kg of four wart-resistant varieties to plant them in wart-infested fields in Gogona. The harvest from Gogona was excellent. This was the beginning of commercial production of potatoes in Bhutan.

At present, Swiss potatoes are household names in all potato growing areas of Bhutan. Potato, being a high altitude crop, is grown in subalpine and alpine areas of Bhutan. Though Bhutanese do not consume potato as much as the Europeans do, potato curry known as "kewa datshi" (potatoes with cheese) features in Bhutanese diet quite often. But, besides potato appearing as an occasional menu, it is a cash crop for the Bhutanese farmers. It is an important export item from Bhutan, both for the table and as seeds. India is the sole market for the Bhutanese potato. The annual export revenue in 2005 was Nu. 182.50 million (FCB), earning much needed cash for the farmers. Though there is fluctuation in production from year to year, there is an increasing trend, both in terms of quantity and export revenue.

The subalpine and alpine areas of Bhutan produce potato of high quality for the table. In addition, these places being in high and pristine areas, seeds are free of diseases. Therefore, the potato from Bhutan finds ready markets in India and fetches a good price. Phobjikha and Bumthang valleys are the major suppliers of potatoes to the export markets. The economy of these places has transformed from a subsistence mixed farming to potato dominated cash economy. Potato has brought a sustained stability to the livelihood of the people where no other cash crop can grow. Potato has given opportunity to poorer people to improve their living standards.

During a micro credit review in a few Dzongkhags, it was found that potato was the major cash crop and farmers invested their borrowings in potato farming, indicating the farmers' confidence to invest in potato. Potato growing farmers are slowly undergoing a change in their lifestyles. They build better houses to live in, send their children to schools and enjoy better nutritional intake. These changes have been made possible through cash income from potato. Therefore, potato is playing a significant role in alleviating poverty in rural Bhutan. With the present trend in development, potato has the potential to further contribute in reducing poverty in rural areas where potato has a comparative advantage.

In Kürze

Fritz von Schulthess hat die ersten Saatkartoffeln nach Bhutan gebracht in der Annahme, dass sie in dem alpinen Klima ebenso gut gedeihen würden, wie in der Schweiz. Ob er geahnt hat, dass die Kartoffel zur besten Waffe im Kampf gegen die Armut werden würde? Die Kartoffel hat nicht nur den Speiseplan der selbstversorgenden Bauern bereichert, sie gedeiht so gut, dass sie im Überfluss geerntet und exportiert werden kann. Die Kartoffel ist die einzige Frucht, die in Mengen exportiert wird, mit der die Bauern zu Bargeld kommen. Die immer weitere Verbreitung der Kartoffel, das Wachsen der Ernten, drängt die Armut zurück. Die Leute bauen bessere Häuser, können es sich leisten, die Kinder zur Schule zu schicken.

En bref

Fritz von Schulthess a importé les premières semences de pommes de terre au Bhoutan, supposant qu'elles pousseraient aussi bien dans ce climat de type alpin qu'en Suisse. Mais se doutait-il que la pomme de terre deviendrait le meilleur moyen de lutte contre la pauvreté? La pomme de terre n'a pas seulement amélioré l'alimentation des Bhoutanais. Cette culture pousse si bien au Bhoutan qu'elle est également exportée en grandes quantités, offrant ainsi une source de revenu monétaire aux paysans. L'expansion de la culture de la pomme de terre et l'augmentation de la production fait reculer la pauvreté. Les gens construisent de plus belles maisons et peuvent envoyer leurs enfants à l'école.

75

Once upon a time a humble potato tuber...

by Erwin Koenig, former Co-manager BNPP, former Resident Co-ordinator Helvetas/SDC, written in the "International Year of the Potato"

Did you know?

- Potato produces more food per unit area and time than cereals.Potato requires 800-1000 kg of seed tubers per acre (rice 30 kg).In Bhutan potato thrives from the plains to heights of 4'500m.The potato cash crop belt is located in the elevation range of 1600-3200m.
- Since 1970 potato consumption grew by a factor 10, to reach 40 kg/person in 2006. Since 1975, potato production grew by a factor 5 and broke the limit of 60'000 t. in 2005. Over the same time export grew from about 3'000 to 22'000 t.
- Bhutan's favorite potato dish is Kewa Datshi.Most common varieties are Desiree, Kufri Jyoti and Yusikap.

Arrival and adoption of the potato

The potato following the Himalayan trade routes might have reached the region of today's Bhutan as early as the late 1600's or as late as 1775 (Georges Bogle). Until the 1900's information on the adoption and use of potato remains scant. In any event, the potato graduated from a kitchen garden crop to a cash crop with the construction of the first roads in the 1960's. Thereafter the farmers rapidly capitalized on the opportunities offered by road access to Indian markets. First government sponsored interventions were initiated in 1973 when the Food Corporation of Bhutan (FCB) started buying potato from the farmers for export. By 1974, the area of production had increased dramatically, but the yields remained low and time had come to gradually replace the degenerated local varieties by modern ones.

Early developments

On a very pragmatic base, the Department of Agriculture (DoA) and the Swiss Technical Assistance imported 4 new varieties from India and Europe. In the early 80's healthy seeds were produced on three government farms and also with farmers in the districts of Paro, Bumthang, Mongar, Luntshi and Trashigang. If a seed had been launched, no institution had yet assumed complete responsibility for managing research and national distribution of improved seeds. This situation defined the framework for a National Potato Programme. In 1983 the Bhutan National Potato Programme (BNPP) was launched with financial and technical assistance from Helvetas/SDC.

The cash crop era

A solid start: The participation of the Swiss Potato Programme/Nepal in the planning of BNPP allowed solid experience and best practices to flow into the project. Prior to the launch of BNPP, CIP had researched key aspects of the marketing of potato, initiated applied research and built up an initial stock of healthy potato seeds. This preparatory work allowed BNPP to concentrate on training the extension service, select and intensively train the registered seed growers and adequately plan its first seed multiplication and seed distribution campaigns.

Development driven by interest and will: Bhutan's healthy working environment with dedicated civil servants and virtually no corruption was decisive in the development of BNPP and its sustainability over time. Throughout the potato belt, the district agricultural offices played a key role in the introduction and adoption, by the farmers, of the new varieties. Training on specific cultural practices, conducted by a dedicated extension service, also equipped the farmers with the necessary skills to exploit at best the yielding potential of the new varieties. Last but not least, the capacity of the DOA to discuss, and endorse plans and proposals was critical to efficient and timely work. I think all of us just wanted this project to work.

Listening to the farmers: During the seasonal training sessions the farmers were encouraged to share problems and best practices. This approach brought along rapid progress in labour saving cultural practices and technical improvements of locally developed "earthing and digging" implements pulled by draft animal.

The key role of FCB's auction-yards: The opening of auction-yards (1982) in Phuntsholing and Samdrup-Jongkhar has been instrumental to the development and marketing of the potato crop. They handle about 90% of the export and the potato producers appreciate the system because of the prevailing transparency, the access to a pool of traders and assured payments. For ages, the auction-yards begged the farmers to grade their potato and not to rush all together to the auction yards without success. The battle was finally won in 2005, when FCB announced separate auctions for small and large sized tubers and started to regulate the quantities to be auctioned daily, so that supply does not overtake demand and negatively affects pricing.

Potato brings changes in production systems and comfort: In the 1980's, potato was for many farmers the only source of cash income. Overtime, the potato cash crop became the main force driving the change from subsistence to market-oriented agriculture. Regular rural income generated by potato cultivation impacts positively on poverty alleviation and quality of life. More recently, rural to urban migration and high rates of urbanization are emerging as major problems in Bhutan. The combination of road access and potato cultivation certainly slows down the progressing rural-urban migration. Many potato farmers admit that "without potato they would have to seek off-farm employment in larger townships".

Challenges and open questions

By 1989, BNPP could present very encouraging results. In amazingly short time, an important research activity and a relevant production of potato seed had been established, while the main focus was put on marketing and on training and advising at all levels (Joint RGOB/Helvetas mission 1989). However the 1990's proved more difficult. The political turmoil and rebel problems along the Assamese hampered the potato export in Samdrup-Jongkhar. The introduction, by the Ministry of Agriculture, of cash payment for all inputs by the Dzonkhags lead to a sharp drop in the demands. BNPP fell in a very critical position when the already produced seeds lied unsold in the stores (Annual report 92). In 1993, a self-evaluation recommended to adjust the seed production to the new realities and consider informal seed production with self-reliant Seed Potato Growers Groups (SPGG). These groups were initiated in 1994 in Trashigang and taken over by Druk Seed Corporation (DSC) in 1995/96 while BNPP's research, training and marketing activities were split among the concerned departments of the recently reorganized DOA. Out of 123 seed groups formed 63 remained in 2004. Their average seed production is 500 tons per year. One of the major problems encountered by SPGGs is that the demand for seed potatoes from various Dzongkhags, often arrived late, leaving very limited room for the groups to plan their production and marketing activities. The question which arises is the following: Could the SPGGs have become the backbone of today's seed production, if their set up had been started earlier in time? Or had their self-reliance and economic viability been better if they had been mandated to produce seed for domestic and export demands? In 2006 the Bhutan Potato Development Programme sponsored by the International Potato Centre and the Common Fund for Commodities was launched to specifically look into the validation and dissemination of seed production models. Maybe the SPGGs will be given another chance, if their organisational and managerial skills are strengthened.

tumbled wealth upon humble households

Back to the future

In the years to come, potato production is expected to continue to grow, driven by Bhutan's growing urban population and India's demands for offseason fresh potato. Further expansion of farm roads and better access to rural credit may set the yearly production increase at 7-10%. In addition there are good prospects for exporting quality seeds to India and Bangladesh, if the dormancy related problems can be resolved. Finally, it is expected that farms which relay too heavily on potato production, may respond to increasing urban demands for dairy products. As potato and livestock complement each other well, the risks linked with a renewed tend towards cash crop monoculture may lessen.

In Kürze

Eine gesunde Arbeitsmoral, engagierte Beamte und das Fehlen von Korruption haben das im Jahre 1983 gestartete Nationale Kartoffelprogramm zum Erfolg gemacht. Die Bauern wurden ermuntert, ihre Erfahrungen auszutauschen, regionale Auktionen garantierten die Abnahme von Ernten und erleichterten den Export. Der erfolgreiche Kartoffelanbau hat massgeblich dazu geführt, dass sich Bhutans Landwirtschaft von der Subsistenz- zur Marktwirtschaft entwickelt hat. Ein regelmässiges Einkommen hat erheblichen Einfluss auf die Lebensqualität der Landbevölkerung. Auch könnten die Bauern, die einseitig auf die Kartoffeln setzen, in die Milchwirtschaft diversifizieren, weil die Nachfrage nach Milchprodukten aus den urbanen Zentren rasch ansteigt.

En bref

Le programme national de la pomme de terre, qui a démarré en 1983, a été un succès en particulier grâce à l'engagement dévoué des collaborateurs, à l'absence de corruption et à une morale de travail irréprochable. Les paysans ont été encouragés à échanger leurs expériences, les ventes aux enchères régionales ont assuré l'écoulement des récoltes et facilité l'exportation. Le succès de la culture des pommes de terre a favorisé la transition de l'agriculture bhoutanaise de la subsistance vers l'économie de marché. Un revenu monétaire régulier influe significativement sur la qualité de vie de la population rurale. Les paysans qui se sont spécialisés dans la culture de la pomme de terre ont la possibilité de diversifier leur production en s'engageant dans la production laitière, répondant ainsi à une demande croissante des marchés urbains.

76

Rural development training

by Dr. Saamdu Chetri, Dy-Resident Co-ordinator Helvetas / SDC, 1988-2006

The basically free education rose to tenth standard class and the policy of the government to encourage every child to attend school has led to a very high enrolment level in the schools. Consequently, the need for additional training facilities in various field increased to provide employment opportunities to many more youth, either passing school or dropping out early for family and personal reasons. Until now, the government stands as the single largest employer and the private sector is just developing. There are limited opportunities for school leavers to be employed in either of the sectors. Today the jobs in the modern sector require specialised skills and knowledge, which is not provided at school. Due to the opportunities of employment, there is annually 1.3 percent of rural-urban migration. The agriculture sector, which consists of 75 percent of Bhutanese workforce, is being slowly drained leaving behind the sick and the old. It is a serious and growing threat to the achievement of self-reliance and food security. Therefore, in agreement with the royal government, the Swiss decided to develop a programme to operate under the decentralised concept of the Rural Development Training (RDT) project at Zhemgang.

Its aim is 'to work towards providing and enabling environment for rural employment with the ultimate goal of enhancing rural livelihood through an increased social and economic security.'

The main objectives of the RDT are: a) to enhance skills and knowledge on agriculture production and rural development, b) to contribute towards creation of employment and income opportunities, c) to support market-oriented farming through appropriate production methodologies, and d) to support institutional strengthening of producers' group (e.g. cooperatives and associations).

The outputs will be achieved through a decentralized, practical and theoretical, multi-disciplinary training at various levels, depending on the need of the existing target groups (young school leavers, farmers and community leaders). A coordination centre for all these activities exists in Zhemgang town. Without losing time, the project began to address one of its components through the facilities of the College of Natural Resources at Lobesa to provide on-and off-farm training for income generating activities; poultry, piggery, mushroom and vegetable production, etc. When the project agreement was signed in autumn 2003, the project began its temporary office at Lobesa from where they began to recruit and train the faculty members. Simultaneously, the infrastructure development at Zhemgang was contracted and the curriculum development and demand-based decentralised training began to be organised in the fields. RDT is now functioning from Zhemgang complex, which is another landmark of Bhutan-Swiss cooperation.

The training programme will consist of: a) an agricultural apprenticeship, complemented with basic theoretical and practical training (mainly for early school leavers), b) farm business training for farmers, providing in-depth practical and theoretical knowledge about subjects with economic potential, c) training in rural development support services, e.g. how to organise producer groups.

The future challenges for RDT will consist in meeting the increasing demand for training with decentralised training concept, building a pool of certified trainers, using available information and data bases to inform the farmers about the recent trends and future perspectives, providing training on specific crops and livestock production technologies for sustainable and improved production from a centrally and easily reachable site, networking the farmers and farmers groups from different geographical regions and farming enterprises to share and learn from their experiences, facilitating the collaboration of farmers to work together as groups leading to larger groups to benefit from the economy of scale and the strength of groups, and creating opportunities for the youth to discover the potential of agriculture as a source of livelihood and systematic presence in media with positive examples of agriculture as source of income and livelihood.

77

In Kürze

Immer mehr und besser ausgebildete Schulabgänger, das verlangt nach immer mehr Arbeitsplätzen. Noch ist der Staat der wichtigste Arbeitgeber, die Privatwirtschaft noch unterentwickelt. Die Arbeitsplätze in beiden Sektoren sind viel zu knapp. Auf der anderen Seite droht die Landflucht den Agrarsektor auszubluten, in welchem noch immer 75 Prozent beschäftigt sind. Die Schweizer haben ein Projekt auf die Beine gestellt, mit dem Jugendlichen bessere Perspektiven in der Landwirtschaft geboten werden sollen. Sie werden ausgebildet und unterstützt, damit sie wirtschaftlich erfolgreich Landwirtschaft betreiben, ein Auskommen und soziale Sicherheit finden können.

En bref

Les jeunes en fin de scolarité sont de mieux en mieux formés et toujours plus nombreux, ce qui demande un nombre croissant de places de travail. Aujourd'hui, l'Etat reste le principal employeur, le secteur privé étant peu développé et le nombre d'emplois encore largement insuffisant. D'un autre côté, l'exode rural risque de priver l'agriculture de ses forces vives, un secteur qui occupe encore 75 pour-cent de la population active. Les Suisses ont mis en place un projet dont le but est d'offrir de meilleures perspectives pour les jeunes dans l'agriculture. Ils sont formés et appuyés afin de pouvoir pratiquer l'agriculture avec succès, y trouvant revenu et sécurité sociale.

Journey of a Tangpa

by Tashi Pem, Programme Officer, Helvetas, Thimphu

The landscape in Bhutan holds many secrets. Bumthang in central Bhutan is home to many of them, from divine imprints to concrete traces of our past. The approach to the Tang valley in Bumthang is almost like uncovering a mystery. Past the Flaming Lake, the dirt road meanders through narrow valleys and brief openings. Almost at the base of an imposing glacial mountain is a gentle hillside dotted with modest homes in the midst of pines and fields of barley and wheat. One of these was the home of a boy who went to the Swiss Federal Institute of Technology. In Tang where cattle are a vital part of living, the boy was soon a little herder playing his part in the network of family interdependency. Even as life closely followed in the footsteps of generations before him, important changes were taking place beyond Tang. Bhutan was emerging in the international scene, planned development activities (first five-year plan from 1961) were instituted and modern, western form of education was begun in the 1950's. Not far from this village, a community school was set up. But a pair of helping hands, however small, was too high a price to pay for a modern education. Before long, the advocacy from the government encouraging parents to send children to schools made an impact in Tang. As a few neighbours began sending one or two children to the community school, the little boy's sister also joined that small group. However, a classroom setting proved far less interesting than the freedom of the hill, and she kept away as often as she possibly could. And so the family decided to send the little boy to replace his sister in school.

The Tang valley is the rural and more reclusive counterpart of Chamkhar. Long after Bumthang assumed a diminished role as the seat of political power in Bhutan, Chamkhar continues to be the administrative and urban centre within Bumthang. It was here that the timid little boy from Tang made his first contact with a tall, burly and pleasant Swiss doctor and began his first profession with Helvetas – as a part-time medical kit carrier. Standing next to the doctor one day, a patient was being operated on a lump on his forehead. As the gory side of the profession became apparent, the little boy fainted and came up with a decision - the medical field was definitely not his calling.
From hence began a long list of association with the Swiss. The capacities of these associations changed with time. When the projects initiated and supported by the "Foundation Pro Bhutan" were handed over to Helvetas in 1975, activities in the Renewable Natural Resources sector in Bumthang were integrated into a comprehensive Rural Development Project. It was in this project that the boy from Tang became a research assistant, and later a research officer in the fodder research centre in Bumthang under the guidance and friendship of another tall, hard-working, and welcoming Swiss. Here the task was more than a kit on the back, as he became responsible for starting the first grassland research centre in the country through Swiss assistance.

Over time, from the hillside of Tang to the Canterbury Plains of New Zealand, the man from Tang traversed and learnt and came back in different capacities within the Ministry of Agriculture. It was around this time that he met a stately and diligent Swiss Professor who was to become a mentor, guardian, and host in the commercial and cultural centre of Switzerland. Henceforth, the prospects stretched even further. He headed the planning and policy division of the Ministry of Agriculture – the core of rural development in the country and the major partner of Swiss assistance in Bhutan– and went on to head the Policy and Partnership Development activities and as Senior Natural Resources Policy Specialist in the Nepal-based International Centre for Integrated Mountain Development. After the first important job with a Swiss, the medical kit carrier was the Deputy Resident Coordinator of Helvetas/SDC Coordination Office in Bhutan, working together with the Swiss he had kept in touch with for advice, constant encouragement and discussions for more than a decade. And today it appears that the journey of the Tangpa has only just begun in so many ways, now being the Minister for Agriculture.

78

In Kürze

Ein kleiner Hirtenjunge aus dem Tang Tal erhält die Chance zum Schulbesuch, weil seine ältere Schwester die Schulbank nicht drücken mag. In Chamkhar trifft der aufgeweckte Junge auf einen Schweizer Arzt und wird dessen Gehilfe. Jedoch: er kann kein Blut sehen, wird ohnmächtig und weiss, Medizin ist nicht sein Fach. Aber es war sein erster Job für Helvetas. Und in dieser Organisation machte er rasch Karriere. Er wird an die Eidgenössische Technische Hochschule (ETH) geschickt, durchläuft eine interessante Laufbahn im Ministerium für Landwirtschaft und ist heute Landwirtschaftsminister.

En bref

Un jeune berger de la vallée de Tang a la chance de se rendre à l'école car sa soeur aînée n'aime pas l'école. À Chamkhar, ce jeune homme éveillé rencontre un médecin suisse et devient son assistant. Toutefois il ne supporte pas la vue du sang, perd connaissance et comprend que la médecine n'est pas pour lui. Mais c'est son premier emploi pour Helvetas, une organisation au sein de laquelle il fera carrière. Il fréquente l'école polytechnique fédérale de Zurich (EPFZ) puis il poursuit un itinéraire professionnel intéressant au sein du ministère de l'agriculture. Aujourd'hui il est Ministre de l'agriculture.

Farmers from Pemagatshel and Bumthang in Switzerland

by Rangsime Tsojay, Pemagatshel and Jangchuk Tsheten, Bumthang

79

80

81 Rangsime Tsojay and the Pflugshaupt's

The Society Switzerland-Bhutan organized several trainings of young Bhutanese farmers on Swiss farms. Personal accounts.

My first host family

My host family for two months was Ernst Pflugshaupt and his wife Elisabeth with three children (1st July to 30th August 2006 in Bertschikon). They are a hard working and a happy family. They were so helpful and kind and I enjoyed very much my stay with them. They used to call me Sammy because they could not pronounce my name.They own 50 acres of land, a poultry farm for meat and 30 cows. They do not produce cheese and butter as we do in Bhutan. They sell the milk. The cows are kept clean, fed well and one cow gives 25 litres of milk per day. The milking is done by machine and one person milks 30 cows quickly. From this family I learnt different kinds of working methods such as making hay, grass cutting, weeding, planting, harvesting, packing etc. and also riding a bicycle.

My second host family

My host family for one month was Martin Pfister and his wife Elisabeth with two children (1st to 30th September 2006 in Birkenhof). They are kind and generous. They also have a big farm, 70 acres of land and 70 milk cows. With this family I got the chance to learn how to process different kinds of Swiss cheese and yoghurts in their factory for processing milk products. I enjoyed working with this family and I even had a chance to show them how we process cheese and butter in Bhutan. I had also nice colleagues, Dominik Marconi and Daniel Stahel. We used to joke every time and laugh although we had communication problems. On the last day they even invited me for a drink.

In addition, to the opportunity to learn farming, we got the opportunity to go on cultural, sightseeing and hiking tours. For instance, on 29th July, guided by Erich Oberholzer and Tshering Altherr we went around Zurich which was fascinating for me to see different kinds of transport systems and in the zoo we saw many different animals which I had never seen in my life. On 30th July, Erich Oberholzer took us to the mountains and we saw the way of farming in the Swiss Alps. On 1st August with Erich Oberholzer we went to the Technorama Museum in Winterthur. There we saw different kind of machines that were used about 50 years ago. On 27th August we went with Erich Oberholzer and Kinley Dorji to the village of Marthalen. Erich Oberholzer explained us the history of this village and he showed us the oldest oak forest in Switzerland. We were lucky because Erich Oberholzer is the forestry expert and he explained us a lot about forestry and how the forests are ecologically conserved and used. During our free time, Namgay and we went from time to time to visit Kinley Dorji and his family, because they were living near our place and were kind. They invited us to attend the teachings of Gangtey Trulku Rimpoche in Switzerland. We all went with Gho and Kira.

Our final excursion was on 23rd September to Muri. We were invited together with Kinley Dorji for a barbecue and to see the farm where our collegue Jangchuk Tsheten worked.

I had everything in Switzerland, European farming and Swiss sight seeing, support from Bhutanese friends and blessing from a Rinpoche.

Finally I would like to thank the Swiss-Bhutan Friendship Association for giving me an opportunity to increase my farming knowledge.

I really learnt a lot and I got many new ideas which I can try now on my little farm and moreover I can share these ideas with other farmers to improve farming methods in Bhutan.

Kadrienche La!

82

Swiss kids remember Jangchuk Tsheten

Sari, 5 years old, kindergarten.
Ronja, 8 years old, second school year.
Jan, 10 years old, fifth school year.

Jangchuk Tsheten has been working in summer 2006 with our father, also a farmer. We don't know exactly what they did. But we remember the following events:

Ronja:
Jangchuk was a very good cook. He made small funny looking cakes. But then he added spices. We couldn't belive that Bhutanese kids do like that.

Jan:
He even went to a turkish shop to buy red capsicum and he pretended that it is not at all very hot. But it was very, very, very hot....

Sari:
After dinner I went to sit on his knees. I told stories and he told stories and we both understood each other very well.

Jan: We made together a bow, and he taught me to shoot the arrow.

Ronja:
And he knew a lot of clever tricks with cards. But I forgot his tricks. He should write a book about that.

Sari: He was a very good friend. I have been sitting on his shoulders, mountains up and mountains down. He laughed and I have been singing.

Jan:
Up on the Alps, we have seen marmots. In wintertime they sleep in their holes. In summertime they sit in the sun. If there is a danger, the chief of the family whistles very very loudly and all of them disappear in their holes within seconds.

Which credits should we give to Jangchuk?
Sari: I give him an eighty twenty.
Jan: That does not exist.
Ronja: The best mark is a six.
Sari: Not in the kindergarten. Hundred is the highest mark.
Ronja: No, no, no, it is a six.

There isn't any consensus. It doesn't matter, his score is anyhow much more than six, and this is the best mark you get in Swiss schools...

83

In Kürze

Immer wieder sind junge Bhutaner auch in die Schweiz eingeladen worden, um hier ihr theoretisches und praktisches Wissen zu erweitern. Einer von ihnen aus Pemagathsel erinnert sich an seine Gastfamilien in Bertschikon und in Birkenhof, wo er vieles lernte, was er zuhause an seine Freunde und Nachbarn weiter vermitteln kann. Er hat aber umgekehrt seinen Gastgebern auch demonstriert, wie in Bhutan Käse und Butter gemacht werden. Sein Kollege hatte offensichtlich viel Spass mit den Kindern der Gastfamilien, die ihn mit Bestnoten verabschiedeten..

En bref

De jeunes Bhoutanais sont régulièrement invités en Suisse pour y élargir leurs connaissances théoriques et pratiques. L'un d'entre eux, originaire de Pemagathsel, se souvient de sa famille d'accueil à Bertschikon et à Birkenhof, où il a appris un grand nombre de connaissances qu'il a pu transmettre à ses voisins et amis. De son côté, il a pu montrer à ses hôtes comment on fabrique le fromage et le beurre au Bhoutan. Son collègue a eu visiblement beaucoup de plaisir avec les enfants de la famille d'accueil, qui ont dû le laisser partir avec regrets.

Forestry

BHUTAN:
The importance of the forests for a continous development of human ecology in high mountain conditions

by F. Fischer
Institute of Sylviculture,
Swiss Federal Institute of Technology
Zurich, Switzerland
1971/1976

The author, on the basis of his impressions, observations and investigations concerning the country's northwest, considers the present state of the forests to be extremely precarious.

Continuation of deforestation at the present speed would result in the country's widespread destruction within 50-100 years.

Forest development

by Lyonpo Chenkyab Dorji, former Minister of Planning; Secretary General, South Asian Association for Regional Cooperation

I was the first Bhutanese to be trained as a forester. After graduating from Dheradhun (India) I went to Zurich (Switzerland) to study forestry management at the ETH in 1967. It was not easy to start the Department of Forest in Bhutan, because people were not aware of the conservation aspect. We were also lacking both the legislation as well as the working procedures. So the Forest Act was passed in 1969, which was followed by the forestry policy in 1974. These were two basic documents on which we tried to manage our most valuable asset.

Bhutan being in the heart of the Himalayas with its very fragile eco-system, maintaining the forest in a very healthy condition is very important for our survival. Over the years we have been able to establish a system with various specialized fields. Nevertheless, while we have achieved a good success in the form of regenerating through natural process, educating our people across the country to sustain this continues to be difficult as we still have an acute shortage of well-trained manpower to look after all aspects of the forestry.

Timber is a basic need of our people both for construction well and fuel. People have the right to this resource for their legitimate uses. The policy of the Royal Government, from the beginning, was not to maximize revenue from the forest by way of export but rather to see that we are able to meet the local demand. On the other hand, emphasis was also given towards saving the forest and to use it in the most sustainable way by converting logs into sawn timber. There were no saw mills back then and without saw mills the wastage was as much as 70% compared to hand-sawn methods. It was therefore necessary for us to introduce sawmills and wood-based industries so that we could reduce the pressure on the forest. However it is clear that these wood industries and the sawmills are not functioning as efficiently as they should. Even though we have 72% forest cover, these industries are still struggling to meet the local demands, primarily because of the rising demand from rapid development. There is still the inherent problem of shortage of supply of sawn timber.

When we look at the development that is taking place in Bhutan and particularly in the construction industry we see concrete jungles coming up. As a cold country there is a big scope for wooden houses instead of using cement and stone or import bricks, which is a big drain on government resources. Besides insulation materials are rarely used. I guess somebody could spearhead in introducing this technology, because it also depends on the attitude of the people. One basic problem is, of course, the lack of skilled workers in the field of construction. We have to import workers from outside and along with them we import ideas from tropical areas. We have to improve the quality of construction and the use of indigenous raw materials, which are very good in terms of insulation like wood and mud.

In Kürze

Er war der erste Bhutaner, der zum Forstingenieur ausgebildet wurde, in Indien und an der ETH in Zürich. Dann übernahm er das Forstwirtschaftsdepartement. Sein Start war schwierig, die gesetzlichen Grundlagen fehlten ebenso wie die Erfahrung zur nachhaltigen Bewirtschaftung von Wäldern. Auch heute noch mangelt es an Fachleuten vor allem in der Bauindustrie. Die importierten indischsen Bauhandwerker verwenden mehrheitlich Beton mit sehr schlechter Wärmedämmung. Verbesserte Baumethoden und einheimische Baumaterialien müssten angewendet werden.

En bref

Il a été le premier Bhoutanais à être formé comme ingénieur forestier en Inde et à l'école polytechnique fédérale de Zurich. Ensuite il est devenu directeur du département des forêts. Ses débuts furent difficiles, les bases légales faisant défaut tout comme l'expérience d'une gestion durable des forêts. Aujourd'hui encore, il manque des experts, notamment dans le secteur de la construction. Les entrepreneurs indiens utilisent essentiellement du béton avec une très mauvaise isolation thermique. Il faut introduire des méthodes de construction améliorées et avoir recours aux matériaux locaux.

84

Forestry programme

by Dr. Saamdu Chetri, Dy-Resident Co-ordinator Helvetas / SDC, 1988-2006

Swiss cooperation in the forestry sector dates back to 1969, when Lyonpo Chenkyab Dorji (then Forest Director) was invited to study Swiss forestry policy. The Bhutan base for forestry was begun in the mid 1970's. Critics write in their personal reports that unlike the livestock plan, the forestry did not produce concrete results in the same period. The forestry programme is a long-term programme, therefore one needed to study and take stock before putting a concrete plan on the ground. The real inputs only began with the posting of the forestry experts to Bhutan and especially at Lamegompa at Bumthang, where the Logging Training Centre was established. The Swiss can proudly say that 300 personnel were trained before handing over the programme to the government in 1988. Assistance in the forestry also began through the multilateral mechanism in the early 1980's, the success of which encouraged the Swiss Development Cooperation and the World Bank to launch the second phase in the Eastern six Dzongkhags of Bhutan. This multilateral project had as major components social forestry, afforestation, capacity development, and institutional strengthening. It began in the mid 1990's and ended at the beginning of 2000.

Under the direct bilateral Swiss support, the Integrated Forestry Development Project (IFDP), which was phased out in 1998, engaged in the establishment of forest management units, forest road construction, implementation of management plans, logging operation on a sustained yield basis, silviculture research in conifer forest and training. The last phase concentrated on the consolidation and self-financing mechanism in order to sustain necessary investments (e.g. in forest roads) from the income of timber sales. The concept of ecologically and economically sustainable forest management through decentralised forestry units has proved to be viable for integration into local structures and expansion to other areas.

Preconditions for this were continued availability and further training of Bhutanese staff at all levels as well as a financial plough-back mechanism, which enabled financial and decentralised management. As IFDP was able to prove over many years, the forest in the conifer belt can be exploited without damaging the ecological balance of the environment and can be profitable without being detrimental to water catchment areas and water resources.

The Swiss bilateral cooperation accepted a bid from the World Bank to execute the project in 2000 to enhance the forestry capacity, assist in development of the five-year plan, and consolidate the social forestry component. Following this project, the Swiss built on the Participatory Forestry Management Programme (PFMP) that started in July 2002 and was financed by SDC. The goal of the project is to contribute to sustainable forest management and improve rural livelihood in Bhutan by strengthening the capacity of local communities to utilize and conserve forest resources, with an emphasis on poverty alleviation and the equitable distribution of benefits. This is also a major project that addresses strengthening of local governance directly and indirectly. PFMP pursues three immediate objectives; a) strengthening the capacity of the social forestry division that is mandated to provide technical support to the Dzongkhag forestry services, b) supporting implementation of PFM activities in 14 Dzongkhags, increased from 7, and c) increasing the capacity of the department of forests to monitor and evaluate PFM activities at all levels – gewogs, dzongkhag and national.

Forests are very important for the rural communities, as they supply products like timber and fuel wood, and serve as grazing areas and vegetation. Currently, there are 42 Community Forests (CF) covering an area of 2,749 hectares; they are managed by 1,560 households. The CF programme in Bhutan is the most likely bridge to strengthen the link between people and forests, thus making a significant contribution to livelihood improvement, environmental conservation and sustainable use of forests. There are more than 20 CF in different stages of preparation (application process, resource assessment, writing the management plan, or going through the approval process).

The progress of the CF programme was delayed mainly due to the suspicion that it would hamper the conservation policy and that there was no evidence for its success. Today, the progress is rapid and as many as 97 private forestry certificates have been issued and many more are in process. The community and private forestry owners can implement the plan as per management description of the CF plan, which means that they can harvest forest products (including timber) on a sustainable basis, without going through the normal (lengthy) procedures.
The beginning is made and if it is going well, there will be many more CF and PF in the years to come. Yet, to strengthen the base, it will be essential to give more attention to harvesting and marketing of timber and non-wood forest products.

The Swiss donated 5 million Swiss Francs to the Bhutan Trust Fund for Environment Conservation (BTFEC) at the end of 1995. BTFEC had been established to fund national conservation efforts through annual financial grants to Bhutanese conservation agencies. The aspiration of the Trust Fund is to contribute to the conservation programme in the entire Renewable Natural Resources Sector by systematically involving local communities and promoting livelihood practices consistent with biodiversity conservation and its principles of sustainable utilization. It has helped to incorporate environmental awareness and education into education system and to continue to reinforce conservation ethics and knowledge in local communities through informal education.
This programme complements many of the Swiss programmes in the RNR sector and converges with the policy of sustainable management of the environment. Although Swiss cooperation was not in the board, it has kept a close relation with the BTFEC programmes.

In Kürze

1969 wurde der bhutanesische Forstdirektor eingeladen, sich die eidgenössische Forstwirtschaft anzuschauen. Damit begann eine lange, erfolgreiche Zusammenarbeit. Holz wächst langsam, forstwirtschaftliche Projekte benötigen Zeit. Bis zum Jahre 1988 hatten die Schweizer Experten 300 Waldarbeiter ausgebildet und konnten ihr Ausbildungszentrum in Lamegonpa an die Regierung übergeben. Sie hatten den Beweis angetreten, dass der Nadelwald bewirtschaftet werden kann, ohne das ökologische Gleichgewicht zu stören. Heute gibt es schon 31 kommunale Waldgebiete, und auch immer mehr private Waldbesitzer, die ihre Wälder nach den Regeln nachhaltiger Forstwirtschaft bewirtschaften.

En bref

En 1969, le directeur bhoutanais des forêts fut invité en Suisse pour voir l'économie forestière suisse. Cette visite a marqué le début d'une longue coopération fructueuse. Le bois pousse lentement, c'est pourquoi les projets forestiers demandent du temps. Jusqu'en 1988, les experts suisses ont formé 300 bûcherons et ont pu remettre au gouvernement leur centre de formation situé à Lame Gompa. Ils ont apporté la preuve que les forêts de résineux bhoutanaises peuvent être exploitées sans perturber l'équilibre écologique. Aujourd'hui on compte 31 forêts communales et un nombre croissant de forêts privées exploitées selon les principes de l'économie forestière suisse.

85

Bhutan Forest Service – Close to nature, close to people

by Erich Oberholzer, former Co-Manager IFDP, Consultant since 1986

86

Throughout the long Swiss-Bhutan collaboration in the forestry sector, one of the main objectives was to provide practice-oriented training to all members of the forest service. Basic technical knowledge learned in a training institute is of course an important precondition for a good professional work. However, theory is not good enough in daily work in the forest, practical training in different forest types is also required.

Initially, the Lame Gompa Training Institute Bumthang provided the necessary training to loggers and cable crane operators, but the institute collapsed after being handed over to the government. In the following years, the Swiss contribution to the forest education was twofold. On one hand, the Swiss supported Integrated Forestry Development Project in Bumthang, offered short courses, mainly in silviculture and harvesting operations. On the other hand, the Natural Resources Training Institute (NRTI) started to train extension people for the RNR sector, among them foresters who in the first year also got a basic training in agriculture and animal husbandry. Field attachments were an important part of the 3 years of training, making sure that the young graduates would be capable of doing their jobs.

Behind all Swiss inputs into forestry training there was also the idea to shift over time from a Forest Service concentrating on police functions to a Forest Service taking its role as a competent partner of the rural population in all forestry and agroforestry related matters. Through better-educated people all over the country and through introducing democratic rights to all Bhutanese, the inhabitants started to look critically at the traditional forest police function. The forest service needed to improve its image in the rural population, not longer based on uniforms but on field-related professional competence.

Therefore, the Dzongkhag forest services, with one forest officer integrated directly in the district administration and NRTI-graduates posted in the Geog Renewable Natural Resources RNR centres, have been established. The young RNR advisers soon realized that the villagers have an excellent indigenous knowledge about sustainable management of the forests in their vicinity. The growing number of community forest management groups became demanding target groups, but the training sector was not aware of these field needs and even deleted the field attachments for NRTI-students. This resulted in new batches of Geog forest extension agents (GFEA) no more self-confident enough to give good advice to people on how to manage the forest resources.

In this situation, the Participatory Forestry Management Project started with practical training in silviculture for GFEA. The one-week courses were always held in one of the recently established community forests. 70 % of the training was held in the forest, together with members of the user group. The trainings were extremely successful in building up self-confidence, in motivating the participants to work closely together with villagers and in enabling them to give advice in simple language. With great satisfaction the participants realized that the villagers started to place strong confidence in them, because their dedication to do an excellent job with the objective to help to improve the livelihood of the local population became evident.

My conclusion: The long term Swiss involvement in the forest sector contributes successfully to meet the overall objective to make the forest service competent for the sustainable management of the forests in harmony with the people.

Participatory Forest Management Project (PFMP)

Phase I 2002–2007
Phase II 2007–2012

Objective
To contribute to the improvement of rural livelihoods and their natural environment by empowering local communities and strengthening their capacity to manage forest resources on a sustainable basis.

Results of phase I
- 42 community forests (CF) in 16 districts approved.
- Successful capacity building activities by numerous in-service trainings and a post-graduate programme.
- CFs are implemented according the approved management plans in close collaboration with the forest extension staff.
- Community participation in management of forest resources provides success stories of decentralized decision-making and management.

Expected outcomes phase II

Outcome 1:	Enabling institutional environment to establish 300 CFs throughout the country based on demands received from communities and technical feasibility.
Outcome 2:	Capacity built at all levels to ensure sustainability.
Outcome 3:	Community Forestry programme contributes to poverty reduction.

Feedback of participants

- This training is of very high importance to us as extension agents; we need to apply it but up to now most of us were not very confident about it.
- A journey of thousand miles starts with a single step. I am a more enlightened forester than before that training.
- Now I am loaded with good knowledge that I can proudly share with my friends and user groups.
- No doubt to implement in the field whenever required and share my experience with other staff.
- Such field exercises should be applied to NRTI. Then NRTI graduates would not need such extra training.
- Now I am able to choose the right silvicultural options, which is very important for sustainable forest management.

In Kürze

Das wichtigste Ziel der Zusammenarbeit in der Forstwirtschaft war die praxisorientierte Ausbildung. Nachdem das Lame Gompa Zentrum an die Regierung übergegangen war, fiel das Programm auseinander. Die Schweiz konzentrierte sich in der Folge auf das Bumthangtal, die Regierung betrieb die Ausbildung im Institut für Natürliche Ressourcen in Paro. Die Theoretiker, ohne Felderfahrung, erwiesen sich als zuwenig selbstbewusst, um die Einheimischen in den Gemeinden unterstützen zu können. Darum wurden Wochenkurse in praktischem Training zusammen mit den lokalen Forstarbeitern organisiert, in denen die Studenten Selbstvertrauen aufbauen konnten und auch lernten, wie Anweisungen in einfacher Sprache zu geben sind.

En bref

Le principal objectif de la coopération forestière a été la formation pratique. Après la remise du centre de formation de Lame Gompa au gouvernement, le programme a été démantelé. La Suisse s'est concentrée sur la vallée de Bumthang alors que le gouvernement faisait la formation à l'institut des ressources naturelles de Paro. Avec une formation théorique mais sans expérience pratique, les étudiants n'avaient pas les compétences requises pour conseiller les propriétaires forestiers et les communes. C'est pourquoi des cours de formation pratique d'une durée d'une semaine furent mis sur pied, conjointement avec les ouvriers forestiers locaux. Dans ces cours, les étudiants ont pris confiance et ont appris à transmettre leurs connaissances dans un langage simple.

87

Education and Culture

88

Education for all! – Education for what?

by Prof. Dr. Martin Menzi, Co-Founder of Helvetas, Senior Advisor to the RNR-sector from1976-2006, Co-Director NRTI 1992-1994

Formal education is one of the most impressive success stories of Bhutan's recent development. Starting off from a few monastic learning centres, a quite extended and fairly close network of public schools has been established and developed in less than 50 years. In hardly more than one generation's time, adult literacy rate has gone up from a one-digit figure to more than 50% and primary school enrolment has reached almost 90%. Now, even in remote places, children get access to basic education, and a few years ago the national education system has been complemented with the foundation of the Royal University of Bhutan. Entering pre-primary in a far out community school opens up the way to a university degree some 15 years later – an exciting prospect, indeed – and a problematic concept as well – he who does not reach the academic summit is a "drop-out".

The most commendable and rather fast built-up of the public education network has been driven by the slogan "education for all"- a noble vision, no doubt. However, even education is not a purpose in itself, it has to enable 'the educated' to find their own way in life and to become a more useful member of human society. But national economies and human societies are, of course, quite complex multi-dimensional systems. They are not in need of academic graduates only; they equally depend on people with diversified qualifications in various fields and at different levels. Evolving decentralised structures of local governance calls for well targeted inputs into large scale human capacity development: "Education for all". Yes, but education policy also has to answer the question "Education for what?". Particularly in a fledgling democratic society and a national economy in the take-off stage, functional and manual skills, social competence and commitment, self confidence and socio-political common sense are probably the most needed qualifications - they are the ingredients of a Capable, Honest, Enterprising, Efficient, Empowered and Responsible Society (CHEEERS).

A diversification and 'de-academisation' of the formal education and, probably even more important, a revaluation of 'non-white collar jobs' in society might pave the way to a promising further development of the national education system. Not only an academic degree shall be the dream of a primary school student – many options at different levels should offer ample chances in various fields of professional activities. 'Drop-outs' are only those who do not find their proper place in a multidimensional, diversified society.

Helvetas/SDC have been strongly involved in the education sector, not only in primary education and teachers training, but also in vocational training, professional RNR education and, last but not least, in rural development training. Helvetas will continue to be a partner in human capacity development, manly focusing on farmers, village communities and local governance structures.

In Kürze

Das Programm "Bildung für alle" ist ein grosser Erfolg. Fast 90 Prozent der Kinder in Bhutan besuchen heute die Primarschule, haben theoretisch Zugang auch zu höherer Bildung. Wer es nicht in eine weiterführende Schule schafft, gilt schon fast als Versager. Für Martin Menzi, Gründungsmitglied von Helvetas und hochgeschätzter Experte in Fragen der Entwicklungszusammenarbeit, stellt sich damit die provokative Frage: Bildung wozu? In einer gerade flügge gewordenen Demokratie, in einer jungen Volkswirtschaft darf ein akademischer Titel nicht der einzige Traum eines Primarschülers sein. Dienstleistung und Handwerk sind gleichwertig zu fördern, ebenso wie soziale Kompetenz und Pflichtbewusstsein.

En bref

Le programme "formation pour tous" est un grand succès. Aujourd'hui, près de 90 pour-cent des enfants du Bhoutan fréquentent l'école primaire et ont en principe accès à une formation supérieure. Ne pas accéder à une formation supérieure est déjà presque considéré comme un échec. Pour Martin Menzi, membre fondateur d'Helvetas et expert reconnu de la coopération au développement, il se pose dès lors la question provocatrice suivante: à quoi bon la formation? Dans une démocratie qui vient de prendre son envol, dans une économie encore jeune, un titre universitaire ne doit pas être l'unique rêve d'un élève de l'école primaire. Les services et les activités manuelles doivent être encouragées d'égale manière, tout comme les compétences sociales et la conscience professionnelle.

We want to learn!

89 .

PEP, PITT and STEP

by Dr. Saamdu Chetri, Dy-Resident Co-ordinator Helvetas / SDC, 1988-2006

The Swiss Cooperation began its support of the education sector through the multilateral support to teacher training back in the 1970's, many years earlier than recorded. The very first direct support provided by Helvetas in the early 1980's was to build the Multipurpose Hall for Jakar Higher Secondary School and to recruit a Swiss teacher, Peter Moser, to teach Swiss children in Bhutan. The main objectives of the Swiss support in this sector were the qualitative and quantitative improvement of the education system, the fostering of cultural cohesion, skills and management development at different levels, and the strengthening of small-scale enterprises.

Primary Education Project

In 1985 the government reached an agreement with the World Bank concerning Primary Education Project (PEP), which was focused on maintaining and expanding both quantitative and qualitative aspects of basis education and on the improvement of teaching learning processes. Swiss Cooperation endeavored to enhance the capacities of educators with the help of Human Resource Development (HRD) and training. While the project was implemented by the Department of Education, the Swiss were mostly providing the monitoring and the supervision with the World Bank. In 1987 Prof. Dr. Uri P. Trier and Prof. Dr. Walter Furrer brought up the idea of partnership at the Teacher Training College in Paro, as they were sharing their knowledge with Lyonpo Thinley Gyamtsho, the then Director General, and Dasho Jigme Zangpo, who at the time was in charge of PEP. They decided to call it Partners in Teacher Training (PITT). The institutional partnership between the Teacher Training Center (TTC) in Paro /Samtse and the TTC in Zurich was not that easy to put into practice, because the idea of partnership was about doing everything together; communicating, caring, sharing/valuing, etc.

Partners in Teacher Training

The project Partners in Teacher Training (PITT) was designed to assist the development of a batch of teacher trainers. The cooperation they agreed on regarded practicing a teaching method which they had seen in the Swiss system and which they were impressed by. The first step then was to select and train associate teachers in order to ensure a close link between theory and practice in the Bhutanese teaching curriculum. They agreed on addressing the project's aims through seven principles:
- to aim strictly at PEP and Secondary Education Project
- to ensure mutual learning
- to yearly review the benefits and problems and adjust accordingly
- to strive for individual and institutional cooperation
- to establish workshops alternating between Switzerland and Bhutan
- to put up joint planning
- to set up cost-effectiveness governing selection of tasks.

The two phases of PITT encompassed collaborative work in three fields: a) the development of school guidance and support (resource centers), b) the development and consolidation of teacher education courses, and c) multigrade teaching. The last point implies the development of teaching/learning materials, quality control of pre-service teacher training, continuous assessment, production of educational materials, as well as the use of Internet and E-learning. The PITT ended in 2003, followed by the Second Education Project (SEP).

Second Education Project

SEP was started in May 1998 and was mandated by SDC to Helvetas as the executing agency, a joint undertaking with the World Bank and the Royal Government of Bhutan (RGoB). The project aimed to reduce the acute shortage of school infrastructure by increasing the number of Primary and Secondary School teachers and expanding school enrolment. RGoB wanted to achieve 95% primary school enrolment by 2002, which was extended later to 2007. However, given the rapid population growth more effort is needed to progress that far. The Depart-

90

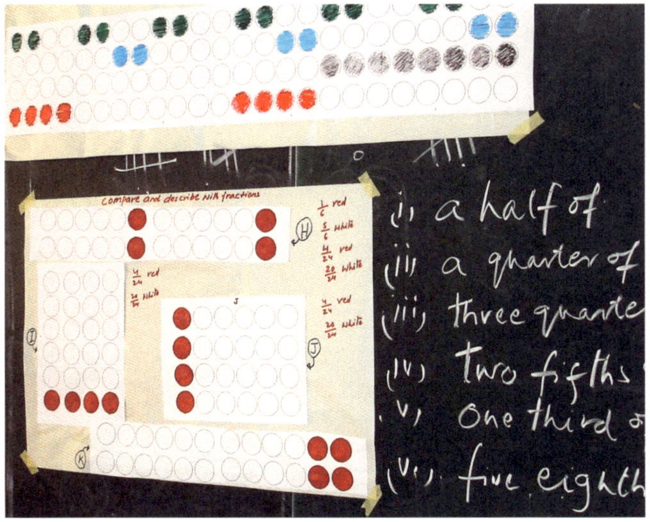

91

92

ment of Education implemented SEP with four components: a) improving basic facilities through the construction and upgrading of 11 Junior and High Schools, b) increasing the number of teachers, c) improving the teaching-learning processes, and d) strengthening the management as well as the administration at the central, district and school levels. Simultaneously, the expansion of the national education institute in Paro, funded by Swiss Cooperation, increased the intake of Primary School teacher trainees from 150 to 300. Including 133 day-scholars, the institute housed 444 Primary School teacher trainees in 2000 - overstraining its capacity. With the completion of the forth phase of expansion it is expected to house over 900 teacher trainees. It is encouraging to notice that the majority of the teacher trainees were young and motivated women.

The Support for Teacher Education Project (STEP) was actually the third phase of support to the education system and is supposed to end in 2008. This project is entirely executed and manned by the Department of Education. Its goal is to contribute to the development of the Colleges of Education in Paro/Samtse and provide quality teaching/learning services to teacher students and teachers. Their aim is to make them proficient in imparting relevant skills, knowledge and attitudes (including new areas of Youth Guidance & Counseling and Information & Communication Technologies) to the youth, which thus gets better opportunities for shaping their lives.

The education sector will not be complete without youth and culture. Great stress was laid on representing the interests of youth and culture under the sector and a number of programs were started under the RNR, benefiting directly the youth: the College of Natural Resources, the Rural Development Training Centre, the College for Education, a skill development training, and many ad hoc youth sports and publication supports.

93

94

In Kürze

Die Regierung von Bhutan setzte sich das ehrgeizige Ziel, bis zum Jahre 2007 für 95 Prozent aller Kinder einen Primarschulplatz anbieten zu können. Helvetas unterstützt das Programm vorwiegend im Bereich der Lehrerausbildung. Die Studienplätze für Lehrer wurden auf 300 Plätze verdoppelt. In einer vierten Phase wird die Kapazität auf 900 Studienplätze erhöht. Zur Freude aller Beteiligten bilden junge und hochmotivierte Frauen die Mehrheit der Studierenden.

En bref

Le gouvernement du Bhoutan s'était fixé comme objectif ambitieux de pouvoir offrir une place à l'école primaire à 95 pourcent de tous les enfants. Helvetas soutient ce programme essentiellement dans le domaine de la formation des enseignants. Le nombre de places pour la formation des enseignants a été doublé pour atteindre 300. Dans une 4ème phase du programme, ce nombre sera augmenté pour atteindre 900. À la joie de tous les concernés, ce sont des femmes jeunes et hautement motivées qui représentent la majorité des effectifs.

Teacher training – Working together

by L.N. Chhetri, National Institute of Education, Paro, and Otto Stern, Pedagogic Highschool, Zurich

It began in March 1991, when Dr. Otto Stern from Teacher Training Center (TTC) Zurich met L.N Chhetri from TTC Paro, to strengthen the Teaching Skills course offered in TTC Paro, and looking back, we feel that we worked together in a true spirit of partnership. For six months the modus operandi was on discussion, brainstorming, research, working by insight, referencing in the library, seeking suggestions from other colleagues and so on. It was all about work, work, work! - Once we even had to break the lock of the duplication room in TTC Paro, because Otto could not live without photocopies, even in the evening, when all other TTC staff members were busy either playing games or spending time with their families.

However there were also great moments of fun and entertainment like fishing trouts, dining together on weekends, or Otto trying to get rid of nasty fleas in his bedroom or noisy pigeons on top of the bedroom ceiling.

Many challenging tasks awaited us: The first one was to establish Teaching Experience (TE) at TTC Paro, the practical part of Teaching Skills. For TE to be successful it was necessary to train Teaching Experience teachers from selected schools from Paro valley. Obviously, a large number of TE teachers were required in order to coach all the thirty-five trainee teachers who were the first Partners in Teacher Training (PITT) batches of TTC. Thus the key concepts of TE such as Pre-conference and Post-conference were born.

Furthermore, the TTC lecturers were required to adapt to the new ideas of mentorship and conducting TE supervision purposefully. In order to establish Teaching Experience slowly but firmly, a series of workshops were conducted at TTC, Paro.

The second task was to strengthen and consolidate the existing Teaching Skills curriculum. The simple laws of Teaching & Learning that originated from the PITT programme were implemented in model lessons to provide a practical base for each teaching skill. The preparation of the model lessons was indeed based on equal contributions and offered some of the most pleasant moments of working and teaching together. Yes, we did team-teaching! When Otto faced thirty-five Bhutanese trainee teachers for the first time, he could not refrain from sweating, but, luckily, the critical eyes of L.N. from the back of the classroom provided some relief. Of course, Otto was over-prepared and could only finish half of the lesson!

Another incident we remember vividly is related to the notorious power cuts. Of course, we always relied very much on the regular supply of electricity and prepared whole lessons on transparencies. But during one of the teaching skill lessons both of us had to rewrite all the information on newsprint paper in turn, due to the failure of electricity supply.

Looking back we feel the quality of our teaching reached a high point during this time of partnership. Meeting other colleagues of the institute and the teachers from the schools enhanced the professional growth. The ideas and skills were shared amongst schoolteachers, student teachers, and the lecturers. The concept of Partnership in teacher training between TTC Paro and Zurich was now a reality, and here is the harvest of working together:
- the concept of Pre- and Post-Conference,
- Information collection by the trainee teachers before planning a lesson,
- the basic laws of Teaching and Learning put into practice,
- Information Input, and how to organize Learning Activities,
- the concept of tutoring a student teacher during Teaching Practice,
- the concept of close collaboration between the schools and the Institute during Teaching Practice.

Writing this text together on both ends of the world almost simultaneously by sending it back and forth on the internet, we felt that the true spirit of working together has come back again for a while.

Source: PITT 1989 – 2003, Partnership in Teacher Training, Marianne Frei et. al. / PHZ, Zurich, 2003

In Kürze

Im März 1991 reist Otto Stern von der Pädagogischen Hochschule Zürich nach Bhutan um zusammen mit L.N. Chhetri die theoretischen und praktischen Grundlagen für die Ausbildung der Lehrer zu optimieren. Es war harte Arbeit, aber es gab auch immer wieder heitere Momente, an die sich beide gerne erinnern. Und vor allem hat sich die Arbeit gelohnt.

En bref

En mars 1991, Otto Stern de la Haute Ecole Pédagogique de Zurich a entrepris un voyage au Bhoutan en compagnie de L.N. Chhetri, afin de définir les bases théoriques et pratiques permettant d'optimaliser la formation des enseignants. C'était un travail difficile mais agrémenté de moments lumineux dont tous deux se souviennent avec plaisir. D'autant plus que ce travail a été fructueux.

95

Looking back and forward

by Dr. Jagar Dorji, Director, College of Education, Paro

The output of this professional partnership has definitely been helpful in improving the teaching both at the institute level as well as at the school level. Unfortunately, such a development like adopting new practices is not visible to the eyes of the occasional observers and can lead to the belief that Partners in Teacher Training (PITT) lessons have been ignored. This is not true, largely because the diffusion of good ideas into classroom practice is very subtle and somewhat difficult to observe and quantify. PITT, therefore, has benefited our lecturers in improving their teaching styles.

I see the existing partnership in teacher training between Bhutan and Switzerland as symbolic as it is an opportunity to learn from each other. We have a relationship enshrined with learning as our main objectives, rather than providing views from those who know to those who know less. While our colleagues at home in Paro and Samtse have learned much from partners in Zurich, I do hope that we have been able to give something in return to you as well.

Most important for me personally is the Intervision Cycle invented through this partnership, which was truly a practical idea of enhancing professional development among teachers at all levels of schooling. This idea seems to work in schools where our head teachers are forward looking and hold a strong professional work ethic. This idea has a lot of potential and it has to be further developed and promoted.

I think the booklets on subject methodologies were also useful to our lecturers at the two teacher education colleges. I sincerely hope that the existing spirit of partnership will be strengthened and even better strategies explored.

Tashi Delek

Source: PITT 1989 – 2003, Partnership in Teacher Training, Marianne Frei et. al. / PHZ, Zurich, 2003

96

In Kürze

Wie Jagar Dorji, Direktor des Nationalen Instituts für Erziehung, schreibt, hat die professionelle Zusammenarbeit der beiden zu einer spürbaren Qualitätssteigerung bei der Lehrerausbildung, und damit auch im Schulunterricht geführt. Die Zusammenarbeit wurde immer als Chance gesehen voneinander zu lernen, sie beruhte nicht einfach auf einem Transfer von Wissen von einem der viel weiss, zu einem der weniger weiss.

En bref

Comme l'écrit Jagar Dorji, directeur de l'institut national de l'éducation, la coopération professionnelle entre les deux a amené une amélioration notable de la qualité au niveau de la formation des enseignants, et ainsi de la qualité de l'enseignement dans les écoles. La coopération a toujours été comprise comme une opportunité d'apprendre de l'autre, il ne s'agissait pas d'un simple transfert de connaissances unilatéral.

Products

by Claudio Zingg, Lecturer in Pedagogy, PH Zurich, in: PITT 1989 – 2003, Partnership in Teacher Training, Marianne Frei et. al. / PHZ, Zurich, 2003

Over the years several guides, brochures and learning materials have been produced. In this chapter a selection is listed and briefly commented upon.

Teaching Skills Handbook for Teacher Training

1993, Chhetri, L.N.; Stern, Otto

A handbook for teacher training with 25 lessons as an introduction to the principal tasks of teaching:

- How to plan lessons
- How to present information
- How to demonstrate skills
- How to organise learning activities
- How to define aims and objectives
- How to question the students
- How to handle the students' questions
- How to introduce and close a lesson
- How to evaluate a lesson

Teaching of Concepts and Skills. Lesson Plans

1994, Frei, Marianne; Furrer, Walter; Stern, Otto; Wanzenried, Peter

This small brochure was intended to be the bridge between the Swiss Leaflet and the Handbooks on Integrated Subject Methodology, which followed its publication. It demonstrates in practical lessons on environmental studies how to involve students through learning activities in the teaching and learning process.

School Based In-service Programme (SBIP)

1995, Chhetri, Gopi; Kinley, Dorji; Karma, Dorji; Stern, Otto; Thinley, Pema

A Model for Teacher Development and School Improvement; The SBIP has been developed to encourage the concept of "Teaching = Information-Input + Learning Activities" throughout the country. The core of the SBIP is an intervision - cycle with the steps of professional input, pre-conference (planning of a lesson), teaching and observation, and finally post-conference (feedback and plan of action). It has been practised in many schools throughout Bhutan since 1994.

Integrated Subject Methodology

1997, Environmental studies lecturers (EVS) at National Institutes for Education at Paro and Samtse, Seminar for basic pedagogic training Zurich (SPG)

Integrated Subject Methodology - A Collection of Model Lessons, Ideas and Theory

Mathematics. Integrated Subject Methodology

1998, Phuntsho, Dolma; Chhetri, Arjun; Kuratle, Armin; Rohrbach, Christian

A Collection of Model Lessons and Ideas

Language. Integrated Subject Methodology

1998, Language lecturers at NIEs Paro and Samtse, SPG Zurich

A Collection of Model Lessons, Ideas and Theory

The handbook on language (English and Dzongkha, Grade 1 to 6 focuses on topics such as reading, writing, grammar etc.

Handbook for Teaching Practice

1999, Teaching Practice Committee, NIE Samtse

The NIE believes in the principle of learning by doing, which is most effectively applied in the teaching practice programme. The Handbook acts as a guidebook for associate teachers and supervising lecturers to support and enhance the professional development of the trainee teachers during teaching practice.

Learning Materials for Primary Schools

2000, Karchung; Rohrbach, Christian; Dhittal, Yentiram; Frei, Marianne; Tobgay, Sonam; Zangmo, Dechen

Idea Folder. The Idea Folder presents 17 different learning materials for self-guided student activities.

Meme Heyley Heyley - In Search of Happiness

1999, Furrer, Walter; Harvey, Barbara; Education Division Bhutan (Choden, Sonam and team) and Swiss TV DRS (Leu, Lotti; Alder, Hansueli and team).

Educational Video: The film is based on a Bhutanese fairy tale about a man who is in search of happiness. There is an almost similar fairy tale in the German speaking culture: "Hans im Glück".

As an educational video, the film is used in Switzerland as well as in Bhutan. It was shown on Swiss and Bhutanese TV.

The video is an inspiration for students to think about happiness and fate. For Swiss students it is also a possibility to think about different approaches to the concepts of happiness and peace of mind. Especially interesting are the statements about the focus of the story from an old man, a merchant woman and a monk, which helps to understand the differences between Swiss and Bhutanese cultures.

97 Kezang and Wangmo, by Marie-Noelle Frei-Pont, 1980

Implementation Handbook for Resource Centres in Bhutan

2000, Dorji, Jagar; Dukpa, Mingbo; Karma, Dorji; Braem, Donat; Rettich, Markus; Zingg, Claudio

Bhutanese and Swiss partners developed the handbook to coincide with the implementation of the first five Resource Centres in Bhutan. It gives a short profile of the main cornerstones of a functioning Resource Centre: aims, location, organisational structure, management and working procedures.

A Guide to Continuous Assessment for Primary Schools

2000, Rinchen, Phub; Lama, A.B., Raika, N.B.; Tenzin, Chogyal; Lop Dorji, Tenzin; Lop Dorji, Ngawan

Continuous assessment that is well performed greatly improves the learning of students. The guidebook was used as a basic document in many workshops held since 1999. The first part gives an overview of the development of assessment in Bhutan and the theoretical foundations of assessment. The second part presents practical examples of summative and continuous assessment.

College of Education, Paro

by Dr. Saamdu Chetri, Dy-Resident Co-ordinator Helvetas / SDC, 1988-2006

98

99

The initially called National Institute of Education (NIE, formally known as Teacher Training College - TTC) has a long history. During the second phase, the Swiss had supported the expansion of facilities at the TTC in Paro through UNICEF. The government, very pleased with the College of Natural Resources, had decided to consider the third phase and requested Helvetas / SDC for expansion, again on a turnkey basis. The objective was to increase the number of teacher trainees to 300 per academic year in Paro, with 150 per batch. The basic aim was to produce enough and competent teachers who were able to teach from pre-primary to higher secondary. The centre was not only aiming to be the centre of excellence in teaching and learning, but was going to act as a centre of cultural, social and civil activity for the people of Paro. It was also to play host for the in-service training of teachers from all over Bhutan during special short courses or workshops. With its proximity to the airport, the college was also aiming at becoming an international centre for conferences and educational dialogue in South Asia.

During the first Round Table Meeting (RTM) in Bhutan in November 2000, the Director of Swiss Development Cooperation, Walter Fust, agreed to finance the fourth phase of the extension of the National Institute of Education (NIE), now College of Education (CoE). He saw the need to expand the teacher's output to address the millennium development goal, "education for all", and to improve the quality of education by reducing the teacher-student ratio. The immediate objectives were: a) construction of an additional infrastructure at CoE Paro and Samtse, b) enhancing capacity of operation and maintenance of infrastructure units at CoE Paro, c) developing the capacity of contractors in construction management (private sector development) for similar constructions in the future.

The signing of the agreement of this project is very historic, since it was the first agreement ever signed at the level of foreign ministers of Switzerland and Bhutan, namely His Excellency Joseph Deiss and His Excellency Lyonpo Jigmi Y. Thinley, in Thimphu on 19th April 2000. The planning was targeted to enhance the enrolment capacity from 450 to 980. The project is being executed again on a turnkey basis with full support from the Ministry of Health and Education. SDC would finance over Nu 250 million for the realization of the project. The construction is foreseen to last until 2009. This phase comprises one multipurpose hall, one administrative building and two library buildings, renovation and planning of the Rimpung complex for class-rooms and science laboratories, re-organising and restoring the existing library as research building, one hostel and development sports infrastructures in Paro and Samtse.

In Kürze

Der "Schweizer Dzong" in Lobesa war so gut geraten, dass die Regierung um die Unterstützung beim Ausbau des Lehrerseminars in Paro bat. Es war das erste Projekt einer langen Zusammenarbeit, das auf Stufe der Aussenminister besiegelt wurde: Am 19. April 2000 unterzeichneten Joseph Deiss für die Schweiz und Lyonpo Jigmi Y. Thinley für Bhutan das Projekt, das bis 2009 fertig gebaut sein soll. Dann werden nicht mehr nur 450, sondern 980 Lehrerinnen und Lehrer pro Lehrgang ausgebildet werden können, was dem Bildungssystem zweifellos neuen Schub geben wird.

En bref

Le "dzong suisse" était si bien réussi que le gouvernement bhoutanais a sollicité la Suisse pour l'agrandissement du séminaire pédagogique de Paro. C'était le premier projet d'une longue coopération au niveau des ministères des affaires étrangères: le 19 avril 2000, Joseph Deiss pour la Suisse et Lyonpo Jigmi Y. Thinley pour le Bhoutan ont signé l'accord pour la réalisation de ce projet dont la construction doit s'achever en 2009. A partir de là, 980 enseignant-e-s seront formés par année au lieu de 450, ce qui donnera à n'en pas douter un nouvel élan au système de formation.

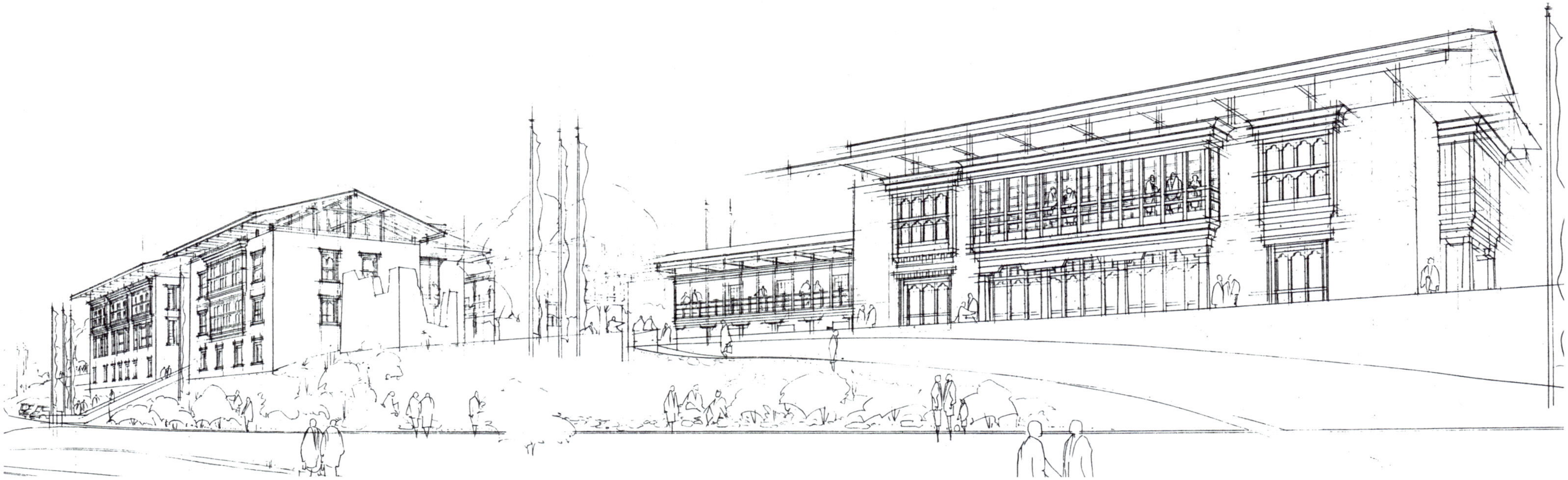

100 Perspective of the residental compound

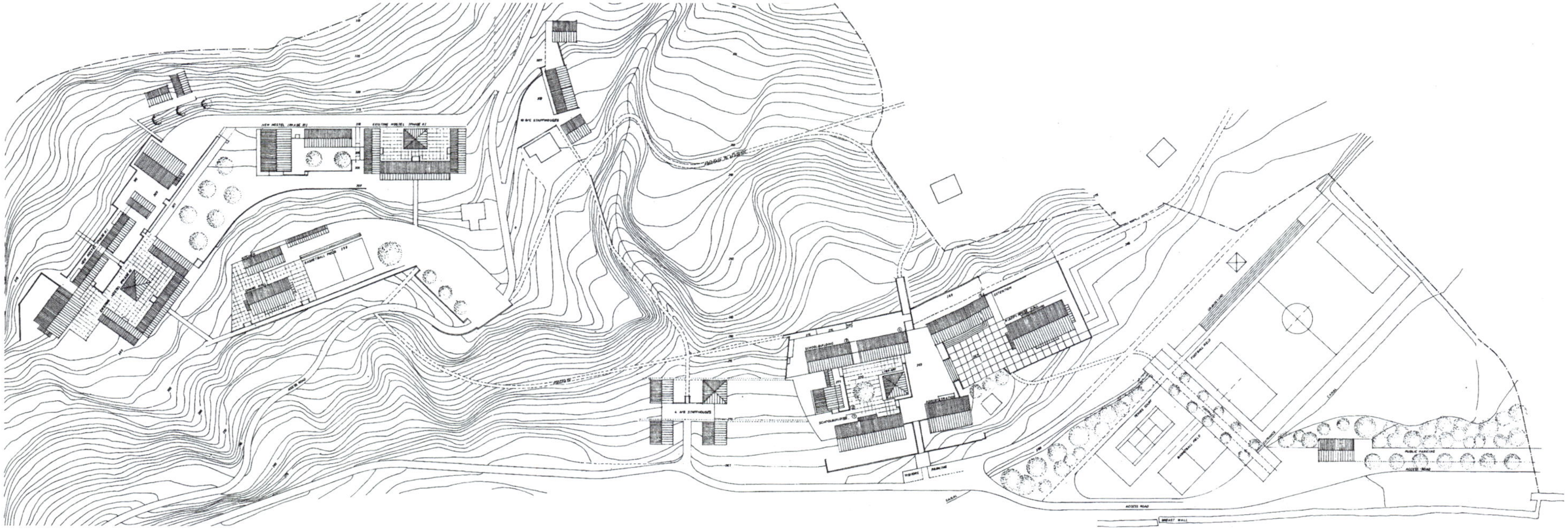

101 Early sketch of the siteplan: residental compound (on the left), academic compound (on the right)

Traditional dyeing methods of Bhutan

by Barbara Bigler, hand-weaver, in: Traditional Dyeing Methods of Bhutan, 2002

102 Madder/Tsö (Rubia manjit) grows all over Bhutan

104 Incrusted insects attached to new host tree

103 Barberry (Berberis asiatica), Robluthang

105 Dyed with lac

Dyeing Recipe from Laya

"We only use Tsö (madder) and Kebitsang (barbery) or Dochur (sour stone)" I was told. On my question what part of the barbery bush they would use, they said "any part, leafs, twigs, and mainly the berries. This did not seem to be very precise. I took some of the berries home and tried them out on wool and yakhair, I added the wool and the yakhair to an equal amount of berries and sufficient water to cover them. After boiling, I let them cool down and rinsed the fibers while rejecting the berries. The same amount of dried madder leaves and stems were boiled with enough water to cover them; they cooled down and were strained. This more brown than red liquid was heated slowly together with the fibers and boiled for one hour. To my astonishment the wool showed exactly the colour of the stripes in the skirts of the Laya women.

Lac/Jhatso Cultivation

Lac is a scale insect cultivated for its dyestuff and for its production of sticklac as well. The insects feed on the sap of different trees and are shifted twice a year from lower to higher places and vice versa. When the dyestuff is harvested the encrustations including the insects are scratched off the twigs they live on, some selected ones for breeding are brought to new host trees where they start a new life cycle.

I was curious to try out all the different pretreatments in combination with Lac. Therefore I submitted a sample of mulberry silk, one of raw silk, one of local wool and one of imported wool to a mordanting with Zhim leaves (light yellow), Zhim leaves with turmeric (yellow), Churpo/sour fruit (brownish), Dochur/sour stone (white) and ashwater (white).

Since 1980 I have been working as a weaver with natural dyes. On my first stay in Bhutan, I noticed that natural dyeing is still alive in this country though competing hard with the ready synthetic dyed yarns imported from India. Knowing that once it is lost, the art of dyeing is very difficult to revive, it was my ambition to note down as much as possible in order to preserve this knowledge.

Through Helvetas I got the opportunity to travel in Bhutan establishing an inventory of the traditional dyeing methods on textile fibres. As I was limited in time and area, I concentrated my enquiries on the northwest, on wool in central Bhutan and on silk in eastern Bhutan. I had to rely on my Bhutanese companions for the places where people could be interviewed as well as on their translations. I tried to note down the recipes as precisely as possible and I collected as much of the dyestuffs as my baggage would allow.

Back in Switzerland I made experiments with the materials I had brought from Bhutan and I dyed yarns following the recipes I had collected. The knowledge of dyeing in the traditional way is very difficult to pass on. These methods require experience that cannot be transmitted by a textbook. They call for all the senses and many of the criteria can only be handed down by an unbroken tradition.I realize also that I have discovered many treasures; many more are left to be found.

In Kürze

In Bhutan ist das traditionelle Färben mit natürlichen Farbstoffen noch weit verbreitet, obwohl die Konkurrenz durch synthetisch gefärbtes Garn aus Indien ständig zunimmt. Barbara Bigler hatte dank Helvetas die Gelegenheit Bhutan zu bereisen und ein Inventar der traditionellen Techniken aufzunehmen – sowohl für Wolle als auch für Seide. Sie hat Rezepte aufgeschrieben und so viel wie möglich an Grundstoffen gesammelt.

En bref

Au Bhoutan, la teinture au moyen de colorants naturels est encore largement répandue, même si la concurrence en provenance d'Inde – avec des fils à la teinture synthétique – se fait plus vive. Grâce à Helvetas, Barbara Bigler a eu l'occasion de visiter le Bhoutan et d'établir un inventaire des techniques traditionnelles, aussi bien pour la laine que pour la soie. Elle a documenté des recettes et récolté autant que possible des ingrédients de base.

Folk Heritage Museum, Thimphu

by Maria Känzig, Technical Consultant; Helvetas, in: Final report, excerpts, December 2001

106 Folk Heritage Museum, Thimphu

107

108

The Folk Heritage Museum was inaugurated on July 27 in 2001. Chief Guest was Ashi Dorji Wangmo Wangchuck, the senior queen, who is in charge of the museum's patronage. As the English press stated: "The opening of the museum designates a further milestone in the preservation of our rich culture." The museum offers six working places. The number of visitors exceeds all expectations.

The aim: to show through permanent and special expositions the rural life in the Thimphu Valley as it was 100-150 years ago. The 3-story house built in the 19th century has been reverted to its former condition through extensive manual work (make of wood and adobe). The fundament of the house, which is made out of stamped adobe walls, has been fixed and the front has been replaced by old wood taken from a house in decay. The corrugated iron roof has been replaced by the traditional shingle roof. It is the first time that such a kind of work has been executed in Bhutan and it attracted great interest. By asking elderly people who were familiar with the house and its former owner, the original condition and its use could be reconstructed. Based on these notes the original floor plan has been re-established and a traditional adobe cooking place has been installed.

Karma Ura developed a list containing all the objects that could have been found in a farmhouse of that time. On the basis of that list all the Dzongkhas were asked to search for those objects. In cooperation with agents of the National Commission for Cultural Affairs the selection was carried out.

The design of the environment has been established in cooperation with the agrarian research station of Jakar and Yusipang. Their employees delivered traditional seeds of plants and tree sprouts. Cypresses (the National Tree) and fruit trees have been planted as well as economic plants, which were used for the production of paper and fabrics, for coloration or for medicine. Adobe construction is well known in Bhutan. Thus the complex has been enclosed by a high adobe wall.

A "living museum" has been the core request. As the press stated: "Besides the exhibitions, the Museum will also undertake small activities and workshops. These enrichment programmes will be designed to give the participants a unique hands-on learning experience about life in rural Bhutan".

109 As another important culture project Helvetas donated a cable crane to help the restoration of the ancient Taktshang Monastery that was destroyed by fire. Taktshang (which means tiger's nest) is one of the holiest places in the country. Guru Rimpoche had flown on a tiger's back and had landed at the place where later the monastery was built. Apart from these larger projects, Helvetas has constantly supported monasteries for water supply and sanitation, contributed to the building of monasteries and temples and its Thangka preparation for Thongdrels.

In Kürze

Helvetas hat auch auf kulturellem Gebiet Unterstützung geleistet. So zum Beispiel beim Umbau und der Einrichtung des volkskundlichen Museums in Thimphu, und beim Wiederaufbau des abgebrannten "Tiger's Nest". Dazu wurde immer wieder Klöstern bei der Wasserversorgung und der Einrichtung sanitärer Anlagen geholfen.

En bref

Helvetas a également appuyé des initiatives culturelles. Par exemple lors de la rénovation et l'installation du musée national de Thimphu, et lors de la reconstruction du "Tigers' Nest" suite à l'incendie qui l'a ravagé. En outre, un appui a été fourni pour l'adduction d'eau et les installations sanitaires de nombreux monastères.

Museum of Ethnography Neuchâtel

by Olimpia Caligiuri Cullity and Marc-Olivier Gonseth, Museum of Ethnography Neuchâtel (MEN)

110 Conch Dung dkar ("white conch") Shell, silver, turquoise, coral. lazurite, wax. 58 x 30 cm.

111 The large conch trumpet encased in gilded silver sounds shrill and loud like a call to eternal life.

In 1968, the Neuchâtel Museum of Ethnography (MEN) received the nucleus of what was to become its Bhutanese collection from the late sovereign of Bhutan, S.M. Jigme Dorji Wangchuck (who reigned from 1952 to 1972). Later, new pieces were added from several members of the royal family as well as others. For instance, King Jigme Singye Wangchuck, the original donor's son, supplied the Museum with some of its finest objects such as the Dung dkar conch, represented in this document. In all, the collection contains more than 250 pieces – including objects of worship, art objects and everyday life items – thus making it one of the largest collections deposited in a foreign Museum.

Switzerland was chosen as a result of King Jigme Dorji's frequent stays at his friends, Fritz and Monica de Schulthess. The couple (who initiated several technical cooperation projects, continued later on by the Swiss confederation and Helvetas) were commissioned by the Bhutanese king to find a museum willing to devote one of its rooms to Bhutan. So, finally, the MEN was chosen.

The permanent exhibition was inaugurated in November 1974 and was reorganised in December 1988 around an important piece of the collection, the tashigomang altar. 10 years later, it was taken down and transferred to Brittany where it topped the bill in a temporary exhibition at the Abbey of Daoulas called "Entre Inde et Tibet, le Royaume du Bhoutan" (Bhutan: a kingdom between India and Tibet). When the exhibition was reinstalled in Neuchâtel in 1999, it was the occasion for a new presentation focussed on representations of the Himalayas in Western imagination. In addition to 25 Tibetan statues and Western objects, the exhibition – still open – presents 74 pieces of the Museum's Bhutanese artefacts. A planned reorganisation of the MEN within the next few years gives rise to hopes for a larger area devoted to the Bhutanese collection.

Bhutan Collection

The relationship between the Museum and Bhutan has been preserved by Marceline de Montmollin's visits to this country as well as her studies. Her first stay at the invitation of King Jigme Dorji took place in 1969 when she took part in the conception of the Paro National Museum. Marceline de Montmollin's research resulted in the first issue of a series dedicated to the MEN collections, Collection du Bhoutan (Collection from Bhutan). Through the years, the number of Bhutanese pieces in the Museum has increased, especially in the area of arts and crafts. The tashigomang acquired in 1987, represents the Museum's last noteworthy purchase. This outstanding piece of which only twenty or so specimens, all ancient, exist in Bhutan, is a portable altar specifically Bhutanese, with "multiple auspicious doors". The tashigomang was specially made for the MEN and acquired by the "Amis du Musée" (Friends of the Museum). Its production constitutes a revival of an artisan tradition whose continuity had been broken. The most recent contribution to the collection consists of a series of bank notes, donated by Dorji Namgyel, curator of the new Trongsa Museum (due to open in June 2008), during his visit to the MEN in the summer of 2007, when he came to study the Bhutanese pieces and discuss a possible future cooperation for an exhibition in Bhutan presenting the MEN's collection.

In the anticipation of this eventuality, what remains to be done is the study of the artefacts initiated by Marceline de Montmollin; for example, field work and the acquiring of contemporary handmade objects for comparison. While objects and practices linked to tantric Buddhism differ little from their well documented Tibetan counterparts, the others – mainly used for domestic use and clothing – are more often specifically Bhutanese and require more investigation.

It is vital that these objects carry on their ambassadorial role in Switzerland. M. Dorji Namgyel's visit enabled the renewal of ties between the Museum and Bhutan through the exchange of knowledge and new concerns. It is to be hoped that this new cooperation develops further in the years to come.

112

113 Portable altar and Tashigomang offerings ("Multiple auspicious doors") Hardwood, silver, gouache on canvas, turquoise and (imitation) coral, painted cast clay.

In Kürze

Die Freundschaft der Familie von Schulthess mit der Wangchuck-Dynastie war die Basis für die Bhutan Sammlung des Ethnographischen Museums von Neuenburg. König Jigme Dorji, der von Fritz von Schulthess schlicht Pön genannt wurde, stiftete dem Museum 1968 die Grundlage, andere Mitglieder der königlichen Familie erweiterten die Sammlung durch zusätzliche Gaben. So besitzt das Museum heute eine der reichsten Sammlungen ausserhalb Bhutans.

En bref

L'amitié entre la famille von Schulthess et la dynastie Wangchuck constituait la base de la collection "Bhoutan" du Musée éthnographique de Neuchâtel. Le Roi Jigme Dorji Wangchuck fit don en 1968 de la base de la collection. D'autres membres de la famille royale ont depuis élargi cette collection par des dons supplémentaires. Le musée possède ainsi une des collection les plus riches en dehors du Bhoutan.

Public Health

114

Public Health

by Dr. Saamdu Chetri, Dy-Resident Co-ordinator Helvetas / SDC, 1988-2006

Health sector programme

If one considered the first Swiss midwife who came and served in Samtse sometime's in the early 1950's, not only the assistance in the health programme but the cooperation itself would be more than 50 years old. However, the Swiss support to the health sector began on a regional mobile basis. The mobile clinic, mounted on a vehicle, failed. Thereafter, the Swiss remained within the valley where they had major project and programme activities. The hospital started in an old house belonging to the royal family, situated next to the Wangdicholing palace in Bumthang. The formal support to health services had begun in 1974 and was phased out in 1994.

Basically depending on indigenous medicine, the people in Bumthang began to shift to modern medicine for two reasons, a) it was cheaper than puja/rimdo/choko and b) there was more hope in getting well soon. In the early 1980's. when the indigenous hospital housed also a modest western clinic, patients could call on either system and doctors referred them to their colleagues, depending on their case.

The main focus of the Swiss was clearly on preventive medicine and hygiene. Thus, teaching and training, from individual training to skill development in management, were prime activities. Several staff members were trained abroad, whereas nurses, health assistants, village health workers, water caretakers and others were trained in the country, either in Gelephu, in the National Institute of Family Health or in Thimphu. One of the most efficient mechanisms was the daily review each morning with the entire crew, planning for the following days. It provided the sense and essence of planning.

Village Health Worker concept

Primary Health Care (PHC) included mother and child health care (MCH) clinics, the village health worker (VHW) programme, and the concept of model village. 20 MCH clinics were monthly visited, aiming at high immunization coverage nationwide for diphtheria, pertussis, tetanus, polio, measles and tuberculosis. The VHW concept was first introduced in Bumthang and later expanded all over Bhutan. 70 functional VHWs were responsible to cater to medical needs and attend to about 200 people each. Female VHWs were trained to attend birth attendance. Each year, there were refresher courses for the old VHWs and fresh courses for the new ones. By the end of 1990, there were no villages that could not be covered within half an hour walk. 19 model villages have shown a good example, promoting the PHC idea. Every model village had safe drinking water supply, waste disposal pits, dry footpaths, and at least a simple pit latrine. Another PHC activity was the school health programme. Teachers were trained as quasi VHWs, delivering for instance practical lessons in tooth brushing. Maintenance of sanitation infrastructure was a continuous challenge; therefore, VHWs were also trained to attend to broken pipes and tanks under the safe drinking water scheme. The many Basic Health Units (BHU) built by Helvetas have been another backbone of PHC.

The Helvetas assistance extended over a zone of three Dzongkhags. PHC was very well managed and it could have served as a field-teaching centre for the health science students to become general practitioners. If it had come through it would have resolved a lot of medicinal problems in remote communities. Helvetas also assisted in herb collections and documentation of this ancient traditional medicinal culture.

It was only during the late 1980's, that Helvetas began to consolidate the health programme by completing the new Bumthang Hospital, sponsored by the Swiss cities of St. Gallen, Winterthur and Schaffhausen. The modern, yet traditionally styled building sheltered basic facilities both of western and Tibetan medicine. Ultimately, the Swiss assistance was phased out in 1994.

In Kürze

Die schweizerische Hilfe im Gesundheitssektor begann mit einem mobilen Ambulatorium, welches bald scheiterte. In der Folge konzentrierte man sich auf das Bumthangtal, wo die grossen Projekte liefen. Ein Haus der königlichen Familie diente als Spital.
Die Bhutaner, die traditionellerweise nur Naturheilmethoden kannten, nahmen die Errungenschaften moderner Schulmedizin gerne an: diese war in der Regel billiger und erfolgreicher. Die Schulmedizin verdrängte die traditionellen Heilmethoden aber nicht, beide Methoden leben zusammen. Das Hauptaugenmerk legten die Schweizer auf Prävention und Hygiene. Man bildete Dorfsanitäter aus – die Frauen auch als Hebammen – die jeweils etwa 200 Personen zu betreuen hatten. Es gab Gesundheitsprogramme in den Schulen, wo die Kinder angehalten wurden, auch ihren Zähnen Sorge zu tragen. In den späten 80-er Jahren wurde das neue Bumthang-Spital eröffnet, welches von den Städten St. Gallen, Winterthur und Schaffhausen gesponsert wurde.

En bref

L'aide suisse dans le secteur de la santé a commencé par un service ambulatoire mobile, un projet voué à l'échec. Par la suite, les efforts se sont concentrés sur la vallée de Bumthang où les autres grands projets étaient localisés. Une maison de la famille royale fut transformée en hôpital. Les Bhoutanais, qui connaissent principalement la médecine traditionnelle, tibétaine, ont su tirer profit des avantages de la médecine occidentale, souvent moins chère et plus efficace. La médecine occidentale n'a cependant pas fait reculer la médecine traditionnelle. Les deux approches coexistent. Les Suisses ont mis l'accent sur la prévention et l'hygiène. Des responsables sanitaires ont été formés au travail paramédical dans les villages et des femmes également comme sages-femmes avec charge de conseiller environ 200 personnes. Des programmes de santé ont été mis en place dans les écoles, exhortant les enfants à également soigner leurs dents. Vers la fin des années 80, le nouvel hôpital de Bumthang a été inauguré, une construction sponsorisée par les villes de Saint-Gall, de Winterthur et de Schaffhouse.

115 Nam Dorji, health assistant, Bumthang

Dorjee and 11 Swiss doctors

by Dr. Saamdu Chetri, Dy-Resident Co-ordinator Helvetas / SDC, 1988-2006

It is difficult to say whether the 11 Swiss doctors survived Dorjee Dukpa or whether he survived them. But it is a fact that Dorjee Dukpa worked relentlessly in Bumthang with 11 of them from 1972 to 1994 under the Swiss health programme. In those days, doctors in Bhutan could be counted on one's fingertips and most of them were foreigners. Suddenly, a certain Dr. T. Tondury appeared in Bumthang from nowhere, adding one name more to Dorjee Dukpa's fingertips. It was learnt later that he was posted by the Foundation Pro Bhutan to nurse the people of Bumthang. The year was 1972, the same year the country was stunned by the sudden demise of our beloved third King.

In 1972, the Swiss started running a mobile medical unit, mounted on a vehicle. It served several districts and had to travel widely to hold medical camps, especially in Wangdue, Punakha, Trongsa, Bumthang, Mongar, Lhuntse, and Trashigang. Another landmark year was 1974, when the dispensary was shifted from Lamegompa to Wangdichoeling. The PWD guesthouse was converted into a small hospital with consultation rooms, patient ward, and a small operating theatre. In those days, if someone was sick, the doctor had to go to treat the patient at home, because the peasants believed that a sick person should not be taken outside their houses. Slowly the people changed their belief and began to accept that they should go to the hospital in case of illness

In 1977, Dr. Peter Leisinger, who was not only energetic, but very innovative, arrived. He started improving the overall health care services, focusing on indoor health care, primary health care and preventive heath care services. He initiated the village health worker programme and piloted the rural water supply maintenance in Bumthang. The medical services and its programmes were extended to three Dzongkhags, namely Trongsa, Zhemgang and Bumthang. At that time, there was no specialization in services offered by the different hospitals. The hospital had to deal with any patient with diseases like leprosy and tuberculosis etc. imported from other districts, especially from Zhemgang and Trongsa.

The two doctors following Dr. Leisinger served only one year each because of personal and health problems. In 1983, Dorjee and his team had to run the hospital and other public health clinics on their own for the whole year. Despite a lot of pressure to maintain the high service standard of the Swiss doctors, Dorjee and his colleagues, Yeshey Nidup and Wangdi, provided good health services. For this, the team is grateful to the unwavering Swiss support, especially from Fritz Maurer and Ernst Reinhardt, the first Resident Coordinator.

In 1984, Dr. Hans Gammeter and his wife, a midwife nurse, joined the project team. He has been described as a diplomatic and hardworking person with leadership skills. The role of health care expanded in providing better services and a lot of emphasis was given to the practical education of the staff. During this time, the planning of a new hospital in Wangdichoeling had begun and was taken up in 1988, during the time of his successor, Dr. Wuest. He further strengthened the work of his predecessor through the model village sanitation program of building toilets in the villages. He was a professional who introduced the daily review meetings and executed everything in a fully planned manner. Dr. Michael Perrenoud, the last Swiss doctor to serve in the Bumthang hospital from 1991 until 1994, succeeded him. Gradually, the hospital had become the district hospital with national staff headed by the District Medical Officer (DMO). Dr. Perrenoud continued to work as advisor to the national staff and assisted in documenting the indigenous medicinal plants.

In Kürze

Dorjee Dukpa – "Barfussdoktor" – hat mit allen elf Schweizer Ärzten zusammengearbeitet, die zwischen 1972 und 1994 in Bumthang tätig waren. Der erste, Dr. T. Tondury kam noch im Auftrag der Stiftung Pro Bhutan. Patienten mussten damals meist zuhause aufgesucht werden, weil die Bauern glaubten, Kranke dürften ihr Haus nicht verlassen. Erst mit der Zeit lernten sie die Vorteile eines Spitalaufenthaltes kennen.
Dr. Peter Leisinger, der 1977 nach Bumthang kam, startete das Programm mit den Dorfsanitätern und kümmerte sich um die Verbesserung der Wasserversorgung. Einer seiner Nachfolger, initiierte ein Programm für die sanitarische Sanierung der Dörfer, die bis dahin noch nicht einmal Toiletten kannten.

En bref

Dorjee Dukpa – "le médecin aux pieds nus" - a travaillé avec onze médecins suisses qui se sont succédés à Bumthang entre 1972 et 1994. Le premier d'entre eux, Dr T. Tondury, avait été engagé par la Fondation Pro Bhutan. A cette époque, le médecin devait visiter les patients chez eux car les gens croyaient que les malades ne devaient pas quitter leur maison. Ce n'est qu'avec le temps que les gens ont compris les avantages d'un séjour à l'hôpital. Dr Peter Leisinger, arrivé en 1977 à Bumthang, a lancé le programme des responsables sanitaires villageois et s'est intéressé à l'amélioration des adductions d'eau. L'un de ses successeurs a initié un programme d'assainissement sanitaire des villages qui, jusque là, ne connaissaient même pas les toilettes.

116 Dorjee Dukpa and outpatients

Health – the little big project

by Dr. med. Hans Gammeter, District Medical Officer, Bumthang, 1984-1987

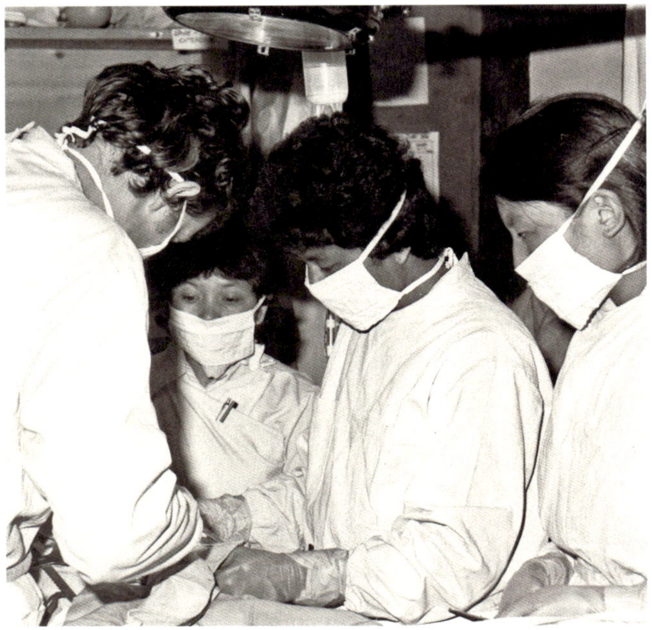

117

118

Project aim?

Over the years the project aim has undergone change which, on the one hand is normal, on the other is the expression of a lack of concept on the part of Helvetas with regard to the health sector. Launched in the beginning as a selective curative service for the local people in the region where Helvetas was actively engaged, the presence of a Swiss medical doctor played an important role in the attractiveness of the work place of the expatriates.

Image building?

Projects in the health sector are popular and endear those running them. In most parts of the underdeveloped world the people, if asked at all about their "felt needs", would list with high priority the need for better health conditions. In saying so they as a rule have curative service in mind rather than their own contribution (drinking water supply; disposal of human waste; avoidance of self-inflicting behaviour such as smoking; improved nutrition etc.) Governments and donators willingly comply with these needs. The commitment of Helvetas in the field of public health over many years has undoubtedly contributed to the good reputation of the organisation and the acceptance of projects in other areas.

The unique case: disadvantages

To my knowledge Helvetas has never managed other health projects outside Bhutan herself. This is the reason why the organisation, although willing and anxious, has been acting with little experience but with a professional approach and with the use of benchmarks. This structurally inadequate project management however allowed the involved medical doctors to leave their stamp which, thanks to their creativity, had also positive aspects.

Primary Health Care: "health for all in 2000"

Why was it possible that the government, in spite of all the difficulties encountered, chose the "Bumthang Health Project" as a model for all districts of the country? Some possible explanations: unlike Helvetas, RGOB in the mid-eighties developed and enacted a clear-cut health policy which, based on WHO models followed the principle of "primary health care". This puts great emphasis on information and prevention, the education of medical staff at the local level (village health-workers) and the operation of small decentralised health units (BHU). In Bumthang conditions for a quick and decisive implementation were favourable. For most of the long-time Bhutanese staff, these ideas were not new, but rather an official outline of subprojects already existing. Many of these employees were held in high regard by the people, especially for their curative know-how which they had attained through the cooperation with the Swiss physicians. Moreover those employees had worked for years in a "flat hierarchy" in a participative working environment (this in contrast to Government Hospitals) and were interested, willing and capable of active and creative collaboration in any phase of project development. Also most helpful was the fact that at the time, the acting District Governor was Dasho Phub Dorje, a Dzongdag with a professional background in health care. Helvetas also provided important support. Because Helvetas set few, if any parameters, the Swiss medic was able to get fully engaged in the Government programme. His role then was mainly that of a teacher/instructor and supervisor. It was important to support the staff in the BHU's in professional, moral and logistic aspects. In those days a chosen few of the Bhutanese staff, both men and women, enjoyed advanced training abroad which served the better understanding of the "primary health care" philosophy, all fully paid by Helvetas. I am privileged to say that I was involved in that project phase.

Good doctors for district hospitals: yet a worldwide problem

In the district hospitals it is the medical doctors who are formative in the way the health system is managed; this in contrast to the "primary health care" system which depends on paramedical staff trained in Bhutan for specified functions. Doctors bring with them their personal experience and role models from the big hospitals where they were trained (in the case of Bhutan mostly in India, to be followed by a few years in an assistant position in Thimphu). Experience in the field of public health (which includes all aspects of "primary health care") is totally missing in that training. Also, the cooperation on an eye-to-eye level with non-academic health experts is not customary and therefore soon replaced by the habitual hierarchy thinking. In the district hospital you will find the whole spectrum of somatic problems in all medical faculties and they therefore require a correct triage or must be solved locally. This of course calls for a fundamental professional knowledge and human experience which a doctor will only acquire in long years. For readers from Europe: this is comparable to the challenges a general practitioner in a rural region has to meet. But just about anywhere a job at the district hospital is unattractive for young doctors, it is a place where they have to mark time before moving on to a career in their particular field of interest in a general hospital. When I worked in Bhutan the government did not have a solution for this problem – whether the situation changed later on, I don't know.

"Prevent the construction of a new hospital"

This was the "instruction" given to me by headquarters in Zurich before my departure to Bhutan. The construction of a new hospital was a wish communicated to Helvetas which recognised that this again would lay the focus in public health to the curative sector. Examples in other countries have shown that an ill-conceived hospital construction could endanger existing and well-functioning facilities of a "primary health care" system. It was only in those years that the discussion started in WHO bodies, which dealt with the question of how the "secondary level" of the district hospitals should be equipped in order to achieve synergy effects instead of competition to the basic care ("tertiary level" are hospitals with central functions that go beyond the basic care). For outsiders it may be difficult to understand why this system should be at the core of many problems. I will list some of them.

The hospital: (only) an architectural masterpiece?

Helvetas, on short notice, decided to take part in the planning and financing of a new hospital after all, following a "threat" by RGOB to hand over the project to another donor. Thus they wanted to make sure that it would fit in as well as possible with the already existing health project. In respect to the architectural standards the RGOB had much clearer ideas than in defining the future function of the hospital and the staffing of doctors. That this type of hospital later on would serve as a model for other districts was also due to its layout and construction method, not because of its functionality. Simply put: the hardware part of it (construction, equipment) was almost perfect, whereas the fitting software (staff, operating process) was lacking in professional know-how, innovation and persistence. For a short time it seemed that, both at the governmental level of the RGOB and with Helvetas, there was an active interest to be responsive to the proposal that the Bumthang Hospital would be used as a training base for general practitioners (meaning doctors to be groomed specially for the requirements of a district hospital). I then had the opportunity to set out my conceptual ideas on this topic in my doctoral thesis. Ultimately the quick "phasing out" of the health project by Helvetas and the staff change at the top level of the ministry of social affairs were detrimental to the realisation.

Sustainability

The core question: what part of Helvetas' engagement for the people of Bhutan has endured? I am not in a position to make a judgement. I would have preferred to ask some of my former indigenous staff; however, due to time limits this was not possible. At best there are – spread over the whole country - some well-trained people in the health sector whose current knowledge and attitude has been influenced by their having been part of Helvetas' health project. Due to conceptual weakness and the little time devoted to it, no lasting impulse to the health system has resulted, this in notable contrast to the impact of Helvetas' projects in the field of agro-forestry.

Indigenous medicine: close cooperation

Helvetas' project was a pioneer one in Bhutan in as much as it integrated the traditional medical system which derives from Tibetan medicine, as early as 1982. It was the widely respected Dungtsho Singay Namgyel who until then had practised medicine in a tsong, now moved in at the small Bumthang Hospital, where he held consultation. Even though the RGOB officially tried to provide even-handed support to both medical systems, there was not an equally close cooperation "under one roof" to be found anywhere else in Bhutan. Notwithstanding the close proximity, everyday life revealed both the distance and difference between the two medical schools. The primary health care approach implies a demystification and simplification of medicine. The primary aim is to empower people to become as proficient as possible in the field of health care. The traditional system, in my view, appears to be less endeavoured, it allows the doctor to play a strong part as a healer. Uncontested attributes of the scientific approach are obvious in the area of infectious diseases (tuberculosis, leprosy), emergency surgery, birth assistance, technical diagnosis (laboratory, x-rays) and prevention (vaccination). On the other hand, cooperation showed the value of indigenous medicine where chronic illness and afflictions are concerned which, in our context, are viewed as psychosomatic reactions. Attempts for a closer exchange of know-how were hindered by the language barrier, job pressure and a rather critical attitude of the Bhutanese staff. Consequently, traditional medicine, to be practised in separate rooms as part of OPD, was included in the planning of the new Bumthang Hospital.

In Kürze

Dr. Hans Gammeter war als Arzt einige Zeit in Bhutan tätig. Er zieht hier durchaus kritisch Bilanz über das Gesundheitsprojekt von Helvetas, das in seinen Augen nicht den gleichen Erfolg zeitigte, wie die Projekte in Landwirtschaft und Forstwirtschaft. Gesundheitsprojekte sind in der dritten Welt beliebt und machen die Spender beliebt. Der Schwerpunkt sollte aber auf Prävention (Hygiene, Wasserversorgung, Ernährung) und nicht so sehr auf kurative Medizin gelegt werden. Bhutan verfolgte ab Mitte der Achtzigerjahre eine vernünftige Politik der Baisversorgung mit dezentralen kleinen Ambulatorien und der Ausbildung von lokalem Medizinpersonal. Helvetas liess sich dann von der Regierung zum Bau eines Spitals in Bumthang drängen, das baulich hervorragend gelöst wurde, im Betrieb aber nicht die erhoffte Wirkung brachte, weil an den Abläufen, der Rekrutierung und Ausbildung von Personal zu wenig professionell und innovativ, und vor allem nicht ausdauernd genug gearbeitet wurde.

En bref

Dr Hans Gammeter a été médecin au Bhoutan pendant quelques années. Il dresse ici un bilan critique du projet de santé d'Helvetas, qui, à ses yeux, n'a pas connu le même succès que les projets agricoles ou forestiers. Les projets de santé sont appréciés dans les pays en voie de développement et suscitent de la sympathie pour les bailleurs. La priorité devrait toutefois se situer dans la prévention et moins dans le domaine curatif. À partir du milieu des années 80, le Bhoutan a mené une politique de santé raisonnable, en mettant l'accent sur les soins de base et de petits centres ambulatoires, et en formant du personnel médical local. Helvetas s'est ensuite laissé convaincre par le gouvernement de construire un hôpital à Bumthang, un ouvrage dont la réalisation a été un succès, mais dont la mise en service n'a pas eu l'effet escompté, notamment en raison d'un manque de professionnalisme et d'innovation dans les procédures, dans le recrutement et la formation du personnel, et aussi parce que la persévérance nécessaire a manqué.

New Bumthang hospital

by Dr. Saamdu Chetri, Dy-Resident Co-ordinator Helvetas / SDC, 1988-2006

119 Laying of the foundation stone

The Swiss assistance in the health programme in the valley of Bumthang and its neighbouring districts was making a good impact, focussing on preventive medicine. But it lacked the right kind of infrastructure to provide adequate services and facilities for the sick, both indoor and outdoor. During 1987, the construction of a 50-bedded hospital in Bumthang began. The Swiss designed it very traditionally, but with all the modern amenities in it. The hospital was a miniature of a complete modern medical centre in itself. It had an equipped operating theatre, x-ray facilities, fully equipped laboratories for reviews and analysis, central heating facilities, 6 private warded bedrooms, and comfortably sized outdoor patient department integrating indigenous medical facilities. The Druk Gyalpo was so impressed that he said this would serve as a model hospital for 20 Dzongkhags and he wished it to be replicated.

The hospital was built at a cost of Nu 14 million, sponsored mainly by the tree Swiss cities of St. Gallen, Winterthur and Schaffhausen. Unfortunately, it has been underutilised from the beginning, since the national policy on referral and district hospitals had changed and preference was given to Mongar and Thimphu. Another reason might have been the shortage of experienced national doctors.

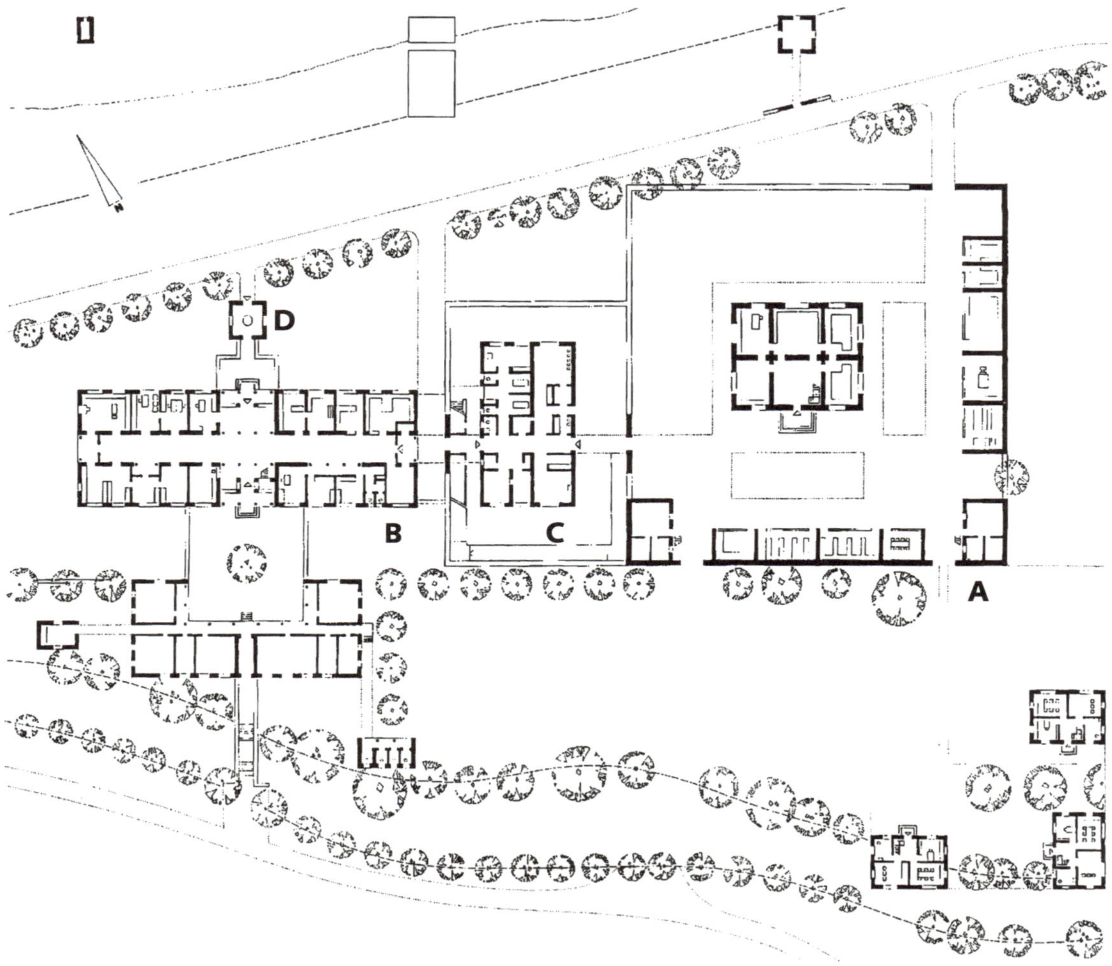

120 A) Old hospital, B) Wards, C) Operation theatre, D) Prayer wheel

In Kürze

Das Schweizer Gesundheitsprogramm hatte ansprechende Erfolge vor allem im Bereich der Präventivmedizin. 1987 begann man mit dem Bau eines 50-Betten-Spitals in Bumthang, das wie eine Miniaturausgabe eines kompletten Spitals ausgerüstet wurde. Der König war sehr beeindruckt und wollte ähnliche Einrichtungen für alle 20 Distrikte. Tatsächlich wurde das Spital wenig genutzt, weil die Gesundheitspolitik den Schwerpunkt auf die Spitäler in Mongar und Thimphu verlegte.

En bref

Le programme de santé suisse a connu un succès évident dans le domaine de la prévention. En 1987 a commencé la construction d'un hôpital de 50 lits à Bumthang, entièrement équipé comme la version miniature d'un grand hôpital. Le roi, très impressionné, souhaitait un équipement similaire pour tous les 20 districts. Dans les faits, l'hôpital a été peu utilisé car la politique sanitaire priorisait les hôpitaux de Mongar et de Thimphu.

Building technologies and materials

by Daniel Schwitter, Architect, Project Manager Bumthang hospital and NRTI construction

121 Prefabrication is traditional

122 Construction site

123 Main entrance

The buildings that Helvetas realized in Bhutan may be denominated as sustainable in as much as natural and locally available materials were used wherever possible. Stones, sand, and timber originate from the immediate surroundings of the construction sites. However, cement, hardware, glass, and sanitation and electric materials had to be imported, mostly from India. Since there was no electric power supply at that time, big construction machines or power-operated tools were unknown. Concrete was only utilized when there was no alternative because its raw material, gravel, had to be produced in a very strenuous manner, and because cement consumption was high, and reinforced steel very expensive. In the 80's, in Bumthang, it took a lorry four weeks to drive to India to purchase cement and get back again. Stones that were used to build the walls were collected in the riverbed and split with a mallet, or mined by hand in the nearby quarries.

Helvetas' buildings are characterized by a very down-to-earth utilization of timber. Supporting pillars, floors of storeys, and roof trusses were built according to the local building style. The Swiss experts optimized the traditional wall elements called „Ekra“, which are fitted together very cleverly without using any metallic connectors, with regard to their thermal insulation and atmospheric impacts. These technical improvements are not visible to laypersons.

One technical novelty in Bhutan was the installation of a floor heating at Bumthang Hospital. A simple hot water tube system was installed in the floor of those rooms in which wood stoves were not appropriate either for hygienic reasons or because of fire hazard. Another novelty was the adoption of windows with rebate frames and a simple metal lock alternative that led to a significant improvement of insulation. A simple construction was developed in the Helvetas' founded Carpentry- and Agro-Workshop that corresponded approx. to the status of technology in Switzerland before double-glazed windows were introduced. Likewise unknown were roof gutters and drain outlets. Nepalese craftsmen made them tediously by hand out of zinc-plated sheet iron. Thanks to the gutters and drains the immediate surroundings of the buildings could be kept clear of mud during the rainy season. The fact that these technologies have all been well accepted and partly even improved gives a great deal of satisfaction.

Many people from Bumthang had never seen a toilet or shower before entering the hospital where the installation of such infrastructure had become necessary for hygienic reasons. A specifically trained team would instruct all entering patients on the correct use of these new devices.

Local artist were employed to carry out finishing work that was done in the traditional building style. Carvers and painters are very sought-after professionals who are usually trained at convent schools. Accordingly, it is quite difficult to recruit such persons. The paints for walls and ceilings are exclusively made of natural materials such as lime, soil, roots, leaves, etc. Each morning, the quantity of paint for a day's work had to be mixed afresh. The dried colour powders were boiled in a binding agent consisting of bone meal and hides, which submerged the entire building site into a cloud of biting stench.

In Kürze

Für ihre Bauten nutzte Helvetas wenn immer möglich lokale Materialien wie Steine, Sand und Holz. Alles übrige Baumaterial musste mühsam von Indien heraufgeschafft werden. Da es keine Elektrizität gab konnten nur konventionelle Werkzeuge eingesetzt werden. In der von Helvetas gegründeten Zimmerei wurden einfache Fenster hergestellt, was die Isolation der Häuser verbesserte. Neu für Bhutan waren auch Dachtraufen und Abflussrohre, mit denen die unmittelbare Nähe der Gebäude trocken und sauber gehalten werden konnte.

En bref

Dans la mesure du possible, Helvetas a eu recours, pour ses constructions, à des matériaux locaux tels que les pierres, le sable et le bois. Les autres matériaux de construction devaient être péniblement acheminés depuis l'Inde. Comme il n'y avait pas d'électricité, seuls des outils conventionnels pouvaient être utilisés. La menuiserie installée par Helvetas a fabriqué de nouvelles fenêtres simples, ce qui a amélioré l'isolation des maisons. Une innovation pour le Bhoutan a été l'introduction de chéneaux et de tuyaux d'écoulement, ce qui a permis de maintenir propres et secs les abords immédiats des maisons.

Rural infrastructure

124

Rural infrastructure for one-way or two-way traffic?

by Prof. Dr. Martin Menzi, Co-Founder of Helvetas, Senior Advisor to the RNR-sector from1976-2006, Co-Director NRTI 1992-1994

125

Bhutan is not only a landlocked country, it was and still is a rather isolated place on the southern slope of the eastern Himalayas. The first motor vehicle appeared in 1962 and it was not before 1983 that Druk Air started operating an air link with Calcutta. Only in the last few decades the national network of roads was steadily growing, but even now many Bhutanese living in remote rural areas have to walk hours if not days for reaching the nearest road point.
Since 1985, Switzerland has contributed to the development of the rural transport network, mainly by supporting the national Suspension Bridge Programme. Cutting forest roads and even erecting a ropeway for giving access to potential places, and more recently also constructing farm roads to remote villages have been part of various rural development programmes.
Roads, bridges and other modes of transport can bring people closer and open up lines of communication and economic interaction – but they can also become 'drainage channels', making it easier for people to move, to migrate, to leave remote areas and to strand eventually in urban agglomerations. Sustainable rural development is a rather complex process: A communication network is one part of it, but health care, education, trade and employment etc. are other equally important components. Therefore, holistic views and integrated approaches to rural development initiatives are required if cutting roads and building bridges have to lead to a well balanced two-way traffic between the countryside and urban centres.

In Kürze

Das erste Motorfahrzeug taucht 1962 in Bhutan auf; erst 1983 nimmt Druk Air regelmässige Flugverbindungen nach Calcutta auf.Strassenverbindungen wurden erst in den letzten Jahrzehnten errichtet. Strassen, Brücken und Transportmittel verbinden heute die abgelegensten Winkel mit den Städten. Aber, – so gibt Martin Menzi zu bedenken - sie dürfen nicht zu Einbahnstrassen der Landflucht und Migration werden. Nur eine ganzheitliche Hilfe, welche die Entwicklung der ländlichen Gegenden einschliesst, führt zu einem gesunden Gleichgewicht zwischen Stadt und Land.

En bref

Le premier véhicule à moteur est arrivé au Bhoutan en 1962; les vols de ligne de la compagnie Druk Air vers Calcutta n'ont commencé qu'en 1983. Les liaisons routières n'ont été achevées qu'au cours des dernières décennies. Des routes, des ponts et des moyens de transports relient aujourd'hui les régions éloignées aux villes. Toutefois, Martin Menzi met en garde: ces liaisons ne doivent pas devenir des voies à sens unique de l'exode rural et de la migration. Seule une aide globale, prenant en compte le développement des régions rurales, peut mener à un équilibre entre les régions rurales et urbaines.

Hardware

by Saamdu Chetri

For many years, Swiss were the only donors who actually gave importance to both types of capacity development, software meaning Human Resource Development/training and hardware meaning buildings/infrastructure. Needs were obviously calling for both. This reflected not only a practical approach, but was also appealing to political realities. However, it must be said that the Swiss cooperation always started off with software, followed by the buildings to house the necessary functions; e.g. offices for forestry, livestock, agriculture, extension centres and workshops to house repairs and maintenance, schools, BHU's etc. Ultimately, true mega projects have been realized.

The Swiss have considered certain aspects in taking up the construction in Bhutan; they systematically strove to create a model for construction, based on the traditional architecture, integrating local materials and skills whenever found functional. Good sanitation facilities to secure hygienic conditions, modern construction and building techniques were a must. A number of large projects that were contracted out to the Bhutanese contractors were sub-contracted to either Indian firms or in smaller parts to local contractors. This way on the job training to the contractors' workforce always became increasingly difficult and finally failed. However, a few of the contractors who were willing to learn have grown to take up large contracts. A unique scenario in Bhutan is that in most cases contractors have failed to deliver the work on time.

Construction time is always linked to money and any delay always adds on to escalating costs. A large number of contractors made up for it through provision of low quality materials and works. However, this is not possible with the Swiss cooperation where most have lost money because they had to deliver high quality (as described in the contract) and due to weak management (that delayed work progress due to bad planning and administration). Therefore, a lot of contractors were always afraid to work with Swiss on turnkey projects. The construction industry represents nearly 20% of GDP and provides a vast field of job opportunities and quality enhancement. It would warrant much more attention of developers, be they foreign or national.

The building sector in Bhutan

by Daniel Schwitter, Architect, Project Manager Bumthang hospital and NRTI construction

The building sector in Bhutan is slowly approximating its structure and technology to the ones of the two neighbouring countries India and Nepal. One can observe that, depending on the type of buildings, construction work is done partly in the traditional way but also quite often, unfortunately, in the „Indian concrete building style with Bhutanese painting works" carried out by various craft and social groups. Activities that involve "dirty" building materials as used by masons, plasterers, tilers, etc., are carried out by people belonging to lower social groups and foreign workers from India or Nepal. Local craftsmen – and convent school pupils in the sacral building sector – carry out building works in which „clean" materials such as wood and paint are being used (carpenter, roofer, carver, painter). Semi-governmental enterprises are responsible for road construction,where mostly foreign workers are employed.

Helvetas' construction projects are assigned on the basis of public calls for tenders. Entrepreneurs submit their offers to so-called „contractors" who possess an official Bhutanese business licence but, in most cases, do not dispose of a professional background in the building sector. The required number of professional staff is being employed only after the contract has been awarded. Indian or Nepalese nationals, who have hardly enjoyed any schooling, do in general the civil engineering and masonry work. Local craftsmen are often contracted only for timber construction work. Medium and more senior technical staff and experts, mostly Indian nationals, are generally employed afresh for each new building. Technical problems that may arise during construction are solved either directly by the awarding authority/building-owner or the workers themselves. In default of specific professional knowledge, the contractors concentrate on logistical and administrative tasks such as purchase of building materials, staff management, and accounting.

Shortly before construction starts, lorries are fetching the workers who often total more than one hundred people when engaged in big Helvetas projects, from the southern parts of Bhutan and neighbouring India. Within two days they set up their camps made of bamboo mats where they dwell together with their families near the construction site. Life in these camps is very hard, and most workers would leave it only after completion of the building, though this may take years. The staple food like rice, millet, and curry is offered by the contractor who puts it at their disposal in daily rations. The workers cook and eat their meals individually in their shacks.
Construction work is not thinkable without the active involvement of female workers who often do the bulk of the work. Women, in lack of cranes and stone crushers, carry out hardest work such as transportation of any kind of building materials from the storing place to the construction site, and cutting big stones with a hammer into small pieces of gravel.
Up to approx. 1990, there were practically no professionals existing in the fields of sanitation and electricity due to the simple fact that there was hardly any electricity supply in rural areas. Running water and toilets were regarded as top luxury. Helvetas has solved the problem by either sending young people to Switzerland for training or by deploying temporarily experts from the Helvetas-run craft school in Kathmandu to Bhutan on an employee basis.
Political unrest in the late 80' in southern Bhutan, where many foreign workers had settled after having been engaged for some years on construction sites in northern Bhutan, represented a big challenge to the building sector. Up to this point in time, resident permits for foreign workers had hardly ever been an issue. Because of the unrests, however, rigorous identity scrutiny of Nepalese nationals had been imposed. As an immediate consequence, there were no more construction workers available, and the whole sector came to a temporary standstill. This led to a number of problems and delays at the beginning of the NRTI construction. Government then provided replacement by recruiting workers from eastern Bhutan, which allowed continuation of the planned construction.

126 NRTI

In Kürze

Lange Zeit war die Schweiz das einzige Geberland, welches sowohl in Ausbildung wie auch in Infrastruktur investierte. Für Bauten wurde ein Modell entwickelt, welches die traditionelle Architektur und die lokal vorhandenen Materialien und Techniken integrierte. Grosse Probleme hatte man zunächst mit den unerfahrenen örtlichen Baufirmen, die den gewünschten Qualitätsstandards nicht gewachsen waren. Sie waren am schnellen Geld und weniger an gutem Baumanagement interessiert. Schweizer Projektleiter achteten genauestens auf Qualität, auf Termine und Kosten. Viele bhutanesische Baufirmen fürchteten ihre Aufträge, weil sie dabei leicht Verluste machten.

En bref

Pendant longtemps, la Suisse a été l'unique pays donateur à investir aussi bien dans la formation que dans l'infrastructure. Pour les constructions, un modèle a été développé qui intégrait l'architecture traditionnelle, les matériaux et les techniques locales. Il a été difficile de collaborer avec les entrepreneurs locaux – peu expérimentés et incapables de fournir la qualité requise. Ils étaient avant tout intéressés à amasser beaucoup d'argent en peu de temps, et moins à une bonne gestion des constructions. Des chefs de projets suisses ont été particulièrement attentifs à la qualité, au respect des délais et à la maîtrise des coûts. De nombreux entrepreneurs bhoutanais craignaient leurs commandes car ils savaient qu'ils risquaient de faire des pertes.

Tashi La – the first and only ropeway in Bhutan

by Karchung Dukpa and Hansruedi Stierlin, Project Managers, in: Helvetas, Swiss-Bhutan Partnership in a changing world, 2000 Thimphu

127

In the late 1960s, Helvetas started a dairy project at Gogona in the Wangdue Phodrang district. Soon the Swiss expatriates working in the project realized that dairy farming and forestry are highly interdependent. They also extended the farming and began to grow potatoes. A forestry consultant from Switzerland first developed the idea of a ropeway to get better access to the national highway. A general accessibility study was made for the three valleys of Phobjikha, the most eastern valley, Gogona in the middle and Khotokha, the most western valley. Even though the Swiss Dairy and Forestry Project shifted its activities to Bumthang, the Royal Government of Bhutan decided in 1979 that the ropeway should be set up from Chuzomsa (nine kilometres east of Wangdue Phodrang) to Tashi La.

The main purpose of the ropeway was to provide access to the Khotokha valley and to transport timber, firewood and agricultural goods. It was planned to open up the vast forest resources of Khotokha and to supply the Wangdue Phodrang area with timber. The survey of the ropeway line turned out to be extremely difficult. The lower third of the total stretch passes through the paddy fields of Bjena area. In the upper two-thirds of the alignment, the ropeway is leading through evergreen primeval forest with a dense undergrowth of bamboo. The survey crew often only managed to penetrate about 20 m per day into this forest. After the survey the corridor for the ropeway had to be cut through the jungle. One full year was needed to complete this work, because all the logging had to be done manually. The machinery, the carriages, the pulley batteries and the saddles for the supports were delivered from Switzerland, whereas the steel ropes came from India. Indian trucks brought the steel ropes to the Bhutan border and dumped them on the ground, but there were no means to lift the heavy steel ropes onto a Bhutanese truck again. The only solution was to dig a big pit, so that a truck would fit in, and then pull the steel ropes onto the truck. A Swiss ropeway expert supervised the whole installation of the steel ropes, the machinery and the wooden supports, which carry the saddles and the pulley batteries. On the occasion of His Majesty the King's birthday on 11 th November 1983, the ropeway was officially inaugurated by HRH Tengye Lyonpo and the Swiss Ambassador with a traditional Bhutanese ceremony.

The most remarkable thing about the 20 years of construction and operation is the fact that, in spite of all the difficulties, which were encountered, there were no major accidents. The ropeway was designed for the transport of goods only, but it was clear from the start that people would also have to be transported. For this reason, the ropeway was later equipped with a carriage indicator, which shows the exact location of the two carriages and which sounds a horn when the carriages approach the station. In 1999, the Royal Government of Bhutan banned the passenger transport for safety reasons, mainly because the skyline cables were then 20 years old. However, for the transport of goods the ropeway is still safe. The hauling cable has to be replaced every 5 years and the supports every 6 - 7 years. During the whole time of construction and later during the operation of the ropeway, Karchung Dukpa, a Forest Ranger attached by the Forest Department, was the responsible manager. In 1990, he was able to buy the ropeway. Since then he has run the ropeway as a private business, bearing the full risk yet making a reasonable profit. Local people benefit most from the ropeway, carrying timber for house constructions and for transportation of their agricultural produce. For about one month in autumn, the ropeway is engaged in transporting the potato harvest to the highway at Chuzomsa.

Immediately after completion of the ropeway, logging operations started in Khotokha. Helvetas financed nine kilometres of forest road, which was constructed in 1984. A comprehensive Forest Management Plan regulates the utilisation of the forest resources. The Forest Management Unit (FMU) comprises 4900 hectares of forest with an annual allowable cut of 6900 cubic metres of timber. Strict protection is applied to the habitat of the black-necked cranes.

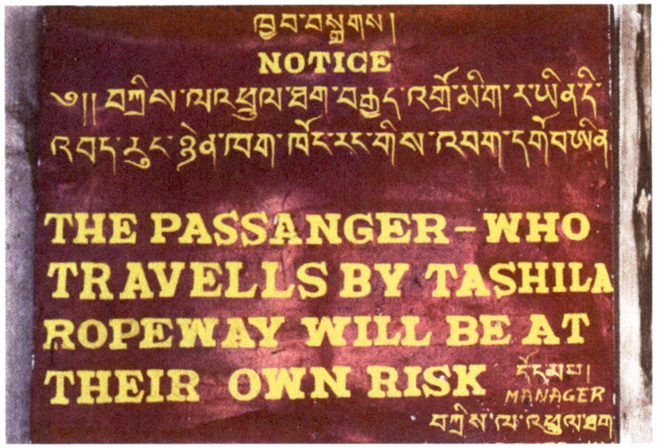

128

In Kürze

Warum nicht entlegene und schwer zugängliche Siedlungen mit einer Transportseilbahn an die Hauptstrasse anbinden? Diese Idee eines Schweizer Forstingenieurs gefiel der Regierung. Der Bau war äusserst schwierig: eine lange Schneise musste durch den dichten Urwald geschlagen werden. Die Seilbahn, die nur für den Transport von Waren gedacht war, wurde ein Erfolg – auch bei den Einheimischen. Der bhutanische Förster, der von Anfang an beim Projekt mitarbeitete, hat die Seilbahn mittlerweile gekauft – und macht damit einen vernünftigen Profit.

En bref

Pourquoi ne pas relier une région difficile d'accès à la route principale par un téléphérique? Cette idée d'un forestier suisse plut au gouvernement. La construction fut très difficile, il fallut faire une tranchée à travers une forêt primaire particulièrement dense. Le téléphérique, conçu pour le transport exclusif de marchandises, a été un succès, y compris chez les indigènes. Le forestier bhoutanais qui a travaillé dans ce projet dès le début a acheté l'installation et l'exploite de manière rentable.

129

Trail bridges – key elements to rural infrastructure

by Dr. Saamdu Chetri, Dy-Resident Co-ordinator Helvetas / SDC, 1988-2006

130 Punakha Dzong (1907)

131 Thangton Gyelpo

132 Iron chain bridge

Historical and religious background

Until recently, transport and travel were highly dependent on foot trails and horses. For centuries, rivers were crossed on wooden bridges of limited span and safety, constructed through local initiatives (cantilever bridges).

The bridge over the Mo Chhu River, the only approach from the west is a fine example of the traditional Bhutanese cantilevered wooden bridge with the beams progressively projecting over the water. The photo was taken before 1908 by John Claude White, a pioneer of photography. Moreover he was the first British political officer overseeing the British interests in Sikkim, Bhutan and Tibet. 1907 he was the delegation leader in Punakha during the coronation of Ugyen Wangchuck, the first king of Bhutan.

Source: Kurt Meyer and Pamela Deuel Meyer, In the Shadow of the Himalayas. A Photographic Record by John Claude White 1883-1908

The Iron Bridge Builder

It is believed that in order to live piously and in happiness, a Bhutanese must build a bridge to link people and valleys; most Bhutanese believe that building a trail bridge is worth one's living. Thus, the importance of trail bridges cannot be explained just in terms of cost effectiveness. Thanks to bridges, the mountain dwellers have also come closer to avail themselves of social, religious and emergency contacts.

The Tibetan saint Thangton Gyelpo, who was also called the Iron Bridge Builder, built mainly iron chain bridges in Tibet and neighbouring countries like Bhutan. Some of these bridges still exist today.

Access to remote areas

The bridge sector has a very important role in the socio-economic realm; the objective being is to assist the Royal Government of Bhutan in attaining a balanced socio-economic development in the country by facilitating access to the remote rural areas.

It would appear that the demand for trail bridges has decreased after the construction of so many of them, but it continues to rise. There is a number of reasons for it, one is obvious: the unpredictable monsoon floods washing away some of the older, less safely built bridges. Growing networks of roads and the wish of the rural people to reduce their walking distance to service centres would be another. A third reason is the development of schools, Basic Health Units and marketing infrastructures.

133 Under construction

134 Pfynwald suspended bridge, built by Bhutanese – a transfer of technology to Switzerland

135 Ambassador Sonam T. Rabgye and State councillor J-J Rey-Bellet. Inauguration at Pfyn, VS, Switzerland

Nowadays, the farmers are demanding larger bridges to enable them to cross with loaded power-tillers for marketing of agricultural produce. Technology has been developed, but it has been decided that no such bridge shall be built in places where bridges on motorable roads in accordance to road master plan will be erected. The sustainability of such a programme is now ensured through the suspension bridge trainings. The respective Dzongkhags must appoint caretakers for the trail bridges. The issue of ownership has been fully understood now, in contrast to a few years ago, when the community still felt that it was the responsibility of the government that has been the giver and the provider, an attitude existing from time immemorial. The Swiss contribution to the trail bridge sub-sector has been substantial, not only in quantity but also in terms of conceptual work such as the development of viable standards, policies and strategies, as well as the strengthening of technical and institutional capacities within the public sector.

In Kürze

Bhutan ist ein unwegsames Land. Flüsse und Schluchten müssen auf einfachen Brücken überquert werden. Eine Brücke ist in Bhutan nicht einfach nur ein praktisches Bauwerk: Wer fromm und glücklich leben will, der baut in seinem Leben eine Brücke. Ganz nach dem Vorbild des tibetischen Heiligen Thangton Gyelpo, der viele Hängebrücken mit geschmiedeten Ketten gebaut hat, die zum Teil noch immer stehen. Heute verlangen die Bauern nach breiteren Brücken, damit sie diese mit ihren Traktoren überqueren können. Die Regierung hat aber entschieden, dass massivere Brücken nur für eigentliche Strassenübergänge gebaut werden sollen.

En bref

Le Bhoutan est un pays difficilement accessible. Les rivières et les gorges doivent être traversées par de simples ponts de bois. Au Bhoutan, un pont n'est pas simplement une construction pratique: quiconque veut vivre heureux et dans le respect de la religion construit un pont dans sa vie. A l'exemple du saint tibétain Thangtong Gyelpo, qui a construit de nombreux ponts avec des chaînes en fer forgé, véritable acier, et dont certains existent encore aujourd'hui. Les ponts modernes doivent être plus larges pour permettre le passage de tracteurs. Le gouvernement a toutefois décidé que seuls les ponts routiers devaient être des constructions massives.

Linking people and communities

by Franz Gähwiler, Civil Engineer, Co-ordinator trail bridge programme

136

137

The building of bridges has a very special meaning to Buddhists: it is said to smoothen obstacles out for everyone! This is one reason why the building of pedestrian bridges in the hills and mountains of Bhutan has a long tradition. During centuries, narrow canyons have been overcome with the aid of simple beam-, rope-, chain-, bamboo- or cantilever bridges. Some of those bridges enabled animals to cross them. The span length was less than 50 metres and the bridges often had to be removed before the beginning of the rains, because otherwise they might have been washed away. Only in the 20th century "modern" pedestrian overpasses became a success in the Himalayan valleys.

In the 1970's the construction department of Bhutan initiated a national Pedestrian Bridge Programme. During the 1980's a successful cooperation developed between the projects for pedestrian rope bridges in Bhutan and Nepal, financed by the Swiss and supported by Helvetas. Experiences have been shared and synergies led to the improvement of technologies and approaches. Newly developed manuals facilitated the establishment of local capacities and simplified the planning, the surveying, the construction and the maintenance of pedestrian overpasses.
From its beginning the suspension bridge programme in Bhutan has been characterized by the villagers' intensive cooperation. The weak or inexistent private sector forced all participants to have most work carried out by unqualified manpower, this under the auspices of the technical staff of the district authorities. The progressive decentralisation allowed the operational work to be shifted from the centre to the districts. An intensive vocational training provided by the project tried to enhance the local capacities in a way that the outsourced task could be assigned and executed in a professional manner.

Until June 2006, 411 pedestrian rope bridges have been built in Bhutan under this programme. This number corresponds to more than half of the 750 river crossovers planned countrywide. According to the currently available capacities, new bridges will be built during the next 15 to 20 years, before the focus will shift from construction to maintenance.

Key data (1987-2006; 20 years)

Average span width per bridge	70	m
Average costs per bridge	21.000	US$
Average costs per meter/span width	300	US$
Average population served	1.500	pers
Average costs per person	14	US$

Bridge construction – a participatory process

by Franz Gähwiler, Civil Engineer, Co-ordinator trail bridge programme, Source: Excerpt from Helvetas Partnership, No. 155, 2/1999

138

For more than 20 years, the inhabitants of the Tading district wanted to build a bridge over the Toorsa River at Taba Ramtey, in the Southwest of Bhutan. The district covers 631 households, 500 of them benefiting from this project. This area is inhabited by the Doyas, an ethnic minority.

They have their own language and have started to open themselves to others only recently.

A bridge for pedestrians and pack animals would allow the villagers all-the-year access to the city of Phuentsholing with its 25'000 inhabitants and institutions such as schools, hospitals, markets, government offices etc. Moreover, the local population would be able to sell their crops, agricultural products such as tangerines, lemons, nuts and ginger, at the city market.

Extensive Preparation

Extensive preparation included the contact with the authorities, the choice of location, the necessary surveying, the discussion about the population's collaboration and the regulation of rights and obligations.

The agents of the rope bridge programme explained to the villagers that extensive and unpaid contribution of labour is expected during the construction. In the case of the Taba Ramtey bridge the Bhutanese engineers estimated that approximately 8000 days of work were required to do the job.

The choice of location became another central issue. The population, of course, preferred a crossover as close to the village as possible. However, they accepted the fact that the circumstances did not allow for such a solution, since the span width of the bridge would have become too large. After discussion the bridge site was fixed about 30 minutes upstream.

Heavy labour

The administration of Thimphu took over the planning part, while the population was responsible for the actual work including carrying cement bags, pieces of steel and the necessary tools, "only" four hours of distance on foot of course. This is no exception in Bhutan, where in certain areas several days' marches are common for such constructions. The heavy work also included the excavation of the foundations, hacking rocks with the air hammer or manually and mincing stones to gravel, again manually.

Well-organized collaboration

The challenge to organise the population's contribution was the "Lachap"'s task, an elected agent of the village who, together with a few households, decided which agent - not excluding female ones – and when he or she had to work. Usually, such a commitment lasted 15 days and after that the next labourers where called up. Such accomplishment could be difficult for smaller households, since it is not possible for them to work in the fields during this time. Richer households employ others to act on their behalf. 2 Swiss Francs are paid per day/person, which approximately equals the customary wages for unskilled workers in Bhutan. Altogether, 9'935 hours of work have been performed in this case.

Learning by doing

The management of the suspension bridge programme decided to organise training for site managers at the Taba Ramtey site. During one month, 22 participants from all over Bhutan learned how to build a bridge and how to organise such a site in cooperation with the local population.

This huge effort led to more cohesion among the people. They immediately filed an application with the government for another bridge to cross a creek of the river Toorsa.

In Kürze

In den 70er Jahren beschloss die Regierung ein nationales Programm für Fussgängerbrücken. In den 80-er Jahren suchte man die Zusammenarbeit mit der Schweiz und Helvetas. Bis Juni 2006 wurden 411 Fussgängerbrücken gebaut. Von Anfang an wurde die lokale Bevölkerung einbezogen. Die Bauern durften mitentscheiden, wo die Brücke hinkommen sollte, sie mussten in Fronarbeit aber auch selbst Hand anlegen. Auf einer Baustelle richteten die Schweizer Fachleute ein eigentliches Ausbildungsprogramm für Baustellenleiter ein, die dann anderswo im Lande die lokale Bevölkerung beim Bau einer Brücke anleiten konnten.

En bref

Dans les années 70, le gouvernement a décidé de lancer un programme de construction de ponts pédestres. Dans les années 80, il a sollicité la Suisse et Helvetas. Jusqu'en juin 2006, 411 ponts suspendus ont été construits. Dès le début, la population a été impliquée, les paysans ont ainsi pu décider où les ponts devaient être construits, et ils ont participé au travaux. Sur un chantier, les experts suisses ont mis en place un véritable programme de formation pour contremaîtres qui ont ensuite pu diriger eux-mêmes la construction avec la population locale.

Puna Tsang Chhu bridge, Wangdue Phodrang

by Dr. Saamdu Chetri, Dy-Resident Co-ordinator Helvetas / SDC, 1988-2006

139 Puna Tsang Chhu Bridge (1962)

The site and the history

The bridge over the Puna Tsang Chhu below Wangdue, is the most important bridge linking east and west of Bhutan. The location where the bridge has been built is a very historic site with full of mesmerizing stories on how the wooden cantilever bridge „Bazam" (meaning wooden bridge) was built in 1684 by Dakpala under the command of Tenzing Rabgay known as the precious prince. A hundred years later in 1783 when Samuel Davis visited Bhutan, the Bazam was still in a very good shape. The bridge was regularly maintained and lasted until it was washed away by the floods in 1917 and 1968. The following year, a "Bailey" bridge, a temporary iron modular construction, replaced it.

Bridges and legends

Karma Ura tells the story of a mysterious river maid who tried to destroy the bridge-work they built in 1684 in dark nights. People living there knew that the rivermaid liked mask dances. So they arranged dances every night. The maid enthousiastically watched and forgot therefore to destroy the bridge...
And the bridge resisted to all water attacks till 1917.

And a Swiss story goes alike: at Schoellenen in a narrow gorge on the important Gotthard trade route to Italy, only a bridge could open the road. But nobody knew how to go about it. Thus, the people negotiated a deal with the devil who promised to do the job. As an award, he only wanted the first soul crossing the bridge to be his. Fine, the locals sent a goat as the first soul. The devil got terribly angry and left the place within seconds...

Design criteria

The government requested the Swiss to design and build a new bridge serving the increasing traffic on this most important national link. The two-lane bridge should carry 32 tons with a span over 120 meters and should incur low-cost maintenance. The Swiss builders submitted three designs: wood, steel, and concrete. While the Swiss favoured a wooden bridge, the government preferred the concrete one. The project was designed by WGG Schnetzer Puskas Engineers, Basle, Switzerland. The design, taking into account the history, blends aesthetically with the surrounding environment, the old remnant pillar and guardhouse, Wangdue Dzong overlooking it.

In Kürze

Paradestück der Schweizer Brückenbauer ist der Bau der neuen Brücke für die wichtige West-Ost-Transitachse. Nicht nur bautechnisch eine Herausforderung; es galt auch auf die Situation und ihre mythologische Bedeutung Rücksicht zu nehmen: Die alte Holzbrücke aus dem Jahre 1684 wurde über die Jahrhunderte gut unterhalten, bis sie im Jahre 1917 und dann endgültig 1968 von den Fluten weggerissen wurde. Die Schweizer hätten gerne wieder eine Holzkonstruktion hingestellt, die Regierung aber verlangte nach einer Betonbrücke mit zwei Fahrspuren, die 32 Tonnen tragen kann.

En bref

Le pont le plus en vue des constructeurs suisses a été le nouveau pont de l'axe routier de transit est-ouest. Ce n'était pas seulement un défi technique, il a également fallu tenir compte de l'importance historique du site: l'ancien pont en bois construit en 1684 a été bien entretenu pendant des siècles, jusqu'en 1917. En 1968 des inondations l'ont définitivement emporté. Les Suisses auraient volontiers reconstruit un ouvrage en bois, mais le gouvernement a exigé un pont en béton à deux voies, supportant une charge de 32 tonnes.

140 Puna Tsang Chhu Bridge (2002)

Report of the supervising engineer

by Hans Pfaffen, Consulting Engineer VDI

Building the Puna Tsang Chhu bridge was a real challenge to all parties involved. This bridge which has a total length of 120 m and a width of 8,80 m, and the arch of which has a span length of 96 m, required 2445 tons of concrete, 232 tons of steel as well as large quantities of timber. It generated over 2000 tons of loads at each end of its arch.

The biggest problems, however, lay with the contractors. As a matter of fact, the consortium consisting of Indian and Bhutanese entrepreneurs did not dispose of much experience, or rather any at all, to carry out successfully such an ambitious construction work. The basic idea of benefiting from an exchange of experience and knowledge did hardly work since the Indian partner alone did more than 95 percent of the entire work. In addition, recruiting Bhutanese workers was illusive, due to the extremely high requirements from the civil engineering viewpoint.

The consortium was awarded the tender because it had submitted the cheapest offer. The Project Management and the implementation obliged the constructor to take over various tasks at his sole responsibility and management. For instance, intensive coaching and mentoring of the construction firm had to be ensured. Furthermore, the survey and control of quality, execution of construction work, technology, accounting, ascertainment of the measurements, negotiations, and payments were also part of the construction site management's tasks. Helvetas and the Project Manager were responsible for all the afore-mentioned activities. This was an enormous job and a big challenge, which, however, gave way to great satisfaction after the inauguration of the bridge.

Time and again, we were astonished by the Indian workers' ability to deliver good quality despite the fact that they had only very simple tools at their disposal. For instance, when displacing concrete elements they used ropes and bamboo canes, taking advantage of the mechanical principle of the lever arm, and succeeded in processing and shifting the heaviest elements accurate to a millimetre. Accuracy was the primary maxim to act on. At the construction site, the bridge was regarded as the world's largest thermometer, since its arch stretched and rose by a couple of millimetres in hot weather. These micro motions were measured daily.

The bridge arch required a simultaneous placing of concrete from both sides in order to maintain balance and symmetry. At times, work went on around the clock.

Sometimes, up to 400 workers were busy on the construction site, but luckily only two minor casualties occurred. The fact that wearing hard hats was compulsory as well as further safety measures have certainly contributed to a positive result. Unexpectedly high flooding had led to a major settling of two supports of the scaffolding, which temporarily put in jeopardy the construction of the bridge arch. This called for rapid action and special measures had to be taken. One of these was a 72 hours shift-work that had to be put in place a couple of times.

It was noted with great satisfaction that the construction workers formed a strong and highly motivated team. These Indian workers have really done a great job. They were mainly skinny men of short stature, but in groups of two or three or more they were able to transport, move, and process very heavy materials and parts.

The construction of the arch bridge has made it clear in an unequivocal way that engineers in Bhutan are not yet in a position to plan and build bridges on their own. Nevertheless, the Roads Department is well capable of building technically less sophisticated bridges. Yet, there is still a lack of capacity in carrying out the necessary technical planning and calculations from an engineer's viewpoint. Therefore, standardized bridges of a span width between 3 m and 72 m have been developed. The complete sets of drawings for such road bridges are with the Roads Department in Thimphu.

Anyway, building this bridge was a incredible experience, and walking over it after its inauguration was a huge pleasure giving a great deal of satisfaction to all parties involved. The Bhutanese are rightly very proud of their bridge, which has already been immortalized in the form of a postage stamp.

In Kürze

Die Brücke ist 120 Meter lang, 8,8 Meter breit, der Brückenbogen hat eine Spannweite von 96 Metern. 2445 Tonnen Beton, 232 Tonnen Stahl und jede Menge Holz. Das Hauptproblem aber waren die Unternehmer: Ein indisch-bhutanisches Konsortium gewann die Ausschreibung, kaum jemand hatte die nötige Erfahrung. 95 Prozent der Arbeiter waren (wie so oft in Bhutan) Inder. Damit hatte Helvetas für einmal keine Chance für einen Know how-Transfer an die Einheimischen. Das gelungene Bauwerk erfüllt die Beteiligten gleichwohl mit Stolz.

En bref

Le pont mesure 120 mètres de long et 8,8 mètres de large, l'arche a une envergure de 96 mètres. Il a fallu 2445 tonnes de béton, 232 tonnes d'acier et une grande quantité de bois. Le principal problème a été celui des entrepreneurs: un consortium indo-bhoutanais a gagné le concours, mais pour ainsi dire personne n'avait l'expérience requise. 95 pour-cent des travailleurs étaient d'origine indienne, comme c'est souvent le cas au Bhoutan. Dans ce cas, Helvetas n'a par conséquent pas pu profiter de former des Bhoutanais. Malgré cela, l'ouvrage fait la fierté de tous les concernés.

141 Temporary trusses for arch construction

142 Formwork arch foundation

143 Temporary false work for arch

144 Steel fitters at work

145 Concreting on top of prefab elements of the arch

146 Reinforcing of parapet walls

147 Centre point of the bridge with temporary support

148 Deck slab under construction

149 New and old temporary bailey bridge

Small Enterprise Development

150

Workshop management – Concept and financing

by Dr. Saamdu Chetri, Dy-Resident Co-ordinator Helvetas / SDC, 1988-2006

The workshops have initially been built as suppliers of the development projects. Later, they catered to the needs of the local population. Helvetas wanted them to be privatised under a loan scheme. Neither were the banks prepared to venture the deal nor was any project harbour ready. In 1985, the Minister for Planning, Lyonpo C. Dorji, gave Ernst Reinhardt, the first Helvetas/SDC Resident Coordinator in Bhutan, the backing to set-up a revolving fund to plough back the loans. The objective was to back the capable and dedicated rural youth who wished to get self-employed. They needed contacts and collaterals, but they did not have access to the local financial institutions.

The scheme was simple and straightforward:

a) the trained managers became proprietors
b) investment costs were fixed at the present value in local currency
c) Helvetas gave a loan to finance the investment
d) land and building, raw materials, semi-finished and finished goods provided collaterals
e) moderately subsidized interest rate
f) repayment within max. 10 years into a Helvetas governed local revolving fund
g) proper accounting by the managers
h) management support by local Helvetas staff

Helvetas financing was targeted towards micro entrepreneurs only.

The repayments of the privatized enterprises were pooled in an account. Out of this funds four more loans to different private start-ups were financed; a sawmill, two vehicle workshops and the apple cider export. Others were set at different regions of the country and in varied business lines: cable cranes, forest road construction units, milk processing, fruit processing, guest houses, mini power corporation and a rope-way. All these units were privatized after 1991. Out of 19 privatized enterprises under this scheme, there was only one case with bad debts.

151 Karma Tobden, Agro-mechanical workshop, Bumthang

In Kürze

Kleinkredite: Ein probates Mittel zur Entwicklung der Privatwirtschaft.Man schult die interessierten Leute und unterstützt ihren Start als Kleinunternehmer mit günstigen Darlehen. Werden diese zurückbezahlt, fliesst das Geld in neue Projekte. Helvetas hat mit dem Fond, der 1985 von Ernst Reinhardt ins Leben gerufen wurde, vielen Bhutanern den Start in die Selbständigkeit ermöglicht. Und sie hat auf diesem Wege etliche von ihr lancierte Projekte an Einheimische abgeben können. Von 19 Projekten, die nach 1991 privatisiert wurden, hat nur ein einziges das Darlehen nicht zurückgezahlt.

En bref

Petit crédit: un moyen éprouvé pour le développement de l'économie privée. On forme les personnes intéressées et les soutient pour le démarrage d'une petite entreprise au moyen d'un prêt avantageux. Lorsque celui-ci est remboursé, l'argent peut être réinvesti dans un autre projet. Avec le fonds mis en place par Ernst Reinhardt en 1985, de nombreux Bhoutanais ont pu démarrer leur projet et devenir indépendants. Et de nombreux projets lancés au moyen de cet instrument ont pu être remis en mains bhoutanaises. De 19 projets privatisés après 1991, un seul crédit n'a pas pu être remboursé.

Karma Tobden

Entrepreneur, former machinist, Agro-Mechanical Workshop, Bumthang

The apprentice

Born in 1959, I come from a very remote village in Bumthang. I had a difficult background too and hence, when I started my career as an apprentice in the agro-mechanical workshop, I never imagined that one day I would own the agro-mechanical workshop. The year was 1979 when I landed in Bumthang with few coins in my pocket. I had completed Kharbandi Technical School. Trained as a machinist I had expressed my desire to work for the Swiss project. I had returned to Bumthang mainly lured by my friends Jambay Nidup and Ugyen Dorji who had joined the project one year earlier. Bumthang was a difficult place and the authorities in Thimphu who were managing the human resource in the country, happily sent me to where I wanted to go.

The time as an apprentice was an eye-opening experience and I made the best of every moment of those years. I learnt to work hard, be dedicated and take initiatives. I was working all the time trying to be the best in everything I did. Later when I took over the workshop, I could supervise and advise with ease. I knew every aspect of the production at the agro-mechanical workshop.

Entrepreneurs and pioneers

One of the peculiar aspects of the Swiss project, which is different from other development projects of other donor countries is the entrepreneurship factor. No other project produces entrepreneurs. Everyone wants to build monuments and hardly any tangible benefit is felt by the people directly. Hence in 1984 when they started talking about privatising the project infrastructures in Bumthang, we were quite surprised. I couldn't believe when I was offered to take over the agro-mechanical workshop. Although I was happy, deep down I also feared that if I failed I would ruin the image of our country.

Today I must say I am very comfortable running the workshop that has been turned into a successful manufacturing unit producing a wide range of products such as cooking stoves, solar water heaters, boilers etc. We have designed smokeless stoves that use less firewood, thereby avoiding deforestations while at the same time improving the health conditions of the people. We have also designed and produced steel cooking stoves that have been supplied in every school and monastery in this country. The World Food Programme and the Ministry of Education are some of our regular clients. UNDP and the Royal Society for Protection of Nature often take our products to every corner of Bhutan, because they are environmentally friendly products. Bumthang bukharis (heating stoves) have become a brand in itself for quality.

We were pioneer businessmen because Bumthang has been basically a land of monks and farmers until the Swiss project brought some development and cash economy. I started one of the first tourist lodges and today there are 35 such places sprawling all over the valley, catering to a large number of tourist who are increasingly visiting Bumthang.

Challenges

Life, of course, is not without challenges. Finding capable people continues to be a problem in as much as trained people are leaving for greener pastures. In fact new recruits take a long time to learn the trade and when they finally do, they leave and start their own businesses. In a way, of course, I don't mind that, because entrepreneurship development will always be good for Bhutan.

Furthermore, there is the problem of getting raw materials. The cost of materials often goes up without prior notice. This makes it difficult to market the products.

Memorable moment

I carry lots of fond memories of my association with the Swiss. Among those memories one still makes me laugh, is an incident that happened to me and one Swiss expert, Fritz Loppacher. In those days, the road condition was very bad and to add to the woes, there were very few Indian jeeps for the project. To maximise the utility the jeeps had trailers attached. Once we were travelling from Bumthang to Thimphu and when we reached Nobding, Loppacher noticed a dark object rolling in front of the jeep. He realised that it was the rear tyre of the trailer. In an instant, he jumped out of the moving jeep, grabbed the tyre and got back to the jeep with the tyre. I couldn't help laughing and appreciating his agility, his swiftness and his reflex. This incident is what I remember of most Swiss people I have worked with. They were the best, whatever life or fate required them to do.

In Kürze

Bumthang war ein Land von Mönchen und Bauern, bis die Helvetas-Projekte neue Möglichkeiten für Schulabgänger eröffneten. Karma Tobden konnte in der Werkstatt für landwirtschaftliche Maschinen eine Lehre machen. Die Schweizer lehrten ihn hartes und effizientes Arbeiten. Heute ist er ein erfolgreicher Unternehmer. Die Qualität der schweizerischen Projekte liegt für ihn darin, dass sie die Entwicklung von Selbstverantwortung und Unternehmertum fördern. Andere Geberländer investieren dagegen oft genug in Prestigeprojekte, von denen die lokale Bevölkerung wenig profitiert.

En bref

Bumthang était une région des moines et des paysans, jusqu'à ce-que les projets Helvetas offraient de nouveaux chances de travail. Karma Tobden faisait ainsi un apprentissage dans l'atelier mechanique. Il a appris à travailler dur dans le cadre de la coopération avec les Suisses est devenu un entrepreneur couronné de succès. Pour lui, la qualité première des projets suisses a été le renforcement de la responsabilité propre et de l'esprit d'entreprise. D'autres pays donateurs investissent souvent dans des projets prestigieux dont la population locale ne profite que marginalement.

Gembo Tensing

Entrepreneur, former store keeper Agro-Mechanical and Vehicle Workshop, Bumthang

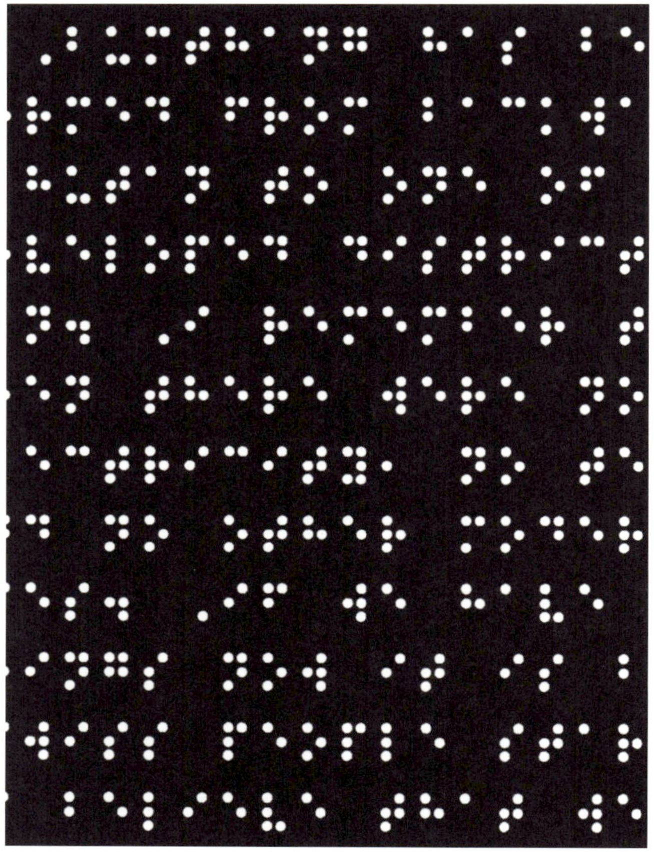

152 Gembo, store-keeper and Tandin, chief-mechanic, vehicle workshop, Bumthang

Meeting the Swiss

My encounter with the Swiss people was rather in a very tragic context for me. When I was studying in Jakar Junior High School, I was attacked by a bear, which completely destroyed my face, including my two eyes. That was in the autumn of 1979 and I was just fourteen. As I lay helplessly in Thimphu hospital, some Swiss people took pity on me and tried to do something. His Royal Highness Prince Namgyel Wangchuck also came to know about my condition and then together with the Swiss people they arranged to send me off to Switzerland for medical treatment at their expenses. I spent ten months in Switzerland undergoing a series of plastic surgeries to reconstruct my face. While my face came to some shape I realized that I would never see again which made me, of course, feel very miserable, depressed and hopeless. The love, care and concern I got from so many people there gave me a reason to be alive and be optimistic.

I came back to Bhutan in July of 1980, and when I was pondering about my life and was facing a very uncertain future, His Royal Highness and the Swiss guys encouraged me to go to what was popularly known as Khaling Blind School. I obeyed them and off I went to carry on with my studies.

Getting a job and my life back

I completed my school in 1982. However, during that period, there were no jobs or work for blind people in Bhutan. So I returned to my native town of Bumthang where again the Swiss guys, whom I had now taken as my guardian angels, came to my rescue. They not only made me feel normal but also proposed a job for me as the storekeeper at the agro-mechanical workshop. I said to myself that those guys were just kidding. How was I supposed to work and that as a storekeeper? But they assured me that it was possible and again I didn't want to argue or go against their wishes. They have always done what was best for me ever since that tragic incident. So I complied and became one of the first blind persons to get a government job. Ever since then I just didn't look back.

I went on to memorize each and every spare part with just the feel of my hand. The store I was working in was huge with hundreds of spare parts for tractors, generators, cable cranes, jeep, trucks etc. I could pinpoint where and how many vehicle parts were in which section of the store. Soon I became a sensation and what the Swiss believed a few years earlier, my Bhutanese colleagues came to understand much later: a visually impaired person can do normal things and lead a normal life.

When the agro-mechanical workshop was privatized, I even got the courage to resign and start my own business. So here I am in Bumthang running a shop of my own, happily married and a proud father of four children – two sons and two daughters. What more can a person desire and what better friends, which I found in the Swiss people, can a person get?

A Swiss reincarnation?

Reflecting on my life, the tragedy, the meeting with the Swiss people, the various trips to Switzerland and the friendship I have cultivated over the years, I sometimes feel I have some karmic connection to Switzerland. Perhaps I was a Swiss in my past life. But definitely one thing is for sure – I can proudly say Switzerland is my second motherland. Sometimes in my sleep I dream of Switzerland. I dream I could see and I dream of beautiful places and people. And between these dreams and my real life, I am doing perfectly okay with my life. I have no reason to complain.

I learnt many things through my association with the Swiss people. First of all they gave me the courage to move on plus the confidence and the motivation to live. They taught me to be frank, straightforward and honest. We Bhutanese often lack the frankness that is required in various situations or circumstances. We beat around the bush and we are diplomatic where we were not required to be so. Working with the Swiss people I have learnt to be honest about my feelings and to be practical all the time.

Bumthang has been transformed from backwaters of Bhutan to one of the most developed districts in Bhutan. I remember those days when there were no roads, no electricity, no telephone and no other modern amenities. If we have these things now, it is because the Swiss people started making us believe that we can work and earn all these amenities.

153

Democracy and my prayers

We are going through exciting times with historic changes taking place faster than we can digest. And I am happy to be living through these defining moments. When the whole country started talking about democracy a few years back, I wondered whether we, the visually impaired people, would be able to part-take in this historic process. So a few months back when I received the Braillecopy of the voter's education manual, I was extremely happy. I realized the government didn't leave us out. I am sure His Majesty the King would have personally taken care to include us.

I went back to my native village in Tang to cast my first vote. Due to the electoral regulations, we have to be accompanied by one person whom we can fully trust and ask him to press the voting machine on the candidate of our choice. When we reached the polling station and before he pressed the button for me, I took a moment to myself and in my simple prayers I wished that this one vote of mine be blessed with continued peace, prosperity and happiness for the Bhutanese people and above all that the Superior Beings bless our beloved monarchs who have always been at the service of us the people and especially the handicapped people like me.

I then asked my friend to press the button and the machine sounded:

"beeep!"

In Kürze

Ein Bär hat ihn angefallen und übel zugerichtet, als er 14 Jahre alt war. Er wird in die Schweiz ausgeflogen, wo die Chirurgen sein Gesicht wieder einigermassen herstellen. Sein Augenlicht aber hat er verloren. Sein König und die Schweizer schicken ihn auf die Blindenschule, dann arbeitet er als Magaziner. Später macht er sich selbständig, heiratet und wird Vater von vier Kindern. Vor einiger Zeit hat er die Wahlanleitung in Brailleschrift erhalten; voller Stolz, und Dankbarkeit, dass der König auch an die Behinderten denkt, hat er seine demokratische Bürgerpflicht erfüllt.

En bref

Attaqué et grièvement blessé par un ours alors qu'il avait 14 ans, il est envoyé en Suisse où des chirurgiens ont reconstitué son visage tant bien que mal. Mais il a perdu la vue dans cet accident. Son roi et les Suisses l'ont envoyé dans une école pour aveugles et ensuite il a travaillé comme magasinier. Plus tard il est devenu indépendant, s'est marié et est devenu père de 4 enfants. Récemment, il a reçu le matériel de vote en braille pour les élections démocratiques; fier et reconnaissant que le roi pense aussi aux handicapés, il a rempli son devoir électoral.

Agro-Mechanical and Vehicle Workshop

by Dr. Saamdu Chetri, Dy-Resident Co-ordinator Helvetas / SDC, 1988-2006

During the mid-1970's, the expanding Swiss programme required many supporting services, such as sawmills, a carpentry workshop, mechanical workshops, etc. Later, Helvetas has privatised these workshops. These small-scale enterprises, which are briefly explained below, gave rise to employment opportunities.

In the late 1970's, they established the agro-mechanical workshop, mainly producing agricultural tools and implements in the beginning . Of the few workers, two potential ones were trained intensively on the job in technical and management skills, including bookkeeping. The unit was privatized in 1985. The deal triggered many innovations for agro-tools, but mainly new products such as more efficient heating (Scandinavian design, brought by the wife of the first coordinator, for she feared suffering from the cold…) and improved cooking stoves. The stoves served the dual purpose of cooking and heating and are the most sought-after products in the rural households. The Swiss Army designed tilting cooking pots, meant for schools, hospitals, monasteries, armed forces and others. Since the venture ran profitably, loans were recovered in full before schedule. And a dream of Fritz von Schulthess finally became true, after 20 years…

Similarly, the carpentry workshop, the vehicle workshop and a sawmill were privatized along the same lines. All of them powered by Nepal-manufactured water turbines – another old Helvetas project and a testimony to a successful south–south know-how transfer. It is interesting to note that as early as 1983 about 40 small turbines and solar panels provide electricity to refrigerators for storing medicines, to light school-buildings, to power wireless sets, to drive machinery, were functioning in Bumthang and other sites.

154

Sawmill and Carpentry Workshop

155

156

157

In Kürze

Projekte in Feld und Wald verlangten nach Gerätschaften und Werkzeugen. Schon in den 70-er Jahren entstanden die nötigen Werkstätten: Sägereien, Schreinereien, mechanische Werkstätten für den Unterhalt von Fahrzeugen und den Bau von Öfen. Auch hier wurde immer darauf geachtet, Einheimische zu Fachkräften auszubilden und ihnen die nötigen administrativen Fähigkeiten, wie Buchhaltung, mitzugeben. Betrieben wurden die Werkstätten mit Wasserturbinen aus Nepal. Und schon in den 80-er Jahren wurden auch Solarzellen zur Gewinnung von Strom eingesetzt.

En bref

Les projets agricoles et forestiers demandaient des équipements spécifiques. Dès les années 70, des ateliers ont été mis sur pied: scieries, menuiseries, ateliers mécaniques pour l'entretien des véhicules et la construction de fourneaux. Ici aussi, une attention particulière a été portée à la formation des partenaires locaux, y compris à leurs compétences administratives par exemple en comptabilité. L'énergie de ces ateliers était fournie par des turbines hydrauliques du Népal. Et déjà dans les années 80, des panneaux solaires permettaient de produire de l'électricité.

Ugyen Dorji

Entrepreneur, Carpentry Workshop, Politician, Bumthang

The Swiss and I

I am Ugyen Dorji and I was born 1958 in a small village of Ngashiphel, which is located near the famous Jampey Lhakhang (temple). I studied in Don Bosco Technical School (Phuntsholing), which was then the only technical school in Bhutan, passing out in 1978. I wanted to pursue higher studies but since there was the need for skilled technicians back then, we were sent to work in development projects of our choice. Unemployment was something unheard in those days. When we reported to the Department of Manpower (now the Royal Civil Service Commission) in Thimphu, we were told that two technicians were needed in a Swiss project in Bumthang.

Now, Bumthang in those days was a very remote district and nobody wanted to go there. The road from Thimphu to Bumthang was still not tarred. There was no electricity, no telephone, no health clinic and not even big shops. The weather was severe and people from other parts wouldn't survive here anyway. So after a few days my friend Jambay Nidup (who later became Royal Advisory Councillor for one term) and I volunteered to come and work in our own district. We thought in the worst-case scenario that we would be at home. At best, we could do something for our own community.

So Jambay and I, leaving aside our dreams of attending university or living in more humane places, came back to Bumthang to work for the Swiss project. We came for a trial period of six-months which they used-to call "national service" and was mandatory for every new recruit in the royal civil service. We reported to Walter Roder who was the project officer here and from day one, I must say, I liked working with the Swiss people. So much so that after four months when we were called back to Thimphu to be sent elsewhere, we asked for extension and to carry on working for the project. We were paid well too. Besides the project allowance there was also something called the technical allowance of Nu. 100 (a fortune in those days!!)

I was assigned to the forestry management unit while Jambay worked in the agro-mechanical workshop. There were no sawmills back then and neither was there any forestry staff appointed by the government. We were solely responsible for extracting timbers, sawing them and distributing to the locals as well as exporting to India through the State Trading Corporation of Bhutan. We also put up the first carpentry workshop in Bumthang to make furniture in order to meet the local demand.

There was hardly any road network in Bumthang district and so I conducted many of my official tours on horseback. Mails would be delivered here once every month and sometimes the drive to Thimphu would take a week during the monsoon season. Life was definitely tough but that made us tougher. The Swiss guys were my role models and I am sure that if every Bhutanese worked like them, Bhutan would become developed like Switzerland. I was twenty when I started working and so I did not lack the energy to learn or to walk for days. I am glad I did what I had to do back then. Those were the milestone moments of my life. Something I would cherish for the rest of my life.

When the Swiss project closed in 1985, we were asked to take over to give sustainability to the project. During the same time, the Royal Government also came up with the privatization policy. So I got the carpentry and the sawmill, Jambay and Karma Tobden (who joined few years later than me) were assigned the agro-mechanical workshop and another schoolmate of mine, Tandin got the auto-repairing workshop.

My community and I

Now when I look back I feel it was a blessing in disguise that we were sent to work in the Swiss project. Apart from taking over (buying) a sawmill and cabinet-making workshop, the experience of working with the Swiss people was invaluable. That would define my life and what I would be doing for my community and myself. First of all, the sight of seeing all those Swiss people leaving their homeland and working in my community gave me extra motivation to work harder. I always thought, "If a chillip (foreigner) is doing so much, I must do twice as much." So I learnt the value of hard work and dignity from the Swiss.

Secondly, which is very important, the Swiss were very pragmatic people unlike we Bhutanese who are illusory and idealistic. Everything at our work place was transparent and democratic that when I later became a community leader, which I still am, I always make a point to arrive at a consensus rather than exercise my authority. This value of democratic principles plus the leadership skills are something, which I now find very useful in my daily life. This does not mean to say that our country was not democratic until now.

Bhutan, as we all know, is transiting from monarchy to parliamentary democracy, where working with consensus and harmony are norms and basics which one has to master if one is to achieve anything in life. My working experience with the Swiss people was therefore crucial in some of my modest achievements. I was elected to the National Assembly as a people's representative from Bumthang for two terms and whilst attending to that in Thimphu, I also served in the parliamentary legislative committee, which reviewed all laws and legislations before they were deliberated and passed by the National Assembly.

After my term ended, the upcoming political party, the People's Democratic Party, approached me to head the Bumthang chapter and also be in the National Executive Committee. Coincidently, my friend Jambay is the head of the local chapter for the other party, the Druk Phuensum Tshogpa. So it looks like we are also playing a role in shaping the democratic reforms in our country and living through these historic times. Had it not been for the opportunity to work with the Swiss, I am sure neither of us would have become community leaders, which we are today, at the dawn of a new era in Bhutan.

Minister and I – the most memorable moment

The most memorable moment of my time with the Swiss project was during one of the visits of the then Home Minister late Lyonpo Tamshing Jagar. He was also a native of Bumthang. A legendary figure in modern Bhutanese history. We were twenty-odd Bhutanese people lined up to greet him. As he got introduced to each of us, he kept asking from which part of Bhutan we came. Coincidently all the twenty of us happened to be from Bumthang. I was the last to be introduced to him. So when I finished saying I was from here, he patted on my shoulder, gave a long and warm smile and said, "I am extremely proud of you guys. You Bumthaps are working to develop Bumthang. You all know that people from other parts of Bhutan really dread coming here because of its remoteness. You have all my support and prayers." Lyonpo Tamshing Jagar passed away ten years later. But that incident remains fresh in my menory and would remain close to my heart forever.

In Kürze

Eigentlich hätte er nach Abschluss des Technikums gerne studiert. Die Arbeitsvermittlung schickt ihn aber ins Bumthangtal, wo er bei einem schweizerischen Projekt mithelfen soll. Er sieht das im Rückblick als "grossen Segen". Nicht nur hat er später die Möbelschreinerei mit Zimmerei und Sägerei mit einem Darlehen kaufen können, der Pragmatismus und das Arbeitsethos der Schweizer haben ihn tief geprägt. Heute ist er Politiker und Vorsitzender der "People's Democratic Party" in Bumthang.

En bref

À la fin de son école technique, il aurait bien voulu poursuivre ses études. Mais il fut envoyé dans la vallée de Bumthang pour collaborer dans un projet suisse. Rétrospectivement, il voit ça comme une grande chance. Car par la suite il a pu acheter la menuiserie (meubles et charpente) et la scierie grâce à un prêt. Il a été profondément marqué par l'éthique du travail et le pragmatisme des Suisses. Aujourd'hui il est politicien et préside le "People's Democratic Party" à Bumthang.

158 The first apprentice

Jampel Ngedup

Entrepreneur, Agro-Mechanical Workshop, Hotelier, Politician, Bumthang

Drafted as a student

In 1965 the Bumthang Thrimpon (district magistrate) Dasho Lhadarla drafted me to attend school that had just come up near Jakar Dzong. Modern schooling was unheard of in those days and children were almost evicted from their homes to be sent to school. I was one of them. So much so that out of 13 children who were identified from my village, the more affluent families petitioned to the authorities and some even bribed the officials to let the children go back home. My family, being poor, could not afford the kickback and so I had to remain and study. This, I believe, happened to many families all over Bhutan. Years later when we started receiving the fruit of modern education, families who had not sent their children to school started seeing their fortune turning against them.

I completed the primary school and having nowhere to go I went back to my village and resumed my life as a farmer and cow herder for two years. Then in 1973 I heard of a school in Phuntsholing run by the Salesians of Don Bosco, which was ideal for a poor farmer's son. The school had boarding facilities and thus it was not taxing for my parents to keep me in school. I resumed my studies there - passing out in 1978 with a certificate in electrical engineering.

Back to Bumthang

Together with my classmates, we reported to the Department of Manpower (now the Royal Civil Service Commission) in Thimphu for jobs in the civil service. Those days, people who acquired some education were straightaway appointed in the civil service as modernization of the economy and the state machinery was well under way.

It was there that Lyonpo Jigmi Thinley who was the director then, told us about two openings in the Swiss project in Bumthang. Now for reasons explained earlier, no one wanted to go to Bumthang. People even resigned from the civil service or switched jobs if they were sent to Bumthang. So when my friend Ugyen Dorji and I volunteered, Lyonpo Jigmi was very pleased and asked us where we came from. We said Bumthang and he teasingly remarked, "Then you guys are just going home."
Much of the project activities in Bumthang revolved around carrying out research and feasibility studies for establishing dairy farms, alternative cropping and forestry management. So I felt a little out of place with my electrician background. Besides, there was no electricity in Bumthang in those days. There was a workshop where we repaired and maintained a few types of machinery and that kept me busy until we brought in the first generator and also commissioned the first micro-hydropower plant. So I doubled up as project electrician and manager of the agro-mechanical workshop.

Representative in the National Assembly

I am by nature a very timid person and it was only after working with the Swiss that I started being forthright and confident. The Swiss were complimented with increased dealings with the local people – bringing services and development to them. Thanks to these, my reputation soared. So it was not by any accident that, in 1988, when there was the need for a Bumthang people's representative to the National Assembly, my name was unanimously endorsed by the public. But had it not been my association with the Swiss people or had I not got the chance to work in the project, I do not think that I would have been known in my own locality. I would have been an unknown electrician working in some power plants somewhere in one corner of the country. In all, I served 11 years as a member of the National Assembly and subsequently for three years as a Royal Advisory Councillor and member of the Bhutanese Cabinet.

The Swiss brought life back to Bumthang

Over the years I have seen Bumthang transform in front of my eyes, thanks mainly to the Swiss project and the people. Back then; Bumthang was one of the poorest and most isolated districts of Bhutan. If a person had two sets of clothes, he was considered rich. If a family has one full course meal with rice, they were rich. People dressed in rags and many went barefoot. Even I walked barefoot in the snow and icy waters. As a student we often walked to Trongsa (62 kilometres away) to get a lift or even further south till Zhemgang, some 144 kilometres away. Luckily we had to do this only once a year.

The people of Bumthang used to migrate to warmer places during the winter. To Mongar and Trongsa and even Zhemgang. They would barter their dairy products for cereals and other food items. Only old people who couldn't walk were left back in the villages in Bumthang. Able-bodied people fled Bumthang as winter set in. After the project was launched and some developments started coming in, more and more people stayed back. These days there is no difference between summer and winter in Bumthang. One could thus conclude that Bumthang has now regained its lost glory it once held, when the Royal Court was in Bumthang. In a way the Swiss project brought back life to Bumthang.

Being among the big boys

I was born in 1957 in a remote village of Dhur on the edge of Bumthang district. Now if we consider Bumthang as backwaters of Bhutan in those days, one can imagine what it feels like to be from such a far-flung village. Even in my wildest dreams, I never imagined to be sitting at the helm of the government. Hence, after I got elected to the Royal Advisory Council, the greatest moment in my life happened when I received tashi khadar (ceremonial scarf) from His Majesty King Jigme Singye Wangchuck on 27th November 1998. He formally appointed me as a member of the Cabinet and the Council. This is something I will cherish for the rest of the life.

In Kürze

Zusammen mit seinem Freund Ugyen Dorji meldet er sich nach Schulabschluss freiwillig für den Arbeitseinsatz in Bumthang. Sein Diplom als Elektriker hilft ihm zu Beginn wenig, weil es im ganzen Tal keinen Strom gibt. Das ändert sich mit der Anschaffung eines Generators und dem Bau eines kleinen Wasserkraftwerks. Sein Ansehen bei den Einheimischen steigt rasant, 1988 wird er als Abgeordneter in die Nationalversammlung gewählt. 1998 beruft ihn der König in den Kronrat und ins Kabinett.

En bref

Avec son ami Ugyen Dorji, il s'est annoncé volontairement après sa scolarité pour travailler à Bumthang. Au début, son diplôme d'électricien ne lui a pas été très utile car dans toute la vallée il n'y avait pas d'électricité. Cette situation a changé avec l'acquisition d'une génératrice et la construction d'une petite centrale hydroélectrique. Son statut auprès de la population locale s'est modifié d'un coup, et en 1988 il est élu comme représentant à l'assemblée nationale. En 1998, le roi fait appel à lui et le nomme au Conseil Royal et au cabinet ministériel.

159 Improved heating stoves, the bread-winner

Milk and fruit processing plants

by Dr. Saamdu Chetri, Dy Resident Co-ordinator Helvetas / SDC, 1988-2006

Some of the best-known enterprises that have been initiated by the Swiss and privatised are the Milk Processing Unit (MPU) and the Fruit Processing Unit in Bumthang. MPU produces high quality products, which are then brought to markets in Bumthang and Thimphu. Yet, supplies still fall short of demand. Similarly, the Fruit Processing Unit does a good business with its apple juice, cider, and different kinds of brandy. There was a time when Bumthang was almost identified with peach brandy, but today it is supposed to be honey. The Beekeepers' Association supplied over 15 tons of honey in the 2007 season to the Bhutanese and international markets.

160 Cheesemaking

161

162

In Kürze

Milch- und Obstverwertung sind eine weitere Erfolgsgeschichte. Die Nachfrage nach Milchprodukten auf den Märkten von Bumthang und Thimphu übersteigt das Angebot. Auch die Auswahl an Obstsäften und Spirituosen ist gestiegen.

En bref

La transformation du lait et des fruits est un autre succès important. La demande en produits laitiers sur les marchés de Thimphu et de Bumthang excède l'offre. L'assortiment des jus de fruits et des spiritueux s'est elle aussi élargie.

163 Kadola, the frontman

Bio Bhutan – a pioneer business case...

by Karma Yangzom, CEO Bio Bhutan

Bio Bhutan is a pioneer enterprise specializing in product development and marketing of natural and organic certified products from Bhutan for local and international markets. With a long-term vision of making Bhutan a recognized player at national as well as regional and international organic markets the main goals of the enterprise are to:

- Contribute to the sustainable use of natural resources of Bhutan;
- Improve income and employment opportunities of rural communities and private entrepreneurs;
- Create surplus value for final consumers through healthy and tasteful natural and organic produces from Bhutan;
- Promote the image of Bhutan as a supplier of pure, natural and organic products.

The origin of Bio Bhutan comes from Switzerland. The idea of bio Bhutan came into being during the Swiss Expo of 2002 where COOP displayed fine Bhutanese architecture in the expo (consultant Patrick Vogel).

Business plan and certification

With financial support from Coop Switzerland and through the auspices of the Swiss Bhutan Society in Switzerland – Bhutan and the Bhutan Swiss Friendship Association in Bhutan, a feasibility study and a business plan for establishing a bio label in Bhutan, similar to the one called "Naturaplan" in Switzerland, was conducted by the potential managers, guided by Patrick Vogel. Indocert, an Indian bio certification agency with support of the leading Swiss agency Bio Inspecta, has established the procedures for bio labelling.

Discussions between the Helvetas office at Zurich, Helvetas/SDC Bhutan, members of the Swiss Bhutan Society and the consultants resulted in the decision that it would be most appropriate for the Bio Label Bhutan action plan to operate as a private enterprise. Helvetas, in the form of a soft loan, provided financial support to the enterprise. Renamed as "Bio Bhutan", the enterprise got a loan of Nu. 5.6 million (CHF 150 000) from Helvetas in January 2005 and received its business license from the Ministry of Trade and Industry in June 2005.

The value of a product

Bio Bhutan promotes the concept that the value of a product lies not only in what you see in the final product but also in the people, places and lives involved in the making of the product. Hence, it is a must for our products not only to be of high quality but also to allow traceability.

The following products have been developed and are available for sale in local and international markets so far: 1) organic certified Lemon Grass Oil (Cymbopogon flexuosus), 2) Lemon Grass Air Spray, 3) herbal medicinal plant (Cordyceps sinensis), 4) ginger powder, has just been introduced in 2007.

Bio Bhutan is the marketing agent of products for two farmer groups, the Distillers of the Dozam Community Forestry Management Group in Dramitse, Mongar, Eastern Bhutan and the members of the Milk Processing Unit in Gogona, Wangdue Phodrang, Central Bhutan. Through marketing of lemon grass oil Bio Bhutan helps to generate income and employment for over 35 households involved in lemon grass oil distillation. Marketing Cordyceps sinensis has helped generate income for farmers across many high altitude communities. The establishment of similar business linkages with a third farmer group, the Dekiling Ginger Group in Sarpang, South Bhutan, is currently under way.

Bio Bhutan products have been introduced into the following regional and international markets over the past two years: New Delhi, India; New York, US; San Diego, US; England, UK; Ruefenach, Switzerland; and Helvetas, Zurich, Switzerland.

In recognition of Bio Bhutan's expertise for training farmer groups in organic production and providing marketing services, the Netherlands Development Organisation (SNV) contracted the enterprise in May 2007 to train the Dekiling Ginger Group in Sarpang and facilitate marketing of their ginger.

In Kürze

Bhutan hat eine weitgehend intakte Umwelt mit einer einmalig sauberen und frischen Atmosphäre. Eine heile Bio-Welt, die Marktchancen eröffnet. Und in der Tat: Mit finanzieller Unterstützung durch COOP Schweiz ist analog zu „natura-plan" eine zertifizierte Marke "Bio Bhutan" geschaffen worden. Mit Starthilfe von Helvetas hat ein privates Unternehmen die regionale und internationale Vermarktung von Bio-Produkten aus dem Drachenland, wie Zitronengrasöl oder Ginger Pulver aufgebaut.

En bref

Le Bhoutan a un environnement encore largement intact et la qualité de l'air y est excellente. Ce contexte favorable est un atout certain pour le marché "bio". Avec le soutien de Coop Suisse, un label biologique – Bio Bhutan – a été développé. Avec une aide initiale d'Helvetas, une entreprise privée commercialise aujourd'hui des produits biologiques du Bhoutan, comme des huiles essentielles de citronnelle en spray ou de la poudre de gingembre, sur les marchés régionaux et internationaux.

in the cleanest atmosphere

by Dr. Saamdu Chetri, Dy-Resident Co-ordinator Helvetas / SDC, 1988-2006

Bio-Bhutan is tempted to bottle the clean Bhutanese air. It seems to have a huge future market, maybe not in the conventional business sense. It is because many tourists come to Bhutan to enjoy the breath-taking sceneries, to feel the traditional and cultural spirits of the people and the country, and last but not the least, to take deep breaths of invigorating fresh air. And they all go back home with renewed vitality, derived from the pristine environment and the interaction with the friendly people.

Bhutan is known for its pristine environment, and fresh air is one of its "free" products. This is because Bhutan has maintained more than 70% of its land area under forest cover. In addition, the Constitution stipulates that 60% of the land area must be maintained under forest cover for all times to come. And a large part of the forest, 26% of it, forms the protected areas with another 9% as biological corridors to connect the protected areas. Thus, as one steps out of the plane at the Paro International Airport, one cannot help but take a deep breath and enjoy and appreciate the purity and freshness of the air! One can almost feel the enchanted air scented with natural fragrances of aromatic plants and trees like cypress, pine, lemon grass, and many others. A week in Bhutan not only cleanses one's lungs, but also cures a lot of ailments.

164

Beekeepers' Association

by Dr. Saamdu Chetri, Dy-Resident Co-ordinator Helvetas / SDC, 1988-2006

Along with cheese, honey has become an essential component of morning breakfast in Bhutan. Also at the farm level, besides cheese, honey has become another potential enhancer of rural income and is improving the dietary level of the Bhutanese, which was not in their habits before. Beekeeping in Bhutan dates back to the 1960's and the 1970's, when several attempts were made by the government to introduce beekeeping. But it was a private venture by Fritz Maurer in 1986, who introduced European honeybee (Apis Mellifera L.) in the Bumthang valley. Based on experience gained from private bee keeping, the Royal Government of Bhutan, with aid from Helvetas, initiated a sound base in 1987 for introducing beekeeping in Bumthang. The joint Beekeeping Development Project was launched for the period 1987-1992, focusing on establishment of successful apiary base in the Bumthang district and training of the breeders and technicians on bee husbandry.

After a substantial number of farmers had gained experience in beekeeping, the functionally independent "Beekeepers' Association of Bhutan" (BEEKAB) was officially founded on 21 July 1997, with a proper governing board. The Swiss assistance continued till 2000 and thereafter other donors such as the SNV have contributed to its capital formation. Today, the association consists of 28 beekeepers and produces, processes, and markets more than ten tons of honey (15.5 tons in 2006), providing considerable income to rural households in the Bumthang district. The processed honey is marketed by the association within the country and consumed mainly by tourists and the Bhutanese urban population.

165

In Kürze

Honig ist wie auch Käse zum festen Bestandteil des bhutanischen Frühstücks geworden. Fritz Maurer hatte mit Bienenzucht begonnen, 1987 hat die Regierung mit Hilfe von Helvetas ein entsprechendes Programm gestartet. Im Jahre 2006 haben 28 Bienenzüchter insgesamt 15,5 Tonnen Honig produziert.

En bref

Tout comme le fromage, le miel est devenu un ingrédient indispensable du petit déjeuner bhoutanais. Fritz Maurer a commencé l'apiculture en 1987, dans le cadre d'un programme du gouvernement appuyé par Helvetas. En 2006, 28 apiculteurs ont produit ensemble 15.5 tonnes de miel.

166

Swiss Bakery and Tenzing

by Dr. Saamdu Chetri, Dy-Resident Co-ordinator Helvetas / SDC, 1988-2006

In the middle of Thimphu there is a strange signboard saying "Swiss Bakery." In the middle of the gallery of Bhutanese tradition, architecture, culture, museums and exotic handicrafts items for shopping in the local markets, there is a most sought-after restaurant with fresh bakery products, exuding a taste of Switzerland.

Arthur Christen, a Swiss who later received the name Tenzing Dorji from Her Late Majesty, the Great Queen Grandmother, Ashi Pema Choden Wangchuck, set up the Swiss Bakery in 1972. He had come to Bhutan in 1965 as a wireless expert to set up the Wireless Telecommunication System in Bhutan. The late King, His Majesty Jigme Dorji Wangchuck, had granted him the Bhutanese Citizenship in 1968. Because Tenzing wanted to create a heritage and give a unique kind of gift to the residents of Thimphu, he quickly decided to set up a bakery. He imagined a decent and cosy sitting and eating-place with self-service catering facilities. It seems that the bakery economically broke even only after some years. Its success stems from the service, the quality of products, and the relations it offers to its customers.

Tenzing Dorji never married, but he adopted a son named Nima Dorji, who later was trained by his father as a baker. Until recently, the Swiss Bakery was a family business.

Tenzing Dorji died on 19 August 2000. He was a Buddhist converted from Christianity. Tenzing meditated in front of Chenrayjee at his temple room built in one of the corners of his small house behind the Swiss Bakery. He identified himself as a Bhutanese, although his complexion did not, and he hated to face any foreigner and talk in his mother tongue, the Swiss-German language. For the Bhutanese people the Swiss Bakery stands as a symbol of friendship.

167 A landmark in Thimphu

In Kürze

1965 ist er als Radioexperte ins Land gekommen und hat für den König erste Funkverbindungen aufgebaut. Der König belohnte ihn mit dem bhutanischen Bürgerrecht, die Königin gab ihm einen neuen Namen: Tenzing Dorji; er konvertierte zum Buddhismus. 1972 eröffnete Tenzing Dorji alias Arthur Christen mitten in Thimphu die "Swiss Bakery", deren Backwaren heiss begehrt sind. Am 19. August 2000 ist Tenzing Dorji gestorben. Seine "Swiss Bakery" ist für die Leute von Bhutan ein Symbol der Freundschaft.

En bref

En 1965, un expert radio arriva dans le pays dans l'idée d'installer les premières liaisons radio pour le roi. Ce dernier le récompensa en lui accordant la nationalité bhoutanaise et la reine lui donna un nouveau nom: Tenzing Dorji. Converti au bouddhisme, Tenzing Dorji alias Arthur Christen ouvrit une boulangerie – la Swiss Bakery – à Thimphu en 1972 dont les pâtisseries sont encore actuellement très appréciées. Le 19 août 2000 Tenzing Dorji s'est éteint. Sa Swiss Bakery reste un symbole de l'amitié pour les gens du Bhoutan.

Clock Tower

168 The clock tower in Thimphu blends Swiss technology with Bhutanese craftmanship. Built on the initiative of late Lyonpo Dawa Tshering, then Chairman of the National Urban Development Corporation, the clock was donated by the family von Schulthess and installed and maintained by Tenzing, Swiss Bakery.

SCAP – Evolution of an idea to an institute

by Eric C. Huber, cehphotographer, Thimphu / Berne

The coming to life of the school for commercial and art photography (SCAP)

Why are all photographs about Bhutan taken by photographers from abroad, while at the same time many Bhutanese students with class 12 are looking for training possibilities? Bhutanese can do it as well as foreigners – they can much better show their country with their knowledge of their culture and history. With this thinking I started to look for private financial, intellectual and hardware support that I got from the "Association School of Commercial and Art Photography SCAP" and by many private sponsors and corporations as well. Sponsors came forward since we had excellent counterparts in Bhutan, in particular the National Technical Training Authority NTTA, the Ministry of Labour and Human Resources.

The training started in 2000 with 26 young Bhutanese. Equipment: 10 analogue cameras and one darkroom. The leading idea simply was: Bhutanese should show Bhutan to the world. The first batch underwent a 3-year training successfully, culminating in an exhibition "Bhutan by Bhutanese" in Switzerland, with over 1300 visitors. Presently, 10 students in batch II will soon start their final preparatory semester for the diploma in July 08. Digital equipment is now used systematically. But this is not the only difference to batch one. Today, it is a professional vocational training in photography and new media including basics in information technology and journalism.

Batch two runs in close cooperation with the Skill Training Resource Division STRD under the Department of Human Resources DHR at the Ministry of Labour and Human Resources MoLHR, an excellent partner. In May 2007 another goal was reached: SCAPprojects became SCAP-Bhutan in the hands of Bhutanese citizens with two departments, Institute of Photography & New Media (training) and SCAParchives.

In future, advanced professional studies in media and communication will be offered, photography being a main pillar (photography, media, communication). Candidates should achieve the same professional level and acceptance as e.g. European students.

Objectives, contents and goals of the training

The focus is on the basic competence of realization: development of the idea > concept making > budgeting > the technical tools (photography, computer, video, cross media) > realization > ways of presentation and publication.

A great importance is given to the indispensable knowledge of interactions and coherence of politics, economy, society, science, history and culture, etc.

Three things are necessary to success

After 7 years of work in a private project, we are enjoying the satisfaction that a small project can be successful and sustainable. Three things are necessary for success: 1. Cooperation based on trust with reliable local partners; 2. Students with passion to work, even under hard conditions. 3. Optimism and flexibility, if the "things" don't work as imagined.

As we say: All good things are always three. I had all of them. I would like to thank the sponsors, the local partners and above all, my students, because the students are always the mirror of the teachers and the school.

In Kürze

Warum sind es immer ausländische Fotografen, die Bücher zu Bhutan illustrieren, wo doch die Bhutaner mit ihrer Kenntnis von Geschichte, Kultur und Mentalität des Landes noch viel aussagekräftigere Bilder schiessen könnten? Eric Huber wollte dem abhelfen, suchte nach Sponsoren und gründete im Jahre 2000 eine Fotografenschule. Der erste Jahrgang hat nach drei Jahren erfolgreicher Ausbildung eine Ausstellung in der Schweiz gezeigt, die von 1 300 Leuten besucht wurde. Mittlerweile ist aus dem Projekt ein Institut in den Händen der Bhutaner geworden.

En bref

Pourquoi est-ce que ce sont toujours des photographes étrangers qui illustrent les livres sur le Bhoutan, alors que les Bhoutanais, avec leur connaissance de l'histoire, de la culture et des mentalités seraient en mesure de faire des photographies plus expressives? Eric Huber voulait corriger cet état de fait, chercha des sponsors et fonda une école de photographie en 2000. Après une formation de trois ans couronnée de succès, la première volée d'étudiants a fait une exposition de photographies en Suisse qui a été visitée par 1'300 personnes. Entre-temps, le projet est devenu un institut en mains bhoutanaises.

169-177 Dekey Choden Gyeltshen, senior journalist, Bhutan Times – a sequence of her day's work by Chencho Dema, SCAP Bhutan

178 Daily life – by SCAP photographer Ugyen Pem

179 Spiritual life – by SCAP photographer Samten Zangmo

Groundwork for Good Governance

180

Groundwork for Good Governance

by Dr. Saamdu Chetri, Dy-Resident Co-ordinator Helvetas / SDC, 1988-2006

The Swiss assistance has directly or indirectly contributed to the development of good governance in the country through its programmes and projects. However, it never was a specific project until recently. Yet, the term "good governance" seems to be too broad and it is not exhaustive in its definition. A number of projects have addressed the efficiency and effectiveness of governance through higher education sponsorships in subject matter specialisation, in management of institutions and human resources, in research capacities, in accounting and transparency issues and in the establishment of processes for cooperatives and associations for the rural poor to decide their own development programmes.

Human Resource Development – the key to Good Governance

This chapter shall delve into those elements where the Swiss cooperation has been involved in provision of good governance services. The following graph gives an overview of the kind of importance that the Swiss cooperation had assigned to the Human Resource Development (HRD) as a tool to good governance. The graph is not representative of all Swiss contributions made to the HRD, because all contributions channelled through the multilateral cooperation cannot be reflected here. However, it gives an idea of the state of art in the HRD.

Trainings outside Bhutan

Agencies	Min of Agriculture	Min of Education	Min of Finance	Min of Home Affairs	Min of Works and Housing	Other Ministries	Semi-govt. Agencies	Royal University
Long Term	114	7	28	3	8	0	12	5
Short Term	542	106	383	13	187	29	61	24
Total	656	113	411	26	195	29	73	29

The following graph can confirm the preceding one; the development of expatriate staff has peaked during 1992 with about 20 Swiss families working in Bhutan. Thereafter, most technical and management posts were being slowly taken over by the Bhutanese personnel.

Development of Helvetas Staff

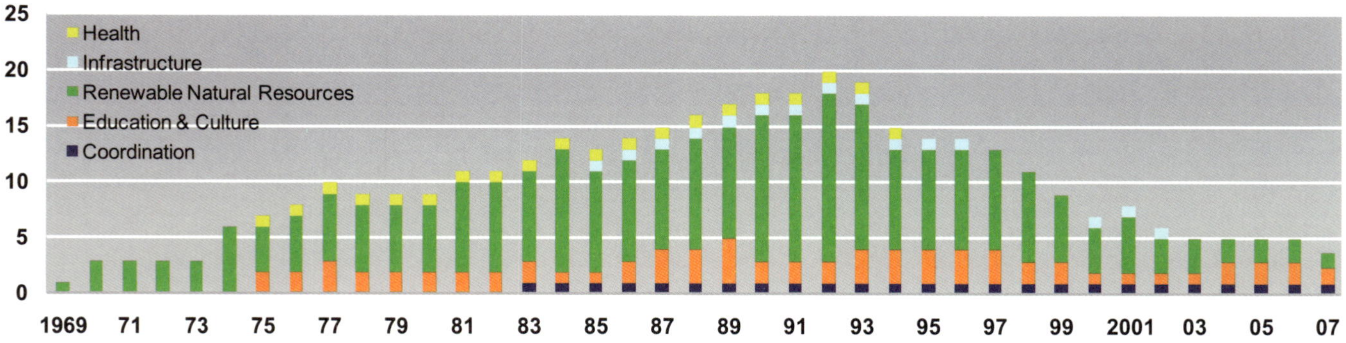

Over 25 years, on average, about 62 slots were provided each year by the Swiss cooperation. There were 184 long-term training/ courses, which ranged from 12 months to 60 months and 1,352 short-term training/courses, which ranged from one month to less than a year. Even if two months were averaged per slot, it would be 124 months of HRD in a year. The major inputs provided has been in the RNR under the Ministry of Agriculture (MoA) with over 656 slots, followed by the Ministry of Finance (MoF) at 411 slots, the Ministry of Works and Human Settlement (MoWHS) at 195, the Ministry of Education at 113, and others.

A large part of the education sector has received Swiss funding through the World Bank and therefore, the HRD from the Swiss cooperation looks lower than it actually was. Furthermore, this graph does not include HRD/training provided in the country to Bhutanese staff and farmers. There could be thousands of courses over the 25 years with an average of approximately 300 a year. It would also be interesting to see the effectiveness of short-term and long-term training in a cost benefit analysis.

Human Resource Development has always received very high priority throughout the entire Swiss assisted programme. Apart from project-related sponsorship, there were specific programmes, like the Human Resource Development support to the Ministry of Agriculture (1992-1999) and the training support to the Royal Audit Authority to promote good governance and controlling in projects (1996-2000), which enabled the capacity development of National Finance Services (2001-2006) to enhance accountability and transparency under the financial systems of all agencies.

Graduates to serve their country

The Swiss have sponsored eight PhD candidates for various subjects specialisation aimed at enhancing the research capacity mainly in the agriculture sector. Most of them are still working in this sector, while some are in management, teaching or out of the system, working in international organisations. Furthermore, over 70 professionals and several chartered accountants were trained under the Audit Authority to enhance their auditing professional capacities, including value for money audit, performance audit, and IT audit for good governance.

Support to the National Finance Services

The project's goal was to strengthen the National Finance Services (NSF) of the Ministry of Finance through development of the required knowledge, ability and skills of the accountants of Ministries, Dzongkhags and agencies for enhancing efficient and transparent public financial management, thereby fostering good governance. After strengthening the capacity of the Royal Audit Authority, the Swiss Agency for Development and Cooperation (SDC) supported long-term capacity development in budget and financial management and professional accounting as well as short-term certificate courses in accounting. Capacity development of Gups (village headmen), Mangmis, clerks and Gewog accountants to enhance decentralisation process effectively was added later.

Three major outcomes can be seen: a) the professional competencies of the National Finance Services financial personnel have improved, thereby increasing its self-reliance; b) a cadre of skilled and motivated NFS personnel is established which effectively and efficiently fulfil its assigned job responsibilities and tasks, thus increasing the quality of civil service; and c) the financial profession is made attractive and professional. List of achievement in 300 in-country training and 45 outside professional courses: 15 Masters in Public Accounting, 10 MBA, 4 Charter Public Accounting, 14 Certified Accounting Technicians, 148 Certificate Courses in Accounting, 75 Budgeting and Financial Management, 403 completed Government Accounting and Financial Management and Bhutan Accounting System (BAS), including training on Dzongkha Unicode Training; 89 National Accounts Service personnel completed the Geog Accounting System (GAS) training. Further 589 Gewog Yargay Tshogchung (block development committee) members, gewog clerks and Mangmis were trained on the use of the GAS, which was introduced to ensure a proper utilization of development funds at the Gewogs.

Since the civil sector officials of the Dzongkhags are charged with the responsibility of providing assistance to the Gewog Yargay Tshogchung members at all levels of development, including book keeping and management, an orientation programme on GAS was provided to 197 civil sector heads to facilitate a uniform budgeting and reporting system.

181

Basic working principles

The Swiss assistance had certain basic principles that it followed in its cooperation; of many, **partnership** was one which they seriously considered from the very beginning. They made sure that in any Swiss assisted project, a Bhutanese counterpart was attached to the expatriate. The whole idea was to sustain the projects/programmes. The cooperation took mostly those projects in hand, which were technically and financially feasible to carry it over several phases until the government was sure to take over. The concept of project management cycles was defined well and everyone responsible was always invited to partake in planning. Participation of the beneficiaries and benefactors was always an important consideration in the project planning and evaluation cycle.

Yet, based on the needs presented, **ad hoc assistance** has also been provided to several organisations in the country, last but not least in terms of Information Technology (IT) support. To begin with the Royal Audit Authority, the Swiss financed an international workshop enhancing IT auditing in Bhutan, aimed at improving good governance for several audit member countries in the world. The Ministry of Agriculture, desirous of improving its planning, monitoring and evaluation systems, received financial support on ad hoc basis. An Information and Communication Technology (ICT) web-based programme was developed to ease reporting and analysing data from the field. Various training programmes were conducted to enhance the capacity of the Information and Communication Section of the ministry, including the maintenance of IT equipments. Support was granted to improve the land records archiving system. The Ministry of Communication wanted to develop ICT for good governance by developing a portal with open access for the public and a platform for all ministries to develop their own ICT units. Another ICT for education was supported by SDC to document experiences in teaching and learning as a mechanism to enhance quality education. The Anticorruption Commission also received ad hoc financing for building capacities of its staff. In addition, they were to experiment with one stop window for applicants, thus improving governance through timely delivery of services.

In addition, the Swiss cooperation in Bhutan spends each year money on **small actions** for publications, youth support, cultural activities and support of women in society. This is all aimed towards improving the systems and/or enabling an ad hoc environment. This small input also gives chance of discovering any interesting concept concerning projects of substantial nature. The Swiss have been **the pioneers in the creation of associations** in a modern form, first starting with the Dairy Association of Gomchens at Gogona, formed sometime's in the mid 1970's. Apolitically, the groups can be very powerful mechanisms in bringing definite positive changes in development and good governance. It is envisaged that at local governance level, the accountability, transparency, and efficiency would be increased due to the dynamics of these groups. Furthermore, the decentralisation and democratisation would be enhanced.

Gender is a catchword in any development cooperation. Unlike the neighbouring Asian countries, equality in Bhutan is far more pronounced. Still, there is lack of women participation in political life and only about one fourth of them is represented in the civil service. The Swiss have observed proudly that in rural trainings for farmers, there have been invariably more than 60 percent women participants.

Aligning projects and programmes to the needs of the government was always a key issue of the Swiss assistance. Its five-year country programmes were jointly designed with the government, the official plans are being closely co-ordinating with the government's five-year plans and concerned ministries' objectives and plans. The Swiss became not only the desired partners of the Royal Government of Bhutan, but they were entrusted with specific sectors for assistance. It was the Swiss cooperation that initiated the first donor co-ordinating meeting under the RNR sector. Thereafter, it was agreed that UNDP would take the lead to coordinate resident donors and an informal mechanism was worked out so that donors meet at least once every six weeks to share information and join efforts in areas that meet and need common interests/efforts.

Bhutan received a medal at Bangkok in 2006 as the best aid coordination country with visible and substantial achievement due to proper utilisation of investments from donors' assistance. The case of Bhutan proved that aid could be better utilised with bilateral funding mechanisms than through the multilateral system.

In Kürze

Das Schlüsselwort nachhaltiger Entwicklungszusammenarbeit heisst „Good Governance – gute Führung. Auch wenn es bis vor kurzem kein eigentliches Programm mit diesem Namen gab, war die Arbeit von Helvetas auf „gute Führung" ausgerichtet. Durch Aus- und Weiterbildung, durch die Vermittlung von Wissen um Verfahren und Administration, damit der Bauer seinen Hof, der Kleinunternehmer seine Bude erfolgreich führen, der Beamte sein Amt im Sinne von good governance verwalte. Das war nie ein Einweg-Prozess, vielmehr ein partnerschaftliches Training am Objekt, von dem – wie wir in einigen Kapiteln bisher erfahren haben – beide Seiten profitierten. Die erste Grafik illustriert wie viele Menschen für welche Disziplinen geschult worden sind. Die zweite Graphik zeigt wie viele Schweizer Fachleute jeweils auf welchen Gebieten eingesetzt waren. Ab dem Höhepunkt im Jahre 1992 nahm ihre Zahl laufend ab, weil mittlerweile immer mehr Einheimische die nötigen Fähigkeiten erworben hatten, das Land unabhängig voranzubringen. Im Jahre 2006 ist Bhutan in Bangkok ausgezeichnet worden als Land, das – weil es die ausländische Hilfe am zweckmässigsten umsetzt – am stärksten von der Entwicklungszusammenarbeit profitiert.

En bref

Le mot-clé pour une coopération au développement durable est „bonne gouvernance". Même s'il n' existait pas de programme de ce nom, le travail d'Helvetas a toujours été orienté sur la bonne gestion. Par des formations ponctuelles et des formations continues, par le transfert de savoir en matière de procédures et d'administration, les paysans ont été formés pour bien gérer leur exploitation, les entrepreneurs pour bien mener leur entreprise et les fonctionnaires pour conduire leur service. Cela n'a jamais été une approche à sens unique. Il s'agissait bien plus d'une formation en partenariat et par la pratique dont les deux parties ont pu tirer profit, comme le démontrent les chapitres précédents. Le premier graphique montre combien de personnes ont été formées par secteur. Le deuxième indique combien d'experts suisses ont travaillé dans les différents secteurs. Le nombre d'experts suisses a atteint son apogée en 1992, date à partir de laquelle leur nombre a constamment diminué, car un nombre croissant de Bhoutanais formés disposaient des compétences nécessaires pour poursuivre le développement de leur pays de manière autonome. En 2006, le Bhoutan a reçu une distinction à Bangkok comme étant le pays utilisant l'aide extérieure de la manière la plus efficace, et profitant par conséquent le plus de la coopération au développement.

Initiatives and impacts

184

Right from the beginning

by Pema Wangchhuk, Secretary of International Boundaries, former Secretary of Ministry of Home Affairs & Director of Agriculture Department

185 Farmer family, 1962

Early years

I come from a very large family of 57 members living under the same roof in Gaselo, a village in Wangdue district. In 1951, when the third King Jigme Dorji Wangchuck married Ashi Kesang Choden Dorji, as a part of the celebration, two schools were opened – one in Thimphu and one in Wangdue. I was in the first batch of students to study in this new school.

In 1955 I finished my school from Wangdue and was sent to Kalimpong (India) for one year in Kumudini Homes and then to St. Roberts High School in Darjeeling. I completed in 1960, what used to be called, matriculation majoring in Arts. In those days there was obviously no motor road in Bhutan so we used to walk to Kalimpong and back along the traditional route passing through Haa, crossing over to Yatung in Tibet and then to India. The journey would take many days.

In 1962 I was appointed as the Assistant Transport Officer in the newly established Bhutan Government Transport Service (BGTS) in Phuntsholing but I stayed there just fifteen days. I followed my friends who were heading for Haa to join the newly opened Wangchuck Military Academy. However, when we reached Paro, Dasho Lhendup Dorji (Lumpay), who was the Secretary General of the Development Wing, didn't release me because of acute shortage of educated people and offered me an internal transfer to any agency of my choice.

It was during those few days in Paro that I met an extraordinary man named Athingla Densapa who advised me to become a horticulturalist. In his view, Bhutan, with varied climatic conditions, had the potential to become a major producer of fruits and other cash crops. I took his suggestion and spent one year in Ranikhet (India) getting trained in horticulture.

Living through Bhutan's development

I started working in 1962; one year after Bhutan launched the first five-year Plan of socio-economic development and modernisation. Sometimes I feel very privileged to have seen the entire modernisation process. After my return from Ranikhet, I was appointed as the sub-inspector for horticulture development and assigned to start the first horticulture project in Yoesipang – seven kilometres away from Thimphu. I was paid a monthly salary of Nu. 80, a respectable sum those days.
What I remember very clearly that first year in Yoesepang was the acute shortage of manual workers for the project. In 1960 Thimphu Dzong renovation had started, in 1961 three highway projects were simultaneously launched between Phuntsholing and Thimphu, Gelephu and Trongsa and Samdrup Jongkhar and Tashigang. These massive projects drained out people from all over Bhutan.

To mobilise such a large labour force, the government introduced the system of chunidom according to which every twelve people were asked to mobilise one person. This was not enough, so the system was reduced to dudom: every person had to pitch one worker. Even this was not enough and finally every three persons in Bhutan had to continuously send one person to work in one of these projects.

Fortunately Lyonpo Sangye Penjore who was then the quarter master general of the Royal Bhutan Army sent 100 soldiers led by one lieutenant. They worked with us and together we built the first agriculture station. Under the same project, we also developed the first apple orchard in Pangri Zampa, north of Thimphu. We didn't have any project vehicles back then and so we ended up walking every day the entire stretch of some twenty one kilometres from Yoesepang to Pangri Zampa .

We would get up at three in the morning, light up a kerosene lantern and just walk in the darkness. Then we would stop working at three in the afternoon and walk back to Yosepang. I had become such a good walker that once my younger brother who was just commissioned as an officer in the army could not catch up with me.

Between 1961 and 1963, the development wing moved between Paro and Samtse every six months. In the warmer months they worked from Paro and as winter approached they moved to Samtse. This was mainly done for practical reasons. First, there were no shops in Bhutan back then. So foodstock and all necessities had to be brought in from Siliguri and one official had to keep making the journey to buy rice, salt, sugar and tea. So Samtse was closer and more convenient. The other reason was servicing the regional offices of Sarpang, Samdrup Jongkhar and Tashigang with financial and technical support. There was no banking system in Bhutan back then.
By 1964, with much of the highway projects completed, the labour pressure eased and twenty people were permanently employed by the project. A year later, in 1965, I was summoned by His Majesty the King to the Royal Palace in Dechencholing to be commanded to move to Paro. I was promoted to the post of assistant director of Agriculture Department under the Development Wing. All sectors such as agriculture, livestock, forestry and education were under this wing. With Thimphu Dzong under renovation, much of the administration was operated from Paro.

Every quarter I had to travel to Alipurduar in India, go to the bank, withdraw the money, come to Paro or Samtse and pay the salary and the bills. Then go to Kokrajar (Assam), withdraw money from there, travel to Gelephu, drop the money and get the quarterly reports. Then go to Gauhati and to Samdrup

186 Stables and staff-quarters at Bathpalithang; Wangdichoeling, Jakar (1978)

Jongkhar and Tashigang and do the same thing. This was a routine until the Bank of Bhutan was established in 1968. My boss, the director Mr. Randhawa, couldn't travel much and so I had to do much of the running of the Agriculture Department. I later learnt that my appointment was mainly for me to take over the department in case no one took up the post. In fact, prior to that, the department had five directors in four years.

In 1968 with Thimphu Dzong rebuilt and consecrated, much of the government administration moved to the capital. The last National Assembly was held in Paro in October 1968. With the closing of the Assembly, the Council of Ministers was also formed with Lyonpo Tamji Jagar (Home Affairs), Lyonpo Chogyal (Finance) and HRH Prince Namgyel Wangchuck (Trade).

The following year, in 1969, His Majesty appointed the two princesses Ashi Sonam Choden Wangchuck and Ashi Dechen Wangmo Wangchuck as representatives of His Majesty in the ministry of finance and the ministry of development respectively. I was appointed as the secretary to Ashi Dechen Wangmo and commanded to move to Thimphu and set up the Development Secretariat inside Tashichho Dzong. I was awarded the title of Dasho (honorific title) and the red scarf in 1972. In 1998, after His Majesty the Forth Druk Gyalpo relinquished the executive powers to an elected Council of Ministers I was appointed Secretary in the Ministry of Home Affairs.

Working with the Swiss

In 1971, I was promoted Director of the Department of Animal Husbandry. The following year in 1972, I also became the Director of Agriculture. That was the time when I came into direct contact with the Swiss people who were working in Gogona Dairy Project.

The Gogona Project was conceived by Fritz von Schulthess in the late sixties. Apparently, von Schultess, on his many trips between Thimphu and Bumthang, had noticed several people from the Gogona area begging for food. Actually, they were not beggars, but gomchens (lay monks) who by tradition led their life praying and collecting food donations. Fritz was really touched by their conditions that he suggested to the King that a dairy farm be started in Gogona, so that the project could sustain these people. The project was directly looked after by HRH Prince Namgyel Wangchuck as chairman.

Fritz Maurer, who has now become a Bhutanese citizen and has settled in Bumthang, was sent there in 1971 as a cheese expert and worked there until the project closed in 1973. A three-member committee was formed to assess the project and hand it over to the local people. I was in that committee together with Lyonpo Chenkhap Dorji who was then heading the Forestry Department.

Off to Bumthang

After Gogona, Prince Namgyel Wangchuck chose Bumthang as the next place to be developed. The reason behind choosing Bumthang is very interesting. Bumthang was the power centre of the country in the early years of the monarchy between 1907 and 1952. The first and the second Kings ruled from Bumthang. But Bumthang was a very difficult place to live in and prosper. Land was almost unusable during winter and except for buckwheat, mustard and wheat, no other cereals grew. Therefore most of the powerful families and courtiers based in Bumthang would have huge land holdings in the neighbouring districts of Trongsa, Shemgang, Mongar and Lhuntse. In winter the people of Bumthang would migrate to these places with their cattle, putting a huge pressure on the local people.
It was thought that unless Bumthang developed and people stayed there all year round, there was no way that the neighbouring districts could be developed. Hence Prince Namgyel Wangchuck suggested to Fritz von Schulthess to do something in Bumthang. The Rural Development Project was thus conceived. Fritz Maurer was then asked to move to Bumthang and start this project. The project was an integrated agriculture, livestock and forestry project and since I headed both the departments, it was very convenient for me to work with Fritz Maurer and other project staff.

Again, since there were very few educated and trained people back in those days, we even agreed that Fritz would also work as the District Agriculture Officer and District Animal Husbandry Officer beside managing the project. As a result, Fritz was highly regarded by the people and they started addressing him as Dasho Maurer. People still call him that way.

If there is one thing that I really take my hat off to the Swiss, this is what they have actually done in Bumthang. They have realised our dream of seeing Bumthang prosper. Bumthang has not only prospered and lessened the burden on neighbouring districts; it has become the centre for horticulture and livestock development in the country. In fact, much of the pasture grass and potato seed and brown Swiss bulls are being supplied from Bumthang. The land in Bumthang has been developed to grow other varieties of cereals, apple orchards adorn the valley, the people of Bumthang have stopped migrating and, above all, it has become the hot destination for tourism in Bhutan.

In the early years of the project in Bumthang. I often had to travel there. We would get a ride till Trongsa and then walk to Bumthang. Sometimes we had to stay overnight in village houses and often people had nothing to offer us. Instead we had to carry our own food and feed the host family. They have come very far and I am proud that I have been a part of the success, assisted by my Swiss friends.

In 1983, Helvetas took over the Swiss projects and development assistance in Bhutan. Ernst Reinhardt came in as the first Resident Coordinator. They were looking for a place in Thimphu to house both the residence and the office. Fritz Maurer suggested several places and Ernst chose one of the houses I own in town, which was then incomplete. Ernst flew in from Switzerland, didn't want to stay even for a night in the hotel and walked in straight with Annegret and their belongings into my house which had nothing functioning. The very next day, he left for a fifteen-day familiarisation tour of Bhutan. It was as if we had known each other for ages. He often wanted things to be improved, to be more functional, in my house and I kept reminding him that this was Bhutan. Ever since then we have always been great friends.

In Kürze

Von Anbeginn hat der Junge aus dem Dorf Gaselo den Entwicklungsprozess seines Landes miterlebt, und dabei Karriere gemacht. Als einer der ersten kann er die Schule besuchen. In Indien lernt er Gemüse- und Obstbau, wieder zuhause startet er gleich als Vize-Inspektor bei einem grösseren Projekt. 1965 schickt ihn der König nach Paro als Assistenzdirektor des Landwirtschaftsdepartements. Zu seinen Aufgaben gehört es alle drei Monate nach Indien zu gehen, um von der Bank Geld für die Löhne der Arbeiter abzuheben. 1971 wird er Direktor des Departements für Viehzucht, ein Jahr später auch Direktor für Landwirtschaft. Das ist die Zeit, wo er mit den Schweizern in Kontakt kommt. Was die Entwicklungszusammenarbeit im Bumthangtal erreicht hat, erfüllt ihn mit grosser Achtung. Bumthang ist heute das Zentrum für Ackerbau und Viehzucht, womit sein Traum für Bhutan Wirklichkeit geworden ist.

En bref

Dès le début du processus de développement de son pays, un jeune du village de Gaselo a suivi ce processus et y a fait carrière. Il fut l'un des premiers à pouvoir fréquenter l'école. En Inde il apprit l'horticulture et de retour au pays, il fut nommé vice inspecteur d'un grand projet. En 1965, le roi l'envoya à Paro en tant que directeur adjoint du département d'agriculture. Selon son cahier des charges, il devait se rendre tous les trois mois à la banque en Inde pour y prélever l'argent nécessaire au paiement des salaires. A partir de 1971 il fut nommé directeur du département de l'élevage et un an plus tard directeur du département d'agriculture. C'est à cette époque qu'il entra en contact avec les Suisses. Ce que la coopération au développement dans la vallée de Bumthang a réalisé le remplit de joie. Aujourd'hui, Bumthang est le centre de l'horticulture et de l'élevage, son rêve pour le Bhoutan a ainsi été réalisé.

187 Bumthang / Jakar (1978)

Bhutan? Bhutan! – A letter to my niece

by Hanspeter Reichmuth, Entrepreneur

Dear niece,

You are about to choose your field of study and you are asking me what are my thoughts on the "economy of development", a field in which you have shown a vivid interest since your journey to India. You are seeking my advice, because, in your view, 50 years of my life as an enterpreneur are equal to the era of modern development cooperation. My experiences – as you know – include eight years in the field in Black Africa and 20 years in the tea trade, which often brought me in contact with Asian cultural circles. But, of course, I can only revert to my own wealth of experience in which acting in a self-governed way was fundamental, and to sum it up I would say: person before function.

Person before function

What I am saying here is from this perspecitve, namely the position of man in success or failure, no matter in which company. It's not the money, not the technology nor the know-how that decide primarily, it's the character. It's the character that makes the difference in any undertaking. To be aware and to develop oneself is just as demanding as to study a country and its culture and the attempt to make a marked contribution to its development. This is my understanding of development cooperation. Was that concept successful over the last 50 years? The answer is: in spite of an army of experts and billions of dollars spent, the degree of poverty has risen worldwide during that time. With the remarkable exception of the Kingdom of Bhutan, which goes to show that there are better ways – there will be more on this at the end of my letter.

What is so attractive in this job? Escape from boredom in a saturated society? Helper's syndrome? Over estimation? Trips around the world and conference talk? Tax free income? Existential crisis? This incomplete list is not my idea, it rather stems from clear-sighted critics in the receiving countries. The list does not contain any attributes needed in order to take on the responsibility in a difficult undertaking, which is certainly the case in foreign cultures. Required are the interest or curiosity in the current situation, intuitition, modesty, persistence and initiative. Expertise can be acquired rather easily but to become an expert in this business, one has first to overcome the language barrier and to have the experience of having put one's foot in one's mouth. It is only then that your are considered to be trustworthy by the people – this being the first and foremost condition before trying to change or build something together.

There are countless examples of entrepreneurial characters in foreign countries, with no obligations but to their own conscience and daringness; clergymen (yes, the often smiled-at missionaries) like the Benedictine Urs Egli from Engelberg, who built a thousand wells in Cameroun. Or Ignacio Ellacurìa SJ, who was shot in 1989 because his speeches and writings in favour of the underprivileged were annoying those in power (to be read in the books of the other Jesuit Jon Sobrino who survived the massacre). Also are to be mentioned medical doctors such as Beat Richner. He is repeatedly attacked, because he supports the people and not the functionaries and their centres of finance and power. And last but not least, the history of emigrants and of many Swiss companies abroad offer character studies.

Person before function is what I wrote. Person, that is the entity the way I understand it, it is commitment that comes from inner conviction. Function, that is a construct that may impart prestige, behind which one can hide, which is open to interpretation, which can be changed and left behind any time. Bureaucracies, whether in a governmental, clerical or economical context, are functionally organized. Their language is abstract, seemingly objective, not touching in any way. It is only when fans, voters, customers and donators are courted that the language referring to the relevance of function and its aims becomes concrete, touching and seemingly visionary. The person sees the problem and is trying to find a solution. The official has solutions and tries to find testing grounds which he then exploits for his own purposes (this is also the focus of W. Easterly in "The white man's burden"). Starting point of this train of thought is the annual budget which should increase and not decrease. Toni Hagen has denounced this in the development cooperation as a form of enforced financial draining. These financial means derive from taxpayers' money.

During your last visit, we were discussing this issue and you where surprised that in a democracy, which means rule of the people, the representatives exercise no control. This certainly shows to some degree the indifference of a wealthy nation that can afford such expenditures as long as ideology and economical interests are satisfied. Hidden beneath, however, are culturally-induced reasons:

Practicable ignorance

Manès Sperber, poet and essayist, once said that every man capable of siring a child and every woman capable of giving birth to a child have believed for hundreds of years that they are then equally qualified to educate their children; and that most people at the very moment they begin to read a newspaper and become aware of political talk feel entitled to enter into the discussion: but just as much as education is one of the most difficult activities of man, so is the acquisition of knowledge and therefore rare to encounter. And this is why he is convinced that one of the most serious dangers for mankind today is the practicable ignorance, more precarious than the ignorance in Socrates' times. I'll give you an example: When I was contracted as project manager in the Sahel by an NGO, upon arrival at the location of my assignment I was introduced as "expert" even though I had no idea of water boring, well construction, agriculture or elementary health care in a culture totally foreign to me. My state of not-knowing was complete, but to my great astonishment it was also practicable. I thus came across a basic rule in this "game", namely that we westerner pretend to know better how the development of other people should be accomplished. This fundamental error is part of an endless chain which keeps in motion the folly with a lot of logic and measured concern.

In 1990 the Neue Zürcher Zeitung (NZZ) published an article with the title "Sense of reality in foreign aid": "One has to be wary of the notion that the industrialized nations are more developed than say the Nepalese or the Indian. The development has taken another course: the Occident is leading technologically and economically but so is the Orient when it comes to spiritual balance. Half of the Nepalese live in extreme poverty but even the needy seem to appear happy and more content than a lot of Swiss who under the burden of affluence surely trail through life." (Here one could start a discussion about definitions of poverty and in this context I recommend you the book "Poverty – wealth of the people" by Albert Tévoedjré, available at abebooks.de). The visionary "Gross National Happiness" of the King of Bhutan expressly puts the well-being of the people in the centre of development.

Visions of society battle for power and influence

Another fact is of collective nature: in high school you have learned that the public has always been the result of given situations of power and authority and that lying in public has nowadays become almost standard in many areas. Where interest groups in an unrelenting way lay claim to their "truth" based on economical, political or philosophical interests, the ethic question determined by the readiness of an open and searching position, plays a modest role. Humaneness is eliminated by the irreconcilability of those who are "absolutely right" and those who by contrast are "absolutely wrong". Visions of society battle for power and influence. The madness of the crusades, for example, portrayed this idea. Those against it were condemned as heretics. Generations to come recognized their irreality, brutality, even the ridiculousness with dismay and surprise. What is your opinion of today's officially enforced solidarity in the light of a balance of the past fifty years in development coordination, looking at the facts and with the sentiments of your generation?

If a young and open-minded panel were to address the issue, then I would like to call their attention to the climate of opinion which is streamlining the current vision of society. All of us are, as Milan Kundera put it, exposed to the "whirl of reduction": The inability to deal adequately with the abundance in the field of consumer goods, information, amusement, work, mobility etc. necessitates simplification. The most ingenious simplification is the binary one, the 0/1-principle, upon which the IT-revolution is based. In its most mundane form, it is used by the media which, in acting as stooges of world history have expanded and channelled the process of reduction. They are spreading worldwide the same simplifications and clichés which are likely to be accepted by as many people as possible. The opposite-pair "poor/rich" has been subjected to this rule by way of reducing it to its economical dimension. Thus having been incorporated in the public opinion, the flow of millions of Swiss Francs of tax money to development bureaucracies has hardly been met with any opposition.

Now, my dear niece, have I discouraged you with my critical remarks? To be sure, my views have an influence on only one part of your decision. The other is that there are also achievements in development cooperation within a partnership frame. One of the most impressive is the one between Bhutan and Switzerland. How was that possible? I will send you the book dedicated to the 50th anniversary which contains all the facts. Beyond that I would like to point out the attitude of the people who made that possible, above all the dynasty Wangchuck and the Swiss entrepreneurial family of von Schulthess.

Should I tell you what kind of a king he was?

When I travelled across Bhutan 20 years ago, I was told the following story: A governor had built for himself a house with three floors – one more than everybody else. The uncle of the king was the Home Minister and it was in this capacity that he visited the provinces as the "ear" of the king. He was asked how it was possible for a civil servant to have constructed such a big house. The king was informed and ordered an investigation which brought to light that public funds had been embezzled for private purposes. The governor was deposed, had to pay back the money and return his sword, the symbol of dignity and power.

Now that is what I call character. That is a clear "no – not that way". It is the honesty upon which trust is based. And therein lies the success of partnership in development which is shaped by the respect and the efforts of entrepreneurs like Fritz von Schulthess and Fritz Maurer, also of people like Martin Menzi, the Reinhardts, E.W. Külling and of the pioneer medical doctors, the forestry- bridge- and ropeway engineers, the architects and instructors as well as their partners in Bhutan, all of which you read in that book.

A lucky case? Yes, and it is also an instructive and inciting comparison. It sharpens the discriminating abilities, which are the instrumental basis of judgment. Another requirement is reading, not so much about development politics, but articles of ideologically independent people who are to be found among poets. I have referred to some of them and you should be able to learn all about their life and works via internet. Finally there is one thing in store for you: personal experience which cannot be substituted by anything. Therefore my advice: delay your plans of studies, go and get involved, get in touch with completely different cultures and life styles. In your academic life, you will then reap the fruits of your practical experience.

Best regards

In Kürze

Eine junge Frau möchte Entwicklungsökonomie studieren und fragt ihren Onkel um Rat. Er ist ein weitgereister, belesener und erfolgreicher Unternehmer. Seine Empfehlung: "Person vor Funktion". Personen erkennen Probleme und suchen nach Lösungen; Funktionäre haben Lösungen, für die sie Anwendungsfelder suchen. Ihre Denkweise ist die des stetig wachsenden Jahresbudgets. Geld, das nur allzu oft von einer Bürokratie zur anderen, oft korrupten Bürokratie fliesst und wirkungslos versickert. Trotz Einsatz eines Heeres von Experten und Milliarden von Dollar hat sich die Armut in den vergangenen 50 Jahren weltweit verschärft. Gleichwohl gibt es erfreuliche Beispiele, eines davon ist Bhutan. Die erfolgreiche partnerschaftliche Zusammenarbeit gründet in der Redlichkeit und dem Charakter der beteiligten Personen – angefangen beim Königshaus der Wangchucks und der Familie von Schulthess.
"Darum liebe Nichte", so schliesst der Onkel seinen Brief, " bevor Du Dich der Theorie verschreibst, geh hinaus, engagiere Dich und lerne völlig andere Lebens- und Handlungsweisen kennen."

En bref

Une jeune femme qui voulait étudier l'économie du développement demanda conseil à son oncle. Ce dernier était un entrepreneur qui avait beaucoup de succès, quelqu'un qui avait beaucoup étudié et voyagé. Son conseil: „la personne est plus importante que la fonction". Les personnes voient les problèmes et trouvent des solutions; les fonctionnaires ont des solutions et cherchent des domaines d'application. Leur mode de pensée est en phase avec un budget annuel en constante croissance. Trop souvent, l'argent passe d'une bureaucratie à l'autre, et disparaît au gré de la corruption. Malgré l'engagement d'une armée d'experts et de milliards de dollars, la pauvreté dans le monde s'est aggravée au cours des 50 dernières années. Néanmoins, il y a quand même des exemples réjouissants, par exemple celui du Bhoutan. Le succès du partenariat dans la coopération au développement est fondé sur l'honnêteté et la personnalité des partenaires, en commençant par la famille royale des Wangchuck et la famille von Schulthess. "C'est pourquoi, chère nièce, avant de te plonger dans la théorie, sors, engage-toi dans le monde réel et apprend à connaître des modes de vie et d'actions différents". C'est ainsi que l'oncle conclut sa lettre.

Good leaders listen to the people

188

189

190

Being consistent in meeting the needs

by Lyonpo Chenkyab Dorji, Former Minister of Planning, Secretary General, South Asian Association for Regional Cooperation

Helvetas had been a very important development partner for many decades. Starting as a private foundation the program grew with the inclusion of Swiss Development Cooperation. My experience working with the Swiss is that they are very cautious planners and rarely do they jump to conclusions. In some quarters of Bhutan, there were even some feelings that the Swiss were rather slow. The long years of collaboration has proved the contrary. The impact that we see today, particularly in the agriculture sector where tangible benefits have reached the farmers of Bumthang or Phobjikha, are successes that can be emulated in other parts of Bhutan. Another landmark achievement is the increased enrolment in primary education.

There are other donor countries operating in Bhutan, beside Switzerland. But it was the Swiss collaboration that saw the first rural development project such as the one in Gogona which was later shifted to Bumthang. Having been in the service of the Royal Government for a long time, I have personally seen the progress, the strategies and all the assistance offered to Bhutan from the government of Switzerland. Helvetas and the Swiss Government have been very consistent in meeting the needs of the grassroots. One salient feature has also been the local capacity building which enabled the sustainability of the project, once the donor left.

Choices and challenges in changing times

Bhutan is going through serious political reforms and even here there are things that could be learnt from Switzerland. For example the relation between the cantons and the federal government could be something Bhutan could learn. The roles of the central government and the local governments could be something similar; there is a degree of autonomy for local governments in Bhutan.

Bhutan has already entered the Tenth Year Plan period and a good education system is being established. The education system is churning out a lot of educated children and graduates. There are also some drop-outs. The planning process should take care of both the educated and the drop-outs, so that every citizen becomes productive. Even though the country has a few big business houses, they are not going to provide enough jobs. Secondly, no government in other parts of the world provides job to all those who come out of education system. The country therefore needs small and medium enterprises to generate enough employment opportunities.

The Swiss way of developing small and medium scale enterprises is also of interest to Bhutan, given that Switzerland has 800 years of experience in this field. Furthermore, the technical and vocational training could ultimately solve the pertinent problem of unemployment in Bhutan and improve the quality of construction.

In conclusion, Bhutan should never be over-dependent on foreign aid. Projects and programs implemented under grants should be sustainable after the donor leaves. Some donors often describe grant aid as "free lunch". But as they say, there is no such thing as a free lunch. I am glad that at least with the Swiss we never had this problem and whatever was done together were projects we could sustain in the long run.

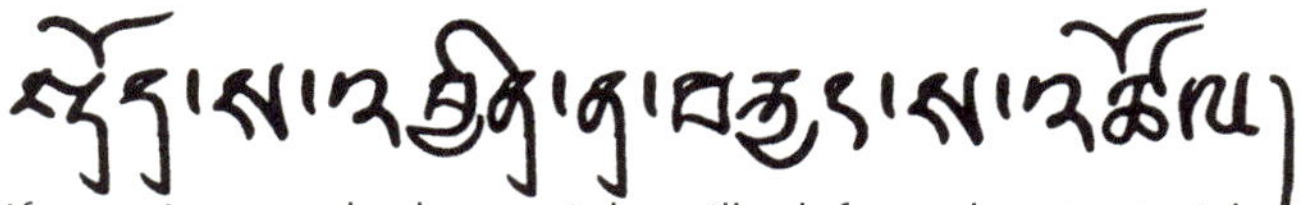

If you give somebody a seat, he will ask for a place to stretch.

Source: Sayings and proverbs from Bhutan, Wisdom and Wit in Dzongkhag Idiom, 1999, Thimphu

191 Lamegompa and Jakar Dzong

In Kürze

Der ehemalige Planungsminister meint, die Schweizer seien sehr vorsichtige Planer, würden nie voreilige Schlussfolgerungen ziehen. An einigen Stellen in Bhutan hätte man sie gar als langsam empfunden. Die jahrelange Zusammenarbeit habe sie eines Besseren gelehrt. Als grosse Stärke der Schweizer sieht er – gerade auch im Vergleich zu anderen Geberländern – deren beharrliche Aufbauarbeit in der Landwirtschaft zum Beispiel, und die Ausbildung einheimischer Kräfte, womit die Nachhaltigkeit der Projekte gesichert wurde.

En bref

L'ancien ministre du plan est d'avis que les Suisses sont des planificateurs prudents, ne prenant pas de décisions hâtives. Les Bhoutanais y ont parfois vu et regretté une certaine lenteur. Mais au cours des années de coopération, ils en ont compris la pertinence. Ils voient une grande force des Suisses – en comparaison avec d'autres pays donateurs – dans la persévérance et le travail de longue haleine, par exemple en agriculture ou dans la formation des collaborateurs locaux pour assurer la durabilité des projets.

Views on the development projects in 1984

by Lisette Müller and Annegret Reinhardt, in: Helvetas, Evaluation report on the Helvetas assisted programmes in Central Bhutan, 1984

Comment

The great majority of the people answering the interviews (82%) are content and happy with the development and change.
The main reason that was given by the people was "easier life", meaning general development, cash and increase of the living standard: "we get whatever we need" and: "due to the national highway we have neither to carry loads nor to walk on foot, we don't get trouble, so we are happy", are indications that some of the daily strains of life have been reduced.
An old couple feels: "although there is no benefit for us old people, young generation will benefit". A young man says: "it is good that we are tracing the path of other advanced countries at least in communication and living standard". "If religious, traditions are not getting lost, I'm happy with development". Other threats are seen by a few individuals and are reproduced in their one words: "With more development, more problems may come along", development creates more wants", "more development seems to bring more laziness instead of making proper utilization of the resources", "the pace of education is not keeping in step with development, it will create social gap and hazards", "rich becomes richer, poor remains the same", "mind cannot be at peace as previously, due to so much tight and odd news and conflicts in the world".
The fact that people are conscious of the weaknesses, threats and faults of development, in spite of conveniences they receive, speaks for the healthy reservedness and pride of the Bhutanese. It shows a potential which, if given proper attention and taken seriously, may be an important control preventing Bhutan from entering the spiral of rampant, haphazard development.

192

"Do you like the way Bumthang is changing, are you happy about it?"

Result	Total		Counter-parts	Decision-makers	Rising class	Honorables	Farmers Villagers
	Nos	%					
Yes	91	70	14	6	15	8	48
More or less	24	18	2	3	3	3	13
Not so much	13	10	5	1	1	3	4
No	3	2	-	-	-	-	3

In Kürze

1984 – also noch im Frühstadium der Zusammenarbeit - haben Lisette Müller und Annegret Reinhardt in Interviews Bhutaner nach ihrer Meinung zur Entwicklung befragt. Wie die Tabelle zeigt, stiess der Wandel durchaus auf Zustimmung. Aber es gab auch Einwände: "Entwicklung schafft neue Bedürfnisse"; "besserer Lebensstandard bringt mehr Faulheit"; "Reiche werden reicher, die Armen bleiben arm"; "die Seele findet keine Ruhe mehr bei all den seltsamen Nachrichten und Konflikten in der Welt".

En bref

1984 – donc à un stade encore précoce de la coopération – Lisette Müller et Annegret Reinhardt ont interviewé des Bhoutanais pour leur demander leur opinion sur le développement. Comme le tableau l'indique, les changements étaient largement acceptés. Mais certaines critiques ont aussi été formulées: "le développement crée de nouveaux besoins"; "un meilleur niveau de vie encourage la paresse"; "les riches s'enrichissent et les pauvres restent pauvres"; "l'âme ne trouve plus la paix, confrontée à toutes les nouvelles étrangères et informations sur les conflits dans le monde".

Change and continuity in Bumthang

by Dolma Roder, Bhutanese student in Anthropology, 2007

The background

The spring before I began my graduate degree in socio-cultural Anthropology, my mother invited me to accompany her on a Helvetas sponsored trip around Switzerland. On the tour, we met Swiss people who had worked with Helvetas in Bhutan. They were almost always nostalgic about their time there. They spoke of Bumthang with a level of intense emotion and even intimacy that caught me off guard. I was an intrigued bystander with no idea on how to make sense of their memories.

Did Bumthangpas remember these people with the same affection and wistfulness? How did Bumthangpas view the 30 years of Swiss experts coming and going in their valley? How did they evaluate and understand the work that these experts had done in their home valley? There were also intensely personal reasons for my interest. My father came to Bhutan in 1973 as a "Swiss development expert" and in 1977 he married my mother, whose family comes from a small village in the Tang Valley of Bumthang. Anthropology offered me an entry point to start making sense of the way other people gave meaning to their lives and their actions meaning. It made complete sense to me to assume that everyday life is best described by those who live it.

Any research topic I pursued about contemporary life in Bhutan would inevitably have to contend with the lived experience of development and change. I quickly learned that anthropological discussions of development were often less then optimistic. Particularly at the turn of the last century, when I began my graduate education, there was a distinct belief in academic circles that development had "failed" or even "made things worse." I was always sceptical of these claims. My experience of development had been up close and personal.

I was aware that in some cases the bureaucracy of development (the endless paper work and meetings and report writing) was prioritized over any tangible actions or results. I also found it disingenuous that so many academic critics accused development experts of ignoring the perspectives of the recipients of development. Many of these same critics wrote extremely abstract articles or books in which they claimed to speak on behalf of people they had never even spoken to.

Source material

So, in the summer of 2005 I returned to Bhutan to conduct semi-structured interviews with about sixty-five Bumthangpas. I knew that Helvetas experts working in Bhutan had traditionally written a final report at the end of their term and I had read a copy of a final report that my father had prepared at the end of one of his own terms. From what I imagined, the final reports were individualized accounts of development in Bhutan from the eyes of the developers. I planned to compare the contents of the twenty-three final reports in the Helvetas Coordination Office in Thimphu to the interviews with Bumthangpas. The final reports are in most cases, intensely personal documents. There are often nostalgic musings on the author's soon-to-end time in Bhutan, last-minute apologies for bad temper, final complaints and disclosures about co-workers (both Swiss and local, both government and Helvetas employed), and even the occasional ill-advised political statement. Even reports that looked and sounded like dry annual reports were personal to the degree that the authors used them as a final opportunity to claim their time and work in Bhutan as their own.

193

194

Both work and personal relationships are central themes in most of these reports. One common thread is constituted by comments and even complaints made by the authors about their Bhutanese counterparts. These frequent observations reflect the consistently asymmetrical relationship between the development aid bringer and the receiver. Despite genuine attempts to try and make the relationship one of partnership, final reports often explicitly recognized inequalities, both economic and political in this relationship.

Imagined audience

Another striking aspect of the reports was their imagined audience. It was clear that Bumthangpas, the target of these various projects, were not the intended audience of these documents.

Not surprisingly, few of the Bumthangpas I interviewed were able to talk about the Swiss and what they had done during their time in Bumthang. The exceptions were people who had worked with the Swiss and the shopkeepers in Jakar, who often claimed that the Swiss and Helvetas had done nothing at all for them. This accusation is not completely without merit, as Swiss projects tended to target landowners and for various reasons most Jakar shopkeepers do not own any land.

Most other people I spoke to regularly confused the Swiss with tourists. When I pointed out the difference, they would usually argue that, since they could speak to neither group, it was impossible for them to make distinctions. Other people, while recognizing the concerns of Helvetas projects (potato variety introduction, renovating the hospital, introducing smokeless stoves and so on) routinely attributed any of the effects of these projects to the Bhutan government or even to the King. "Thanks to the government" was a very common prefix phrase in any discussion of changes that people viewed as positive. Many people did, however, know of Fritz Maurer, a long-time Bumthang resident and the "other" Swiss man who had married into the valley. However, most were unsure about what work he had done and believed that he came to live there because he had married a Bumthangpa woman. The kinds of changes that final reports attributed to Helvetas rarely matched Bumthangpa versions of change. Even the change that I had thought would be easiest to connect with Swiss intervention; the growing importance of potato as a cash crop, proved in retrospect to be an inexact connection at best. They however attributed the introduction of certain export potato varieties to the government.

Conceptions of development

It might not be possible to say that Bumthangpa and Swiss conceptions of development and change in the valley are undeniably linked, but it would also be inaccurate to declare that this is evidence that Bumthangpas were critical of Swiss-initiated development in their Dzongkhag. For Bumthangpas, development is on-going and constant and while projects and individuals come and go, the efforts and presence of the government are always visible and felt.

Whatever the causes of changes in Bumthang, I was repeatedly told that Bumthang had become comparatively prosperous, especially by project staff at the Eastern Central Region –Agriculture Development Project (ECR-ADP), which is funded by Helvetas, but staffed completely by Bhutanese civil servants.

195

196

197

While Bumthang falls within the ECR, the ECR-ADP staff saw far greater need and urgency for development in districts to the south, where Helvetas had not traditionally worked.
Bumthangpas agreed almost unanimously that important changes have occurred in recent decades including "the way we eat and the way we dress." When asked to elaborate, people clearly felt that both their diet and their clothing had significantly improved. The ability to afford rice for most meals was almost always cited, as was the ability to buy nicer clothes and "real" shoes. Bumthangpas, in general, seemed unopposed to most of the changes that the valley had seen, in many cases they welcomed the opportunities it had brought them.

Important changes

Many people over the age of seventy remembered the hardship of taxes, especially the labour tax that saw them spending several days, even several weeks, transporting goods for the government. This was not only a great physical hardship but also a significant economic burden for the household which, albeit temporarily, lost the labour of an able-bodied member. Many of them told me that the removal of this form of taxation was the most significant change that they had seen in their lifetime,
People in and around Jakar were much more likely to talk about education and access to Western medicine as positive changes. In general, people brought up the fact that living in Bumthang gave them access to religious practice and activities that might not be possible in other part of the country. People in general seem to participate in these events and activities at whatever level they can afford.
Both the ability to participate in religious practices and to invest in their children's education were important ways whereby Bumthangpas defined their lives as good ones. People also mentioned cars, electricity and the presence of bigger and better-stocked stores. One woman in her seventies observed that now, as long as you have the money, you can get anything you want. While people further off the road believed that changes are concentrated around urban centres, they too felt that they ate and dressed better than in the past. They were also more likely to attribute all desirable changes to the King, suggesting perhaps that a sense of government presence is limited by road access.
Questions about who benefited the most from development also produced some unexpected results. The most common answer was that everyone was able to benefit equally and that there were no differences. After some probing, however, people often noted that "those who spoke well" or "those who knew how to talk" did better for themselves. Tashi Wangchuck has similarly noted that "oratorical skills (kha) are highly valued in their own right and persuasive debaters are respected. Kha is valued even more than yonten (knowledge)". Eloquent speakers most often have some degree of education and, for a variety of reasons; they are more likely to be men.
Gender often surfaced as an important factor for perceiving and experiencing change. It was also implicated in the sorts of things that stayed the same. Household labour continues to remain in short supply -- a perennial, much-noted problem in Bhutan and an important limitation on the financial success of a household. Most people with land continue to grow buckwheat (a labour intensive crop) for their own consumption, de-

198

199

spite telling me repeatedly and emphatically that daily consumption of rice instead of buckwheat was one of the most significant signs of their improved lives.

Social differentiation

While I saw numerous instances of differences in knowledge, attitude and experience of development in Bumthang based on residential patterns, generational position, land ownership and gender, this diversity was rarely reflected in the Helvetas final reports. There was in some cases, a recognition that road access, particularly in terms of access to markets, was varied but this was most often described as a problem that could be fixed by building a road. Most Helvetas projects targeted farmers and landowners, a focus that left out many of the shopkeepers I spoke to in Jakar who, as I noticed earlier, often did not own land (they were in many cases either Tibetan refugees or single mothers). As for gender differences, not only did they go largely unnoticed, some final report authors went so far as to strenuously reject the idea that gender made any difference in the areas where they worked.

What do these findings mean in the context of the legacy of Swiss work in Bumthang? In a nutshell, my findings were that: Bumthangpa accounts of development and change left out Helvetas, while Swiss accounts are inclined to ignore individual experiences and differences in measuring the success of their projects. However, my paper has attempted to show this discrepancy, pointing out this kind of a disconnection is not useful to understand how people in Bumthang feel about recent changes. I know that like the Swiss that I met on my mother's tour, many Bumthangpas have fond memories of their interaction with Swiss people but this is completely on an interpersonal level. Development and change was seen as the work of the government and evaluated and understood from this perspective. At the same time I know that Swiss experts in Bumthang were often able to make sense of the complex picture that was Bumthang, but this was not reflected in the way that they "did" development. Despite these misconnections, contrary to academic account of development, irrespective of the source of development, Bumthangpas are convinced that important things have changed and important things have stayed the same.

In Kürze

Ihr Vater kam 1973 als Entwicklungsexperte nach Bhutan, heiratete 1977 eine Frau aus Bhumtang. Ihre gemeinsame Tochter, Studentin der Ethnologie, geht der Frage nach, wie die Fachleute der Helvetas einerseits und die einheimische Bevölkerung andererseits die drei Jahrzehnte schweizerischer Entwicklungshilfe wahrnehmen und einschätzen. Sie studierte die 23 Schlussrapporte der jeweiligen Projektleiter und führte 65 Interviews mit Bumthangpas. Ihr Fazit: Die Rapporte sind sehr persönliche, gelegentlich nostalgische Betrachtungen der jeweiligen Amtszeit; eine Gelegenheit, Bilanz zu ziehen über das eigene Wirken. Sie sind für die Bürokratie in Bern geschrieben und nicht für die Nutzniesser der Projekte. So erstaunt es nicht, dass die meisten der Interviewten, die Helvetas-Leute mit Touristen verwechseln (wer mit Helvetas persönlich zu tun bekam, erinnert sich allerdings herzlich gerne an die Frauen und Männer aus der Schweiz). Alle Interviewpartner anerkennen und loben die Entwicklung ihres Tales, die markante Steigerung ihrer persönlichen Lebensqualität. Aber kaum einer sieht einen Zusammenhang mit Helvetas-Projekten. Für die meisten ist es das Werk der Regierung, oder gar des Königs persönlich.

En bref

Son père était venu au Bhoutan en 1973 comme expert du développement et épousa une femme de Bumthang. Leur fille, étudiante en anthropologie, étudie la question de la perception et du jugement porté sur trois décennies de coopération au développement, d'une part par les experts suisses, et d'autre part par la population locale. Elle a examiné les 23 rapports finaux des différents chefs de projets et a réalisé 65 interviews avec des Bumthangpas. Ses conclusions: les rapports relatent des considérations très personnelles et parfois un brin nostalgiques sur leur séjour au Bhoutan. Ces rapports sont écrits pour les bureaucrates à Berne plutôt que pour les bénéficiaires des projets. Ainsi il n'est pas étonnant que la plupart des Bhoutanais interviewées confondaient les collaborateurs d'Helvetas avec des touristes (mais celles et ceux qui avaient collaboré directement avec Helvetas se souvenaient avec plaisir des partenaires d'origine suisse). Toutes les personnes interviewées ont reconnu et apprécié le développement de leur vallée, l'accroissement significatif de leur qualité de vie personnelle. Mais peu d'entre eux y voient un lien avec les projets d'Helvetas. Pour la plupart d'entre eux, cette amélioration est à mettre sur le compte du gouvernement ou même du roi personnellement.

There's a whole lot more to say about that...

Interview with Fritz Maurer by Maria Känzig, in "Helvetas-Partnerschaft" Nr. 162, 2000

201 Fritz Maurer

Fritz Maurer is a master cheese maker and has lived and worked in Bhutan since 1969. Until 1983 he was the team leader of the Swiss Development Assistance Organisation HELVETAS.There is hardly any other country where in three short decades so much has changed so quickly.

In an interview with Maria Känzig, Fritz Maurer recalls times past and present, speaks of pigs and sustainability, of brewing beer and also of development assistance. In German this is referred to by the acronym EZA, which is short for "EntwicklungsZusammenArbeit", or in English: cooperative development work.

Let's begin in 1969, that's when you arrived in Bhutan.
In those days it was customary for cheese makers to go and work at least one year abroad. So, after passing my master examination, I looked for a job outside Switzerland. Just then I read an ad in the Swiss Dairy Paper, our trade paper. It read: "Cheese maker wanted – for Bhutan". I did not have a clue about that country and I had first to find out, in which part of the globe it was located.
But I finally got the job. My employer at that time was a Swiss businessman. He was a friend of the late king of Bhutan. This businessman couldn't really help me with the questions I had about dairy farming in Bhutan. So I just started off on the trip to Bhutan with large expectations and a headful of ideas and in my bag, my return ticket Calcutta-Zurich. It was valid for one year.

Gogona was your very first stop. Tell me more about that.
Let me first go back even a little further. One year before my arrival in Bhutan an experienced Swiss cheese maker had visited Bhutan from Nepal. He was to do preliminary research on how to develop dairy operations there. I was actually intended as his assistant. But because my arrival had been delayed, we could only meet briefly in the capital Thimphu. The outcome of his research was devastating for me: There was no surplus milk to be had in Bhutan. Because of that, I actually felt like returning to Switzerland soon. But Paro Penlop, my Bhutanese boss, who was also the brother of the king, did not agree with me at all. He said simply, "well, you're here now, and if you have no milk, well, go and see how you can get some and get on with it." That wouldn't be so simple, I told him. One would have to develop dairy farming from scratch. That meant most of all that we would need to create the feed base, procure better cattle, etc. I said: All that would take a long time. "Never mind", he said. "We are a poor country and we are a poor people. But one thing we have in abundance: Time! It does not matter how long it takes. At one point, one must begin. Just start, I promise you my full support".

Between us we had a sort of oral gentleman's agreement. I put in the greatest effort in all the necessary tasks at hand, and Paro Penlop kept his promise. He had great patience with this Swiss greenhorn and did hold it against me, if at times out of my eagerness or at other times because of my anger, I forgot the protocol which one uses in communicating with His Royal Highness. He was also of great help in tackling the administrative hurdles, which at that time were controlled by Indian hands. To this day I happily recall an episode from that time! That was like that: For months I had tried to get a few breeding pigs from the government farm: The Indian manager was always very polite, but my request just always seemed to get lost in the heaps of papers on his desk. When I finally put my request to Paro Penlop, he said 'no problem, don't worry!'

The very same afternoon he personally drove me to the farm, where the very appearance of His Royal Highness alone, caused enormous excitement. Paro Penlop came to the point without great ado and suddenly all doors were open to me for the national breeding station for pigs. From one pigpen I selected the most beautiful animals. "And when will you fetch them?" the manager asked. Paro Penlop quietly said to me: "Better take them with you right now, before he changes his mind, when I'm not there. Well yes, but how? In all of Thimpu there were but a few trucks and the National Pig Farm possessed no vehicles... "Do they fit in my car?" he asked to my surprise. "Certainly, but the seat covers, the stench..." "Put them in!" Paro Penlop told the hired farm hands who were watching the scene, while the Indian manager tried to utter some objections. Then the pig transport got under way, with His Royal Highness at the wheel. I can still see the shocked faces of the Indian officials staring in unbelief at our car and its cargo while walking home on the same road we were taking. Paro Penlop found it delightfully amusing and while we turned the corner to his residence, he asked "When can we expect the first sausages?"

202 Gogona

But now to your question about Gogona. We began trying to cultivate the fodder for the animals. The brown cattle, which we imported from Kerala in India, later formed the base of our cross-breeding programme here. That was the beginning of the 'Dairy and Forestry Project', which was later sponsored by Helvetas.

By now you have lived for 30 years in Bhutan. Some things must have changed in cooperative development work (EZA)?
Of course! First, the name itself has changed. In the early days when we talked about our work, we called it development 'aid' or 'assistance' (German: 'Entwicklungshilfe'). Now it's no longer called 'aid' or 'assistance' but 'cooperative development work'. The word 'aid' or 'assistance' has totally fallen out of favour. It's frowned upon, totally scorned. I actually ask myself at times "Why, really"? Development aid or assistance does not need to be one-sided. Some of my Swiss colleagues who worked in Bhutan wrote me later, that they probably 'received' more from Bhutan, than they could actually bring to the country. They probably allude to cultural and spiritual values, which have been lost or at least repressed in some western countries by the increasing emphasis on materialism.

The conditions under which we worked at that time were very difficult compared with today. There were hardly any roads in the country, people travelled mostly on foot. There were no medical facilities in the rural areas and in most things and most of the time we were completely left to our own devices. On the other hand, cooperative development work proceeds more professionally, which is also true for Helvetas, and I find this change to be very positive. But then again, I have some difficulties with the increasing bureaucracy in Bhutan. At some official levels, the willingness to come to a decision has strongly decreased. One prefers to call for international experts and consultants, to organize workshops and seminars about problems, which one could have just as easily solved during a normal working meeting with the actual actors involved. I also don't think much of certain 'buzz words' which seem to be concocted somewhere else and then flung around the globe with missionary zeal. Currently we are riding on the 'participatory' wave. As if it hadn't been observed all along EZA (cooperative development work) is doomed to failure if it is not based on participation from the bottom up. Currently, another such buzz word is making the rounds: 'Sustainability'. We actually had written the concept of 'sustainable development' on our flag long before it became popular. Sustainable development has long been our practice in our forestry work in Bhutan and the country has much to show for it. I could go on about other such buzz words, but maybe we better leave that for later discussion at a seminar or workshop...?

In which areas and sectors did you build up Bhutanese enterprises?
If you put it this way, I immediately think of 'big' names, such as Hayek, Blocher etc... With my name being Maurer, I could most likely succeed in becoming the president of a political party(a person named Maurer being the president of the biggest Swiss party), but since there are no political parties in Bhutan, this road too is denied me... But let me continue in earnest: I have not developed any enterprises; rather, I have assisted in getting small-scale trade and industry started. I promoted them sufficiently to keep them on their feet, - particularly in agriculture, dairy farming and food processing. I also promoted certain trades, for example metal-working and machine shops and wood-processing enterprises.

You too have become a small entrepreneur. What is your recipe for success?
You must be kidding? Before one can issue prescriptions for action, one must be successful. But success, for inexplicable reasons, most often seems to have avoided me. For example, just take the small beer brewery. I had to face the fact that idealism and hard work are not enough to make a go of it. That business is too small, the competition from India too large and the enthusiasm of the native population for my barley juice hasn't been exactly overwhelming; it's been mediocre.

Could you foster alcohol consumption in Bhutan?
Beer is a popular drink in Bhutan and until recently all beers have been imported from India or other countries. My native brew accounts for only a tiny portion of total beer sales in Bhutan. I don't want to minimize the problem of alcoholism in the country. Who knows, my 'Red Panda' beer might even play a small role in diverting people away from the higher percentage stuff? For those affected by alcohol problems I might suggest a more radical cure! They should switch to my cider, which we also produce here.

But, naturally, we also make other products. For example, I'm also active in beekeeping. Bees have interested me ever since childhood. Maybe that's why I'm also a good runner... Today I take care of 50 bee hives. And finally there is the hospitality industry, in which I also have a stake, where we have clear synergies and which we must exploit. For example, few people can serve our guests breakfast with fresh bread, butter, honey and cottage cheese and in the evening there's Raclette with our native beer!

In your experience during the past 20 years, how have the conditions changed for private sector development?
It is stated government policy to encourage the private sector,

especially small trade and commerce. But there's still a large gap between theory and practice. There are many attempts to develop potential small entrepreneurs but then, if someone really shows initiative and wants to build up a small enterprise, then obstacles – probably unintended – get put in the way. For example, take the high interest rates for obtaining a loan and the considerable guaranty which is necessary to get one.
This state of affairs doesn't really foster a favourable relationship between the entrepreneur and the State. The normal Bhutanese citizen sees the governmental administration as a somewhat uncanny and inscrutable entity, which at best one can make use of and otherwise better avoids. Let me tell a story, which is quite typical for what I mean: A former local co-worker recently got quite angry about the taxes he has to pay (30% of profit). 'And what do we get for that?' he asked. I tried to explain to him that the State has quite a few responsibilities to pay for, for example, health and education expenses, the upkeep of the roads, etc… To which my counterpart replied: But don't the international Development Assistance Organisations pay for that?

In your view what would be meaningful projects in Bhutan?
If the question is asked in such a way, one could get the idea that meaningful projects might only be the kinds of 'hardware' projects or structural projects on which you can lay your hands on, maybe a hydro-electrical power plant, which, of course, can be a good thing if it is well planned and fulfils all environmental requirements, etc. But for me, a very important project was the importation and introduction into Bhutan of cancer-resistant potato varieties. We distributed them throughout the whole country and potatoes became in some areas the most important 'cash crop'. Now for me, that kind of project is just as important and meaningful. Or take that nurse who came and worked for many years without pay. Her boundless energy and empathy created trust and confidence among the people. This played an important role in the subsequent establishment of a public health system. I believe that these activities also qualify as meaningful contributions and incidentally, both of these examples didn't start out as a 'project'.

How do you see the future of Cooperative Development Work (EZA) in Bhutan?
Less is more.

Let me ask provocatively: Is there any necessity for Cooperative Development Work in this country?
Let's ask the question the other way around: What would happen if tomorrow we totally stopped development cooperation, any kind whatsoever? In practical terms, this would mean that all sector development would very much slow down. New taxes would be raised. Agriculture would experience a strong revalorization. Self initiative and responsibility would be strengthened as values and prized at a much higher level. A whole sector of the population, which today enriches itself directly or indirectly, would become impoverished or would have to get used to working again. And there's a whole lot more to say about that too…

Do Cooperative Development Work and the culture of a country at times work at cross-purposes?
As far as Bhutan is concerned, both the government and the people are very strongly committed to safekeeping their cultural values. However, one tends to forget the fact that culture is not a rigid factor, it changes constantly. Bhutan cannot turn into a museum; the country has opened its doors. Cooperative development work has long since become a pillar of the culture of this country. And other influences – from other countries as well – television and the new global communication technologies play a far greater role than cooperative development work.

Tashi delek! Thank you very much!

In Kürze
Fritz Maurer, der Käsermeister, der 1969 von Fritz von Schulthess mit einem Einjahresvertrag nach Bhutan geschickt worden war, ist im Bumthang Tal sesshaft geworden. Er blickt in diesem Interview auf bald 40 Jahre Arbeit zurück. Er hat viele Projekte gestartet – vom Futteranbau, über Viehzucht und Milchwirtschaft bis zum Ackerbau. Aus seiner Sicht war die Einführung krankheitsresistenter Kartoffeln einer der grössten Erfolge. Kartoffeln werden heute in vielen Gegenden produziert, in grossen Mengen nach Indien exportiert.
Fritz Maurer hat sich in Bumthang auch selbst ein kleines Imperium aufgebaut: er macht Käse, braut Met, gewinnt Honig von 50 Bienenvölkern und fabriziert Apfelsaft. So geniessen die Gäste in seinem Hotel immer frische Lebensmittel. Er hat mitgeholfen, kleinere Handels- und Industriebetriebe aufzubauen. All die Arbeit bedeutet ihm nicht einseitiges Geben. Wie viele der Frauen und Männer, die in Bhutan gearbeitet haben, fühlt er sich reich beschenkt in kulturellen und spirituellen Werten, die in Bhutan noch nicht vom Materialismus verdrängt worden sind.

En bref
Fritz Maurer, le maître fromager envoyé au Bhoutan par Fritz von Schulthess en 1969, avec un contrat d'une année, s'est installé définitivement à Bumthang. Dans cette interview il évoque près de 40 ans de travail. Il a initié de nombreux projets – de la production fourragère aux grandes cultures en passant par l'élevage et l'économie laitière. Pour lui, l'introduction de variétés de pommes de terre résistantes aux maladies a été l'un des principaux succès. Aujourd'hui, des pommes de terre sont produites dans de nombreuses régions et exportées en grandes quantités vers l'Inde.
Fritz Maurer a également construit son petit empire à Bumthang: il fabrique du fromage, brasse de la bière, extrait du miel de plus de 50 ruchers et produit du jus de pomme. Ainsi les hôtes de son hôtel ont toujours des produits frais. Il a contribué au développement de petites entreprises commerciales et industrielles. Pour lui tout ce travail n'est en aucun cas un transfert à sens unique: il a aussi beaucoup reçu des nombreuses personnes qui ont travaillé avec lui au Bhoutan, sur les plans spirituel et culturel. Car au Bhoutan, ces valeurs n'ont pas encore été entièrement substituées par le matérialisme.

Challenges ahead

BHUTAN'S NATIONAL NEWSPAPER

KUENSEL

THAT THE NATION SHALL BE INFORMED

March 26, 2008 Vol XXIII No 23 [Nu. 8] www.kuenselonline.com

NATIONAL ASSEMBLY ELECTIONS '08

The people have spoken

But what have they said?

BY KINLEY DORJI

The morning of March 24 was warm and sunny. It was one of the quietest days of the year. By nightfall the quiet became a stunned silence as the electorate gave Druk Phuensum Tshogpa 44 out of 47 constituencies, a landslide victory.

Most people, including winners and voters, were somewhat taken aback by the force of the electoral verdict. Observers were assessing the candidates and expecting a close race. They could not predict the most important element in an election... the electorate.

The message was not new. In 2005, when His Majesty the fourth Druk Gyalpo began public consultations on the draft Constitution, people around the country pleaded with him not to abdicate and to delay the democratisation process.

The people have not changed. Thus the resounding message from the Bhutanese voter: Change? "Yes". Complete overhaul? "No".

Druk Phuensum Tshogpa was able to convince the Bhutanese voters that its five former ministers and senior bureaucrats were well groomed for leadership by none other than the fourth Druk Gyalpo. Electorates around the world are known to be conservative, sometimes frustratingly so, and the Bhutanese voters, too, appear to have decided to play it safe.

It is likely that the Phuensum Tshogpa was also able to provide a strong sense of reassurance because it has been more convincing on its commitment to Gross National Happiness. In the absence of clear ideology, the DPT manifesto promised stability on a GNH platform.

DPT also hit a sensitive chord among the

CONTINUED ON 14

Prime minister elect : a momentous moment

DPT - absolute majority

BY PHUNTSHO CHODEN

The Druk Phuensum Tshogpa will form the country's first democratically elected government, having won a surprise landslide victory against the People's Democratic Party on Monday's historic general election.

The DPT, led by party president Jigmi Thinley, won 44 of the 47 seats to the National Assembly. The PDP candidates from Phuntsholing, Gasa (Goenkhatoe-Laya) and Sombaykha constituencies secured three seats in the National Assembly to form the opposition Party.

Of the total 253,012 votes cast, DPT won about 67 percent and PDP 33 percent. A total of four woman candidates and 43 male candidates were elected to the National Assembly.

Almost 79.4 percent of the total 318,465 registered voters cast their votes in the 47 constituencies on March 24. Of the total voters, 235,893 cast their votes on the electronic voting machine in 865 poling stations and 17,119 votes were through postal ballots.

Gelephu constituency had the highest number of voters with about 9,427 followed by Chapcha-Bongo constitu-

A unique journey through time

by Kinley Dorji, Editor in chief, Kuensel

Introduction

If 2008 is an unprecedented year in Bhutanese history, many people would agree that it is a special year in human history as Bhutan continues its unique journey through time.

203

The kingdom will enthrone the fifth King of Bhutan, His Majesty Jigme Khesar Namgyal Wangchuck, and celebrate the centenary of the Wangchuck dynasty throughout the year. Bhutan also saw the incredible transition from a monarchy to a parliamentary democracy in the unfurling of a democratic vision that has been described as "one of the most daring experiments undertaken today".

Poised to move into a new era of history, the Bhutanese people are deeply apprehensive, yet enormously excited.

Background

As history fuses with legend, the Bhutanese experience unravels like Vajrayana true teachings. Bhutan's history was carved by mythological personalities, from Guru Rinpoche to Pema Lingpa and Drukpa Kuenley to Zhabdrung Ngawang Namgyal and then to the succession of dynamic Kings. Now, the fourth King, His Majesty Jigme Singye Wangchuck, who abdicated in December 2006, has closed one chapter and a new chapter was opened by His Majesty King Jigme Khesar Namgyal Wangchuck.

With an uncanny clarity of vision His Majesty King Jigme Singye Wangchuck steered the kingdom through more than three decades of phenomenal progress and concluded his reign with a historic initiative in political transformation. His Majesty, who introduced the concept of Gross National Happiness as an inspiration for Bhutan's development and as a goal for human progress, established the path of good governance in this democratic process.

Having enjoyed unprecedented peace and stability under his reign, the people of Bhutan were overwhelmed when His Majesty announced his abdication in his National Day address in 2005. Men, women, and children asked His Majesty, why?

The royal response, simple and clear, was that a small and vulnerable country like Bhutan must not be left in the hands of one individual who is "chosen by birth and not merit". His Majesty believed that Bhutan needed a strong and unique system of governance and, at this time, a democratic constitutional monarchy was the answer.

The people of Bhutan were apprehensive. The educated section of society proposed that democracy would work better when the population at large was better educated. The rural majority was intuitively suspicious of democracy, having seen democracy bring more instability in many countries in the region and around the world.

The collective question was, why now?

His Majesty the King, who travelled and talked to people around the country throughout his reign, explained that the best time for change is when everything is going well. Bhutan, today, enjoyed peace and stability, the national security was assured, and Bhutan's relations with the world had never been better.

204

As His Majesty the King had emphasized through his reign: "The destiny of the country lies in the hands of the people". This was what His Majesty meant. And the Bhutanese people were thus given the responsibility to take the kingdom into the future.

At a special sitting of the Cabinet on December 14, 2006, His Majesty said: "As I hand over my responsibilities to my son, I repose my full faith and belief in the people of Bhutan to look after the future of the nation, for it is the Bhutanese people who are the true custodians of our tradition and culture, and the ultimate guardians of the security, sovereignty, and continued well-being of lour country."

The transition

2008 is, therefore, a time for reflection. The people of Bhutan, as well as their friends around the world, are reflecting deeply on this change. All Bhutanese citizens are trying to understand their individual responsibilities as well as the changing relationships among civil servants, politicians, media, civil society, private sector, and the community at large.

Some of the government's most dynamic ministers and officials have resigned to enter politics. The rest of society is adjusting to the changing political environment.

This powerful sense of being Bhutanese comes from the essence of Gross National Happiness. Happiness, as it is taught in Buddhism, is an individual pursuit. The people must look inside themselves for happiness because there is no external source of happiness. Therefore, GNH is a mandate of the state, a responsibility of the government, to create the right environment for all citizens to seek happiness.

205

The essence of Gross National Happiness becomes even more relevant in a democracy and places a profound responsibility on all individuals. As two political parties emerged in September 2006, and political activity picked up in the following months, this became very clear. The road to democracy is not going to be easy.

There is no template for democracy, but there is much strength in the Bhutanese system that is an advantage over many other democracies around the world. The clear vision of the leadership, a stable political environment, a growing economy that is carefully being nurtured, and, most important of all, the strong bonds that existed between the King and the people of Bhutan provide a foundation for democratic governance.

A group of civil service leaders from India, who held a workshop on democracy in Thimphu in October, 2007, pointed out that Bhutan was more ready to run a government than India was when India established a democratic government.

The future

People talk about the future. For the people of Bhutan the future is already here. Today's generation of Bhutanese are watching the future unfolding every day. We are a part of the future. We are carving a future out of the past.

206

At the helm stands His Majesty Jigme Khesar Namgyal Wangchuck. As the Monarch who will take Bhutan into the future, his responsibility is to translate today's dreams into tomorrow's reality. In his first address to the nation His Majesty outlined the priorities for the country's future.

"Henceforth, our responsibilities will always be first and foremost the peace and tranquillity of the nation, the sovereignty and security of our country, the fulfilling of the vision of Gross National Happiness, and the strengthening of this new system of democracy," His Majesty said when he addressed the nation on December 17, 2006, only days after he took over the responsibility as Head of State. "To fulfil these aspirations, in this age, we must first build a strong and dynamic economy. And in doing so, we must remember that, as a landlocked nation with a small population, it is vital that whatever we do, we work harder and do it better than other nations. For our small kingdom, excellence must be the only standard."

Personifying the Bhutanese state, His Majesty the King quickly established his credibility as a leader of the future. In October 2007, His Majesty explained that the peace and prosperity of the nation required the hard work from the people. His Majesty said that Gross National Happiness was a shared national objective and that democracy was inherently about values and principles. His Majesty emphasised the importance of building a strong economy as a path to a vibrant democracy and Gross National Happiness.

During the historic celebrations of National Day, 2007, as the nation listened with intensity, His Majesty the King outlined the responsibilities for different sections of Bhutanese society. From the Bhutanese youth, His Majesty asked for hard work, commitment, and excellence. On the civil servants His Majesty placed the responsibility of making democracy work and setting high standards for the population. The politicians, in serving the people in a new era, must set a clear, principled and noble path. To the people, His Majesty said: "You and I, the people of Bhutan, will not fail in our efforts to build a stronger Bhutan."

What His Majesty King Jigme Khesar has established, in the short time as Druk Gyalpo, is a sense of security that the new era will be one of stable creativity in preserving the kingdom of Bhutan as a nation that all Bhutanese people will be proud of. The royal pledge is that today's generation will hand over this legacy, stronger than ever, to posterity.

207

Perspective

Bhutan's journey through time, therefore, is characterized by the sense of continuity as one enlightened King hands over the reins of governance to his heir. In His Majesty King Jigme Khesar's own words, change will be guided by a national conscience that is inspired by Gross National Happiness.

Gross National Happiness is the system of values that kept Bhutanese society together through centuries of change. It carries an enlightened wisdom that this system of values will be Bhutan's strength as it moves into the future.

In the end, as dramatic as today's changes might appear, Bhutan is not replacing the sacred Bhutanese system. We are building on it. Democracy is not the goal. It's a path to good governance, to help us achieve our broader goal of Gross National Happiness.

208

In Kürze

Das Jahr 2008 ist eine scharfe Zäsur in Bhutans Geschichte. Sie war über Jahrhunderte geprägt von mythologischen Figuren. In den letzten hundert Jahren lag das Schicksal in den Händen der Wangchuck-Dynastie. Der letzte und dynamischste unter ihnen, Jigme Singye Wangchuck katapultiert sein Volk quasi vom Mittelalter in die Moderne. Im Dezember 2006 verzichtet er auf den Thron und verordnet seinem Land die Demokratie. Das Volk ist geschockt: „Wir hatten es so gut unter den Wangchucks; warum sollen wir uns jetzt mit Politikern herumschlagen, die überall auf der Welt soviel Unheil anrichten.“ Der König bleibt unerbittlich; als Regent hatte er immer betont, die Zukunft Bhutans liege in den Händen des Volkes. Und langsam wächst die Einsicht, dass auch in der Demokratie das gelobte bhutanesische System der Gross National Happiness weiterbestehen kann.

En bref

L'année 2008 a marqué une rupture dans l'histoire du Bhoutan. Pendant des siècles, le Bhoutan était marqué par des figures mythologiques. Au cours du dernier siècle, son sort était entre les mains de la dynastie Wangchuck. L'avant-dernier roi, et le plus dynamique d'entre eux, Jigme Singye Wangchuck catapulte son peuple quasiment du Moyen Âge vers le modernisme. En décembre 2006, il renonce au trône et ordonne la mise en place d'une démocratie dans son pays. Le peuple est choqué: "tout allait si bien sous le règne des Wangchuck, pourquoi devons-nous nous battre avec des politiciens, alors que partout dans le monde, ceux-ci causent tant de malheur". Le roi reste ferme: du temps de son règne, il a toujours insisté sur le fait que l'avenir du Bhoutan doit être entre les mains du peuple. Aujourd'hui, les gens comprennent progressivement que le principe tant apprécié du Bonheur National Brut peut être maintenu sous un régime démocratique.

The Bhutanese Media – guiding change

by Siok Sian Dorji, Freelance writer and filmmaker, Thimphu

The kingdom of Bhutan is going through historic changes today as the country makes the transition from monarchy to democracy. Documenting these dramatic times and facing their greatest challenges, Bhutan's media are poised for an explosion in their growth.

The media in this Himalayan nation of 630,000 people have always mirrored Bhutan's development. As the country opened up to modernisation, it quickly spanned the centuries and moved from building infrastructure to the information age in four decades. Having built basic infrastructure, improved the literacy rate, increased life expectancy and sustainable livelihoods, the government began to focus on the media to reach people over the landlocked and mountainous terrain. In the age of development communications the government believed that the media could help spur development.

BBS radio, started by youth volunteers, was taken over by the government and expanded in the 1980's. The country's first newspaper rolled off the presses in 1986. Media growth picked up pace in the 1990's as the information age arrived. In 1992, a royal decree from the fourth King of Bhutan made the media organizations autonomous. The tenets of freedom of expression and media are enshrined in Bhutan's Constitution.
Today, the media play a central role for political change.

Profile of the Bhutanese media

The Bhutanese media continue to reach out to the unreached. The Bhutan Broadcasting Service SW and FM radio covers the entire country and beyond. BBS TV (the national TV channel) reaches almost all urban towns and can be viewed globally through satellite. International television reaches people in 46 towns and urban settlements. Two private FM radio stations were started in 2006/2007. There are three newspapers, two of them launched in 2006.
There is an estimated 20,000 computers in the country and online forums and chat sites are becoming increasingly popular. The Bhutanese film industry continues to produce more films every year for a growing audience.
The introduction of television and the Internet in 1999 was an important landmark for media growth. Today, television is the main choice of entertainment and a medium for news and information. Radio continues to have a significant audience, especially among rural listeners, and new FM stations are capturing the youth and the urban listeners. By early 2008, Bhutanese mobile phone users will be able to access Internet on their phones.

The impact of the media

Perhaps one of the most important concerns today is the prolific impact of TV in Bhutan with more than 30 channels beaming into homes across the country. Bhutanese children are now born into homes where TV is on for several hours a day. Most of the stories about people, life, and society are now told, not by parents, schools or elders and others in the community, but by a group of distant media companies driven largely by commercial interests.

Of greater concern is the fact that the Bhutanese community is jumping from an oral society to a visual society without developing a literary tradition. Media studies show that people who did not read much in the first place, are not reading; they are turning to the visual media for their news, information, and entertainment.

Role of the media

The latest challenge for the Bhutanese media is to be an active player in the new democratic government.
Bhutan's media have always been extending the boundaries of public discourse and are today facing pressures from public, politicians, and government. The media's responsibility as the fourth estate - to be a watchdog for society - is now being felt more than ever. Bhutanese media are today facing increasing demands and expectations.

One of the most important roles for media in Bhutan is to foster discourse and to be a public space for discussions on issues vital to an emerging democracy. Bhutan is making the move towards a democratic constitutional monarchy without having had time to develop a vibrant public discourse that is essential for the success of a democracy. As a small country with limited resources, Bhutan needs to envision the kind of media that will enhance the people's well-being without falling into the same pitfalls of the global media – where news and information is being trivialised and overtaken by hedonistic entertainment fuelled by the commercial conglomerates.

Elections in the internet

January 2, 2008, Kuensel online

Gross National Happiness

At a crucial juncture in Bhutan's history, what is the role of the media in nurturing future generations? How can Bhutan's media find its own personality, and mature into a fourth estate that supports the growth and development of a constitutional monarchy? What can media do to empower citizens so that they can actively participate in a democratic society? How can the media draw on the global experience to adopt what is good and relevant? The values of Gross National Happiness can provide inspiration for this vision, as media play vital roles in the pursuit of happiness. If GNH is interpreted as the need for government or society to create an environment in which individuals can pursue their happiness, then Bhutan's media have to help create such an environment.

This means the need to develop public service media as a healthy response to the commercialism of global media. Public service media mean providing the essential information and forums for discussion needed to empower people. It means regarding media listeners, viewers and readers as citizens rather than mere consumers, and it means providing quality content rather than quantity. Media must help develop good taste and culture, promote understanding, spur literacy and development, create informed debate and empower people.

Public service media in Bhutan's context means media that must be independent of state and market controls to truly serve the public. It means giving citizens the education and information they need to develop the critical wisdom necessary to open our minds to the possibilities of enlightened living. Bhutanese media have the responsibility of deepening the discourse on the priorities of a rapidly transforming society, and on GNH.

In a GNH perspective the media must serve the public by informing and empowering the citizen and providing the public space and discourse that will strengthen civil society. If GNH can be embedded into Bhutan's media development, it will provide the best self-regulatory environment for media to grow. Bhutan's media will instinctively provide quality, relevant and inspiring content to enhance Bhutan's search for well-being and happiness.

Bhutan's media function in a small vulnerable society that has survived on the strength of its cultural identity. The media's role is more critical than ever and can empower people to develop the ability to achieve the freedom to attain happiness. The media can be a true guide for change.

Bhutan elected 15 parliamentarians to the National Council on December 31. Another five will be elected on January 29. His Majesty the King will appoint five eminent citizens as members. The 25-member House of Review of Parliament will comprise 20 elected members, one from each dzongkhag, and the five appointed by the King. A total of 147'789 people voted in the first round of the National Council elections representing 55% of the 269'337 registered voters.

Bhutan's border with India was closed and security was present at polling stations, particularly in dzongkhags near the border.

The Resident Coordinator of the UN system, Mr. N. Rosellini, who visited 10 polling stations on December 31, said that he was impressed by the smooth organisation of the elections.

Having watched the mock elections earlier in 2007, when the awareness level was low, he said, he found the people much more self-confident and knowledgeable about what they were doing.

He added that the elections were free and fair, with voters coming from diverse backgrounds.

After observing the elections, the Chief Election Commissioner of the Indian state of Manipur, Mr. R. Rashmi, said that "it is an ideal situation, with no crime and law and order problems, no threats to candidates and voters, like in India. It was free, fair and very good for democracy."

In Kürze

Den Anfang machten Freiwillige mit Kurzwellenradio, bis dieses 1980 von der Regierung übernommen wurde. 1986 erschien die erste Zeitung. 1992 erhielten die Medien per Dekret des Königs autonomen Status – sie werden aber (als service public gewissermassen) subventioniert. Die Meinungsfreiheit ist in der Verfassung garantiert. In drei Jahrzehnten hat das Land den Sprung ins Informationszeitalter getan. Satelliten TV erreicht 46 Städte, Internetzugang gibt es seit diesem Jahr auch übers Handy. On-line Foren und chatsites sind sehr populär. Bhutan ist (wie so manches Drittweltland) im Laufe einer Generation von der mündlichen Überlieferung in die vulgäre digitale Bilderwelt der Neuzeit gestolpert: in Haushalten, die noch nie ein Buch gesehen haben, plärrt heute den ganzen Tag das Radio oder der Fernseher. Die einheimischen Medien stehen vor zwei grossen Herausforderungen: Sie möchten der Tradition des Landes Sorge tragen, und sie müssen die lebhafte und umfassende öffentliche Diskussion organisieren, ohne die eine Demokratie nicht funktionieren kann.

En bref

Au début, ce sont des volontaires qui émettaient par radio sur les ondes courtes, jusqu'à ce que le gouvernement reprenne cette activité à son compte en 1980. Le premier journal parut en 1986. Les médias ont obtenu un statut autonome par décret royal en 1992 – ils obtiennent des subventions en tant que service public. La liberté d'opinion est garantie dans la Constitution. En l'espace de trois décennies, le pays a réussi son intégration dans l'époque de l'information. La télévision par satellite atteint 46 localités, et depuis cette année, l'accès Internet est possible par le téléphone portable. Les forums en ligne et les sites de tchatche sont très populaires. À l'image de nombreux pays en développement, le Bhoutan est passé en l'espace d'une génération de la tradition orale dans le monde vulgaire des images digitales modernes: dans des ménages qui n'avaient encore jamais vu un livre, on entend brailler la radio ou la télévision à longueur de journée. Les médias indigènes ont deux grands défis à relever: ils souhaitent prendre soin de la tradition du pays et ils doivent organiser une discussion publique et vivante sans laquelle une démocratie ne peut pas fonctionner.

Switzerland and its Democracy – a view from inside

by Annemarie Huber-Hotz, Chancellor of the Swiss Government (until end 2007) Fragments of a lecture at Royal Institute of Management, Thimpu, Bhutan, 21. April 2006

209

210

211

The Federal Chancellor – the government's "chief of staff" – is particularly involved in the workings of Swiss democracy. It is one of the important tasks of the Chancellery to supervise the functioning of the instruments of direct democracy. In close co-operation with the cantons and communes, not to mention the committees responsible for the various initiatives and referendums, the Federal Chancellery organises popular votes and elections at national level.

Direct democracy – basic to the Swiss

The political form in which people live is not arbitrary, but is determined by a country's character and its past. This is true for Bhutan and for Switzerland. Switzerland is a multi-cultural country with four national languages. Due to global migration, Switzerland has taken in a large number of foreigners over the last fifty years, and they now make up for about 20% of our population. Switzerland has always been a multi-cultural society and this is even truer today.

Solidarity with minorities

The founders of the modern Swiss state recognised over 150 years ago, that stability and prosperity can only be guaranteed through solidarity and a far-reaching involvement of the linguistic, regional and cultural minorities, both in the political decision-making process and in all key positions of the State.

Network of checks and balances

They created a finely tuned political system with a complicated network of checks and balances between the people and the political authorities, the government and Parliament, the Confederation and the 26 constituent states (cantons).

Limitation of power

No person should hold too much power. There is no permanent head of state, no permanent president of the political authorities. No one should always belong to the majority, just as no one should always be in the minority. Every Swiss citizen is sometimes part of the majority and sometimes part of a minority.

Political rights of the people

It is no exaggeration to say that the situation in Switzerland is reversed. Federal laws are not subject to any judicial control as to their constitutionality, but they are all subject to the scrutiny exercised by the people. All Swiss citizens over the age of 18 are entitled to vote in federal matters. It took Switzerland a long time to give women their voting rights – they had to wait until 1971.

The acceptance or rejection of a proposal is certainly a means of expressing confidence, or lack thereof, in the authorities, but the government remains in place in the event of rejection. We vote for or against the issue at hand and not on something else.

Instruments of direct democracy

Voters' rights in Switzerland are more extensive than in many country. First, as is usual, voters elect the members of the National Council, the first chamber of our Parliament. Then, the members of the second chamber, the Council of States, are elected according to cantonal law. Voters also have direct rights with regard to the Constitution and federal legislation: 100'000 voters can request a total or partial amendment to the Constitution by means of a popular initiative and 50.000 citizens can ask for a referendum on any law adopted by the Parliament. The Swiss citizens have many means to participate in the political decision-making process, and they can vote two to four times a year at national level and even more at cantonal and local level. To sum up, the initiative allows the people to initiate a law, the referendum, to correct the sins of omission of government and Parliament.

Political parties

The political parties play an important role in direct democracy. The power a party has in political life depends either on its size, which allows it to become a part of the governing coalition, or on its capacity to veto government decisions. Since 1959, the four largest parties, which cover about 80% of voters, are represented in the government.The main task of Swiss political parties is to present candidates for parliamentary election – and at cantonal level also for government - and to take an active part in election and referendum campaigning.

212

213

214

The Media

A big challenge for the political parties, and for the government and Parliament, is the dominant role of the media. They influence the forming of public opinion in a decisive way. They contribute to political agenda-setting and make it possible to build up popular candidates for election.

Advantages - disadvantages

Direct democracy is a very important instrument of political legitimisation for government and Parliament. It contributes to the stability of the political system, which is a base for a successful economy and the welfare of society. However, the perfect functioning of this system is not self-evident.

A question concerns the participation of citizens in popular votes and elections: With a voter turnout of under 50%, can it still be said that we have the legitimacy that we are seeking? What can we do to ensure that people not only consider democratic rights as an individual right, but also as a civic duty?

Trust as an important requirement

There is evidence to suggest that trust in institutions – both private and public – has declined over the years. And Switzerland is no exception, due to a number of factors: the political context, globalisation, the state of the economy, the political culture, attitudes to authority, changing values and the media. Mutual trust between the political institutions – government and Parliament – and the citizens is an essential element of the democratic contract.

Promoting values

Politics is part and parcel of society and changes along with it. With this change, politics and in particular governments have a particular responsibility. Government means taking the lead and being a role model. If a government wants to do this with credibility, it must meet specific requirements. First and foremost, it must be honest and humble.

Honesty and humility

It means presenting the decision processes openly and truthfully, saying what we know and what we don't know, admitting that we have not got everything under control and that mistakes can happen. An honest government can admit that not everything can be planned and that there is no such thing as the one and only solution, but that there are always alternatives.

Tolerance and the ability to listen

Tolerance means taking note of other points of view and incorporating them into one's own thought processes. That implies listening to and taking your political opponent seriously. The debate must be on the issues at stake, and must not degenerate into a personal attack.

Unity

It is part of political leadership. A government is only credible if it has a certain amount of internal consistency or if it is at least willing and able to achieve unity under difficult circumstances

Conclusions

Switzerland is often considered as a role model. We are still aware that our democracy cannot be exported as it is, and that improvements can still be made. We understand that direct democracy is a collective learning process, for citizens as well as for political parties, governments and Parliaments.

In Kürze

Beim Einüben demokratischer Prozesse lassen sich die Bhutaner gerne von ihren Schweizer Freunden beraten. Etliche junge Bhutaner haben die Schweiz zu Ausbildungszwecken ja auch schon besucht und kennengelernt. Im April 2006 – kurz bevor der König abdankte – hat Annemarie Huber-Hotz am Königlichen Institut für Management in Thimphu einen viel beachteten Vortrag über die demokratischen Institutionen unseres Landes gehalten.

En bref

Pour la mise en place des processus démocratiques, les Bhoutanais se laissent volontiers conseiller par leurs amis suisses. De nombreux jeunes Bhoutanais sont d'ailleurs déjà venus en Suisse pour y être formés et ont appris à connaître ce pays. En avril 2006 – peu avant l'abdication du roi – Annemarie Huber-Hotz a donné une conférence remarquée à l'institut royal de management de Thimphu sur les institutions politiques suisses.

What makes development cooperation work?

by Karin Reinhardt, Swiss student of Political Science and Anthropology

Introduction

"Development theory" developed in the context of this world struggle, and it is important to note that no development theory proved to be really valid or successful.
Source: MANCALL, Mark (2004): "Gross National Happiness and Development. An Essay". In: URA, Karma/GALAY, Karma (2004): Gross National Happiness and Development. Thimphu, Centre for Bhutan Studies: 1-50.

I agree with M. Mancall in "that no development theory proved to be really valid or successful" But what happened in reality? One could ask:

- What is the value of development cooperation? Does development cooperation contribute to the betterment of developing countries?
- How is good development cooperation defined? What needs to be done to make development cooperation work?

For me, as a Swiss citizen, a further question is interesting:

- Is Switzerland a good partner in development cooperation? What is Switzerland doing and what should the country do?

Development cooperation does not guarantee economic growth.

Changes in politics should not be a precondition for receiving help.

Development aid is hope not expectation.

It is scandalous that a cow in the European Union gets more subsidies than a poor human being.

There is not just one solution when looking for the right way in development cooperation.

Reducing poverty is also in the interest of highly developed states like Switzerland.

Switzerland is a good partner in development cooperation, but it could even be a better one.

More Money, fewer Problems?

I am dividing the most quoted points of criticism into three elements; an economical element, a political element and a social element.
The **economical** element states that development cooperation does not cause economic growth. Many critics point to the fact that countries that have received a high amount of financial and technical assistance are not better off years after. Often this criticism is referring to Africa. It is true that Africa has got huge problems, but this is not generally true for Africa as a whole. Africa is a continent, not a small country! I do not agree with the view that economic growth is the only way to measure the success of development cooperation. This represents the point of view that development cooperation is the input, economic growth the output. What lies in between is not discussed.
The **political** element points to the difficult political situations in many developing countries. Development cooperation with an untrustworthy and shady government is debatable and might even be senseless. One way to avoid money draining away and promises being broken is to try not to work directly with the government, but to strengthen other social groupings. It is the duty of development cooperation to support political reforms when this can improve the life standard, but it is also their duty to deal with present governments and political structures. Changes in politics should not be a precondition for receiving help.
The **social** element, finally, has two main points of criticism. One is that, so far, development aid did not help to reduce poverty and that the really poor people did never benefit from any assistance. Unfortunately, the first point is not that wrong. It is a shame that the real aim of development cooperation – reducing poverty and helping those who suffer the most – is far from being reached. Another argument is that aid causes expectations to receive money and impede people to act on their own initiative and take responsibility for their lives: development cooperation makes people lethargic. As to the second point, I have to say that I do not believe this assumption. It represents a picture of poor people that is, in my view, too negative. It represents the view that people in developing countries are just lazy and wait for money from the North. However, the will to get more than they presently have and maybe to get as much as we have seems only natural to me. At the same time most people do not take pride in being supported financially and are more than eager to get out of this dependency. Development aid is hope not expectation.

Does Money Make the World Go 'Round'?

What is good development cooperation? What needs to be done to make development cooperation work? Every decade has had its own paradigm on how to improve the conditions in the developing world. Theorists often claimed to have found the one and only way to develop the underdeveloped world. Today, these ideas seem to be outdated or even ridiculous and reality and pragmatism is much more important than theory and ideologies. A decision made in the 1970's and reiterated today says that every donor country should increase its budget for development cooperation to 0.7% of the gross national income (GNI). But the experience shows that more money does not necessarily mean more help. However, it must be clear that the amount alone is not decisive, but the actions taken with it. The biggest mistake the industrialized world made was to promise a certain amount and then not to live up to its obligations.

The keyword in the political debate is good governance. Generally good governance means the way how a government uses economic and social resources to develop its country. Good governance includes characteristics such as participation, respect for the rule of law, democratic institutions, transparency and compliance with human rights. I generally support the idea of good governance, because an efficient political environment strengthens a state immensely, which then leads to better service for the people and better economic performance. The implementation of good governance should mean supporting a country's efforts to develop efficient governmental institutions.

I suggest implementing good governance in a way that a receiving country is able to adapt to the political reforms; this means that reforms are incorporating the historical and sociocultural context of a country.

Ownership means that the receiving countries themselves should formulate development policies and strategies. The decision lies within the government, the officials, the economy and the civil society. These policies should be implemented in partnership with donor countries and guarantee development tailored to the users' requirements. I totally agree that development cooperation should be a dialogue in partnership between donor and receiver country. Ownership requires an inclusion of civil society in the process of decision-making and development. This is really important in order to make sure that a majority of the population benefits from improvement. There is not just one solution when looking for the right way in development cooperation.

Swiss Quality?

Switzerland's way of development cooperation is written down in its constitution and follows the principle of solidarity, neutrality and universality. The country's position in the international system as well as its own political system is formative to its development cooperation. Is Switzerland a good partner in development cooperation?

Switzerland invests about 1.5-2.0 billion CHF on official development cooperation (ODA), which approximately corresponds to 0.4% of the GNI. Switzerland's efforts in development cooperation are not only a sign of solidarity with the South but lie also in the country's own political and economical interests. In the age of globalization, the interdependence between states is not only becoming closer, but states are also more vulnerable. Poverty and conflicts in certain states have consequences for other states, e.g. through migration or terrorism. Development cooperation can help to establish stable and good international relations and is a major part of Switzerland's international presence. As one of the most important financial centres of the world, Switzerland has a strong interest in a flourishing world trade. I am convinced that Switzerland's development projects are of high quality. Impressively, the country works together with fragile states. When it comes to politics, Switzerland can count on its experience with democracy and federalism, which are political instruments that guarantee a high degree of participation. Democracy and federalism in Switzerland have also an effect on development cooperation. They restrain the power of the government and increase the possibilities of the Swiss citizens for decision-making. It is therefore decisive to convince people that development cooperation is necessary and useful. Switzerland should pay at least 0.7%. But why? Migration and resulting problems have been often-discussed issues during the last few years; closing the borders – as suggested by some - is in my opinion not a solution. Even in Switzerland the protection from terrorism is high on the political agenda. To a large extend, both phenomena derive from poverty. Therefore, reducing poverty is also in the interest of highly developed states like Switzerland. And due to its wealth, the country has the capacity to help.

I think that Switzerland is a good partner in development cooperation, but it could be an even better one. The country's own interests should be more in the centre of its development efforts, especially in times when development cooperation is often criticized.

In Kürze

Erfolg und Nachhaltigkeit der Entwicklungshilfe sind umstritten – auch in den Empfängerländern selbst. Dieses Kapitel beleuchtet die Wirksamkeit der schweizerischen Entwicklungshilfe aus verschiedenen Blickwinkeln. Die Studentin Karin Reinhardt meint, die Theorien des letzten Jahrhunderts hätten sich überlebt. Gefragt sei Pragmatismus und nicht Ideologie. Das Schlüsselwort heisst "Good governance". Entwicklungszusammenarbeit ist ein Dialog unter Partnern, wo die Empfängerländer unter Einbezug ihrer Bevölkerung die Strategie bestimmen müssen. Die Schweiz ist mit ihrer langen direkt demokratischen und föderalistischen Tradition ein starker Partner in diesem Prozess. Als Land, dessen Wohlstand vom freien Fluss von Kapital und Gütern abhängt, hat die Schweiz ein vitales Interesse an der Bekämpfung der Armut. Und so plädiert Karin Reinhardt für eine Verdoppelung der schweizerischen Entwicklungshilfe.

En bref

Le succès et la durabilité de la coopération au développement sont souvent remises en cause, y compris dans les pays bénéficiaires. Ce chapitre donne un éclairage sur l'efficacité de l'aide suisse au Bhoutan. Karin Reinhardt est d'avis que les théories du siècle dernier appartiennent au passé. Aujourd'hui, il faut du pragmatisme plutôt que des idéologies. Le mot-clé est "bonne gouvernance". La coopération au développement est un dialogue entre partenaires, et ce sont les partenaires dans le pays bénéficiaire qui doivent définir les stratégies, en impliquant leur population dans ce choix. Avec sa longue tradition de démocratie directe et de régime fédéral, la Suisse est un partenaire fort dans ce processus. En tant que pays dont le bien-être dépend de la libre circulation des capitaux et des biens, la Suisse a un intérêt vital à la lutte contre la pauvreté. C'est pourquoi Karin Reinhardt plaide pour le doublement de la coopération suisse au développement.

Switzerland-Bhutan: Dependable partners

by Mario Fehr, Swiss National Councillor, Social Democrat, Zurich, Member of the Foreign Affairs Committee

In the summer of 1989 I travelled to Bhutan for the first time. Further visits followed in the years 2000, 2005, 2006, 2007 and 2008. During those years the country made a powerful development leap. In Bhutan you can now find television and Internet connections, the number of cars has increased tremendously and many Bhutanese men and women own a mobile phone. In the mean time, in cities such as Phuntsoling, Paro and Thimphu, disco dancing is to be found. In Bhutan, the land of the peaceful thunder dragon, the modern world has arrived, so to speak, 'on velvet paws'. The quiet and composure, the fascinating landscape and the peacefulness of the people, however, have remained.

Between tradition and modernity

I was and am impressed by all that which Switzerland and especially HELVETAS have accomplished in Bhutan throughout the years. I am however just as impressed by our partners in Bhutan, who sought a dialogue with us in an open and constructive manner and accepted self-confidently mutual cooperation. Today Bhutan strikes a balance between softly opening up the country to modernisation and democratization while preserving its unique tradition and rich cultural heritage. In this respect, this balancing act succeeds admirably and is, in my opinion, especially true when one views some of its neighbouring countries. Without a doubt, Switzerland has made an essential contribution through its much-appreciated long-term development cooperation.

Democratisation in full swing

Bhutan is in the middle of an extremely dynamic process. The first political parties in Bhutan were established in the year 2007. In 2008, for the first time, general, democratic election for both chambers of the new Bhutanese Parliament were held. For the lower house (similar to the Swiss National Council), 47 representatives are selected, according to a proportional system, with 2 to 5 mandates for each of the 20 districts. For the upper house (similar to the Swiss Council of States), according to the majority system, one councillor has been determined in every one of the 20 districts, and in addition a maximum number of 5 further delegates are appointed by the king. This yields at most 25 national councillors. Also, in 2008 The first national constitution will also enter into force in 2008. In that same year, H.M. Jigme Khesar Namgyal Wangchuck, the 5th Druk Gyalpo has been crowned king, but only within the framework of a constitutional monarchy. The 4th king, H. M. Jigme Singye Wangchuck, has in 2006 submitted his resignation, entirely of his own free will and to everyone's total surprise. The wise monarch initiated the ongoing democratization process not only from above, but has also implemented the changes against much resistance and doubt. This is a truly unique process of democratization from above. As such, it deserves our unrestricted support and correspondingly earns our highest respect.

Switzerland's important role

The long-time cooperation between Switzerland and Bhutan is seen positively and is highly valued by all participants. Switzerland enjoys an impressive standing in Bhutan, based on its successful long-time engagement. Yet this position exceeds by far what might actually accrue to our country if we compare our limited financial engagement to that of other donor countries. Bhutan would like to become the „Switzerland of Asia". The small mountain country "Druk Yul" and its people are indeed very close to the similarly sized alpine country, Switzerland, with regard to its population and its political institutions.
Bhutanese women and men are justifiably proud of the progress achieved by their country in the past years. As regards the approaching democratization, there is much good will and also much scepticism. It remains to be seen whether or not the quick introduction of the democratic structures will really succeed. I was continuously reassured that Switzerland is one of the best and most reliable partners of Bhutan. Switzerland, in many respects, serves as an example to Bhutan and whatever is offered in terms of suggestions or criticisms falls upon open ears.

Consequences for Swiss politics

Bhutan currently finds itself in a highly interesting, but in no way unproblematic phase of its history. The democratization process from above is a unique experiment, and if it succeeds, that success may become a beacon for the entire region and possibly even beyond. Switzerland enjoys a great deal of confidence by the Bhutanese and it should definitely use this bonus. Anyone who wishes to strengthen the democratization process in Bhutan must continue this work through appropriate guidance and supportive projects, at least until after the second general elections, which will take place in 2013 at the latest. It would be reasonable to continue our presence in Bhutan until 2015-2020. Until then, concrete steps can also be undertaken to assist the 30 percent of the population that still lives under the poverty line. Those economically and socially underprivileged persons, especially in the South and East of the country, are often forgotten. Switzerland has the ability even now to offer valuable and purposeful project work in this area.

If Switzerland wishes to continue with Bhutan the political dialogue during which issues concerning the political system, the new state constitution and its implementation as well human rights questions are raised, it must assist in shaping this exciting and ongoing process as a partner and friend. The example of Nepal shows the direction that misguided democratization processes may take; the repair of such failures comes at a dear price. In Bhutan, a unique chance exists to avoid setbacks of this type from the beginning.

Future development cooperation

Switzerland should show a strong presence in Bhutan for at least the next eight to twelve years. It is important that the country's democratization and decentralization efforts be strengthened through concrete local projects. Furthermore, a 'good governance' aspect should be part of all such projects.

Agriculture / long-term food security: Our participation in the sustainable use of natural resources (RNR) must be continued. This is an important, clearly visible and experientially verifiable touchstone of our Swiss-Bhutanese development cooperation. Switzerland is present throughout Bhutan. The results of this cooperation deserve high marks indeed, given that more than 60 percent of the population is working in agriculture.

Rural infrastructure: The building of trail (suspension and suspended) bridges throughout the country is a Swiss hallmark. Because of the country's topography, it is of crucial importance for the people from partially quite distant villages to have quick access to the main arteries of traffic. That program, which profited from the long term experiences in the neighbouring country of Nepal, has so far been successful and must be secured financially and technically in the future.

Forestry / Social and Community Forestry (PFMP): The common use of the forests is of great importance not only ecologically, but also economically for the communities as users of forest and wood products. This common usage also has a positive effect in that it pushes the democratization process along in the affected districts and communes and helps establish further autonomy. The program is increasingly successful and will soon be implemented in all districts (Dzongkhags). Switzerland has been able to utilize and bring to bear many of its own experiences and advances in forestry management.

Regional Development Initiatives in South and East Bhutan (Regional Development Initiatives): These projects help reduce the income disparities (poverty level) in Bhutan. In these regions live many of the 30 percent of Bhutanese women and men who live below the poverty line. In the affected districts and communes, such projects also promote the implementation of grassroots-level democratic processes. The Rural Development Training Centre in Shemgang fulfils an important educational role in this process.

The next eight to twelve years are crucial

The economic development of Bhutan is viewed positively, especially in light of the envisioned income accruing from the future sale of electricity by its hydro-electric power plants. Nonetheless, the resulting large dependency on India must not be underestimated. For the midterm, we can expect increasing self-contributions from Bhutan – given its general population of only 700'000 inhabitants. In this regard the government of Bhutan is prepared to be forthcoming.

In future, the projects to be preferred should directly aid the individual engaged in the decentralization and democratization process and – at the same time - enable Switzerland to support the stated political objectives through the relevant concrete assistance projects. Additionally, good governance aspects should be observed in projects wherever appropriate. It is of decisive importance that Switzerland supports Bhutan in the next eight to twelve years with a substantial development program through the democratization phase. This will also safeguard the previous successful outcomes under the interesting development philosophy called "Gross National Happiness", but this must be secured in a sustainable and long term fashion. The coming eight to twelve years will show if the Bhutanese democratization effort will be considered a success or a failure. Switzerland can and must help shape this crucial process

In Kürze

Wie soll die Zusammenarbeit zwischen der Schweiz und Bhutan weitergehen? Nationalrat Mario Fehr, der Bhutan aus eigener Anschauung kennt, vertritt dezidiert die Meinung, die Schweiz müsse Bhutan in der Demokratisierungsphase über die nächsten acht bis zwölf Jahre substantiell unterstützen. Nicht zuletzt auch, um das bisher Erreichte abzusichern. Die Entwicklung Nepals sollte als abschreckendes Beispiel dienen. Bhutan hat einzigartige Chancen, ein gutes Vorbild für die ganze Region zu werden, wenn ihm seine Partner und Freunde dabei helfen. Schwerpunkte sieht er nach wie vor in der Land- und Forstwirtschaft und der Entwicklung der ländlichen Infrastruktur. Der Schwerpunkt sollte sich allerdings in den Osten und den Süden des Landes verlagern. In diesen Regionen lebt ein Grossteil der Bevölkerung, die noch immer unter der Armutsgrenze lebt. Regionale Entwicklungsinitiativen sind auch geeignet, die Demokratisierung und die Grundsätze guter Führung in die entlegeneren Distrikte und Dörfer zu bringen.

En bref

Comment la coopération entre la Suisse et le Bhoutan doit-elle se poursuivre ? Le conseiller national Mario Fehr, qui a sa propre vision du Bhoutan, est convaincu que la Suisse doit apporter un appui substantiel au processus de démocratisation du Bhoutan au cours des huit à douze prochaines années. Ne serait-ce que pour maintenir les acquis. Le développement du Népal devrait servir d'exemple dissuasif. Le Bhoutan a une chance unique de devenir un exemple à suivre pour toute la région, si ses partenaires et amis l'aident dans ce sens. Pour lui les priorités restent dans le secteur forestier et agraire et dans le développement des infrastructures rurales. Toutefois l'appui devrait se concentrer à l'Est et dans le Sud du pays. C'est dans ces régions que se trouvent la plupart des gens qui vivent au-dessous du seuil de pauvreté. Les initiatives de développement régionales sont également appropriées pour apporter la démocratie et les principes de la bonne gouvernance dans les districts et villages éloignés.

Pillars and approaches of Swiss Development Cooperation

by Ambassador Walter Fust, Director General of SDC

The activities of the Swiss Federal Department of Foreign Affairs are based on the five foreign policy objectives defined in the Federal Constitution:

Peaceful coexistence among peoples
Respect for human rights and the promotion of democracy
Safeguarding the interests of the Swiss economy abroad
Relieving poverty in the world
Preserving the natural environment

Swiss development policy gives the priority to the fight against poverty, in harmony with the Millennium Development Goals (MDGs) of the United Nations. The two other pillars of Swiss Development Policy are: to improve Human Security by reducing systemic risks and to contribute to sustainable globalisation process that favours the development of the least developed countries.

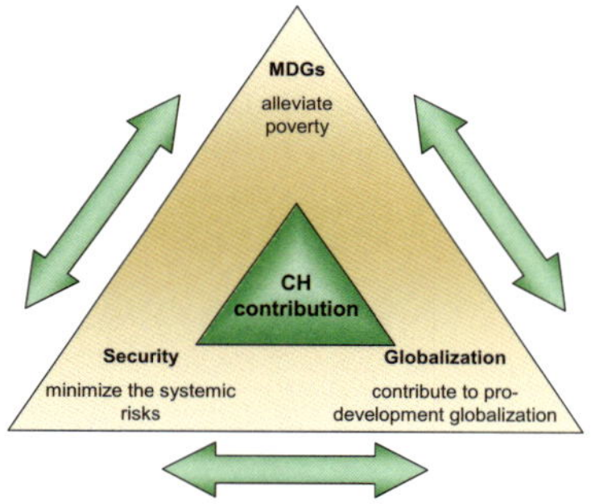

Although this framework does not include any cultural or spiritual dimension, there are many similarities with Bhutan's objective of increasing Gross National Happiness. Good governance, the sustainable management of natural resources and an economic growth that brings benefits to all parts of the population are underlying principles in both concepts.

In 2006, Switzerland provided 2'063 CHF million or the equivalent of 0.39% of its national income (GNI) in official development assistance (ODA). The biggest part of the Swiss development cooperation is shared between two agencies: the Swiss Agency for Development and Cooperation (SDC) (CHF 1'348 million) and the State Secretariat for Economic Affairs (SECO) (CHF 325 million). SDC is responsible for the overall coordination of Swiss development activities. In 2006, 57% of SDC's budget was spent for bilateral development cooperation and 43% of the budget went to multilateral development organisations.

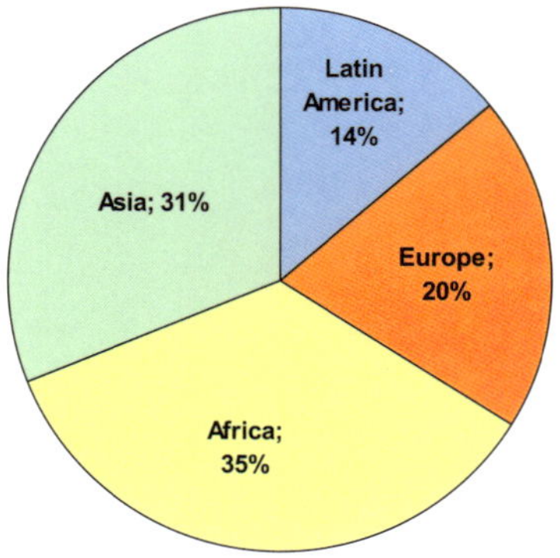

African and Asian countries are supported with about one third of the bilateral budget each, while Latin America and Europe benefit from the last third.

In view of the financial and personnel limitations, Switzerland has concentrated its bilateral development cooperation on 14 priority countries and seven special programmes in the Middle East, Africa, Asia and Latin America. At the multilateral level, SDC collaborates in particular with UN organizations, the World Bank, and the regional development banks.

Very early on, the emphasis in cooperation between Switzerland and Bhutan was placed on agriculture and forestry, rural infrastructures and the education sector. Up to now, Switzerland supports both the country's economy and social progress.

Switzerland is a signatory to the Paris Declaration on Aid Effectiveness of the Organisation of Economic Cooperation and Development (OECD) and is following its five Partnership Commitments on Ownership, Alignment, Harmonisation, Managing for Development Results and Mutual Accountability. These commitments envisage a more result oriented and effective development cooperation. Even if Bhutan is not a signatory of this declaration, the Swiss cooperation with Bhutan is very much following these principles. Swiss cooperation in Bhutan is well aligned with Bhutan's 5-year plans that have been presented since 1961 and the Swiss cooperation with Bhutan has shown very good results. In the education sector, particularly in vocational training, the Swiss apprenticeship system has always been an inspiration for Bhutan and a quite similar system with vocational schools is now successfully operating in Bhutan.

First the introduction of improved potato varieties and later the introduction of a genuine potato seed system to produce locally adapted potato varieties as well as the support in the development of sustainable potato production techniques have had a tremendous impact on the income situation of rural communities. There are many other important achievements that have been possible with the successful partnership between Bhutan and Switzerland, such as the many suspension bridges that were constructed and have made remote areas more reachable or the community forestry approach that is now seen as laying the basis to increase incomes of rural communities.

But all these successes have only been possible because of the great commitment and responsible actions of the various Bhutanese partners with whom the Swiss cooperation agents worked .

Over the past 50 years, Switzerland has supported Bhutan with about 150 million Swiss Francs. Being well on track to reach most of the MDGs, Swiss support has been scaled down to a lower level but will continue for the period of the 10th 5-year plan (2008-2013) and mature into a long lasting partnership of mutual exchange and support. Switzerland is recognising that in this period of big changes (transition from a monarchy to a parliamentary democracy) support of the newly created bodies in the governing system is crucial for succes.

In Kürze

Der Schwerpunkt der Entwicklungszusammenarbeit mit Bhutan lag von Anbeginn im Bereich von Landwirtschaft, Forstwirtschaft und Bildung. Die schweizerische Lehrlingsausbildung hat die Bhutaner immer fasziniert; mittlerweile haben sie ein sehr ähnliches System aufgebaut. Die Schweiz unterstützt Bhutan weiterhin auf reduziertem Niveau vor allem bei der Entwicklung der regionalen und lokalen Verwaltungsstrukturen.

En bref

Dès le début, le point fort de la coopération au développement avec le Bhoutan a été dans le domaine de l'agriculture, de la foresterie et de la formation. La formation par apprentissage a toujours fasciné les Bhoutanais; ils ont entre-temps développé un système très similaire. La Suisse continue son soutien au Bhoutan dans une mesure réduite, notamment pour le développement de structures administratives locales et régionales.

The friendship associations

by Pema Wangchuck, Tshering Wangda and Ernst Reinhardt

Introduction

The Society Switzerland-Bhutan was founded in 2000. It has presently more than 100 listed members. Almost all of them have lived and worked for longer periods in Bhutan under the Swiss bilateral or multilateral assistance programme. We are happy to have among us friends from the very early period .

The Druk-Switzerland Thuendrel Tshogpa, its sister organisation, was established in 2001. Almost all its members have been working in Swiss assisted programmes.
The two Societies endeavour to strengthen their ties even more in the future, based on the signed Memorandum of Understanding.

Memorandum of Understanding

between the Society Switzerland-Bhutan and Druk-Switzerland Thuendrel Tshogpa

Preliminary
The members of the two associations are committed to strengthening and expanding the existing cooperation between the peoples of the two countries in line with mutually agreed priorities. The focus of this association will be 'people to people'. The activities thereby undertaken by the two associations will not overlap or duplicate other existing bilateral development cooperation. Notwithstanding the fields of cooperation identified in this Memorandum of Understanding, the scope of activities may be broadened in the coming years with the consensus of both associations .

Farmers Training
Young Bhutanese farmers can be selected on the basis of their proven commitment to be farmers in Bhutan. They will be selected and sent to work and stay with host families in Swiss farms with a view to augmenting their skills and knowledge in crop, dairy and forestry production and processing.

Sports and Cultural Cooperation
Activities which promote culture and heritage of Bhutan in Switzerland and that of Switzerland in Bhutan will be facilitated by the two associations. This may include support to the preservation of cultural projects, and artists such as musicians, dancers, artists, craftsmen etc. Bhutanese sportsmen, especially with expertise in archery, can visit Switzerland to promote traditional archery. Similarly, Swiss arts and culture could be promoted in Bhutan through visits of artists and organisation of exhibitions.

Exchange of media Personnel and Academics
A well functioning media is particularly important for the growth of civil societies. Training of media personnel as well as academics from autonomous agencies will be a focus of cooperation between the two associations. For the promotion of understanding between Swiss and Bhutanese people, exchange of visits between media and academics will be promoted. There could be institutional partnership between such bodies.

City Partnerships
Urbanisation is taking place in many places in Bhutan. Some cities of Bhutan may be linked with cities in Switzerland in order to seek technical and financial assistance. The two associations will look into the possibility of establishing a linkage programme.

School-to-School Friendship Linkage
Certain schools in Switzerland and rural Bhutan can be linked via e-mail and correspondence as sister schools. Students of the two countries can embark on a programme to write to each other, sharing news and opinions, thus building awareness in other parts of their respective societies. In order to enable the Bhutanese students to undertake this information sharing and friendship building exercise, the schools in Switzerland could consider funding the modest cost of correspondence and communication, which would otherwise hinder the Bhutanese students from doing so.

Funding Arrangements
The two associations will endeavour to explore various sources of funding, including foundations, subscription fees of members, and individual benefactors to implement the mutually agreed activities.

Signed in Thimphu on 12th November, 2001
Ernst Reinhardt, President Bhutan-Swiss Friendship Association
Pema Wangchuck, Chairman Druk-Switzerland Thuendrel Tshogpa

215 The farmer and the Queen, Rigifestival 2004, Switzerland

In Kürze

Die Gesellschaft Schweiz-Bhutan wurde im Jahre 2000 gegründet, Ihre Schwesterorganisation In Bhutan, die "Druk-Switzerland Thuendrel Tshogpa" im Jahre 2001. Beide Vereine haben sich zum Ziel gesetzt, die Freundschaft zwischen den beiden Ländern zu pflegen und zu intensivieren. Sie wollen auch als Kommunikations- und Informationsforen wirken zum besseren Verständnis der beiden Völker.

En bref

L'association Suisse Bhoutan a été fondée en l'an 2000, et son organisation soeur au Bhoutan, la "Druk-Switzerland Thuendrel Tshogpa", en 2001. Les deux associations ont pour but d'entretenir et d'intensifier l'amitié entre les deux pays. Elles veulent également servir de forums de communication et d'informations pour une meilleure compréhension entre les deux peuples.

Vote of thanks

We can look back with joy on 50 years of successful cooperation between Switzerland and Bhutan. Many have contributed to it, and for decades Helvetas had the privilege to be part of it.

Tashi Delek and a heartfelt thank you to:

- The population of Bhutan for its efforts to improve living conditions and for their willingness to adapt to changes involved
- The thousands of Bhutanese who have taken over challenging new tasks
- Our Bhutanese colleagues for their commitment and perseverance
- Our international staff members for their professionalism and their enthusiasm
- The Swiss Agency for Development and Cooperation (SDC) for the financial and thematic support
- All donors who gave their support, both financially and otherwise, and in particular the Family von Schulthess
- All others who made this success story possible

Special thanks go to the Society Switzerland-Bhutan for their initiative and their immense efforts to publish this memorable book.

Helvetas,
Swiss Association for International Cooperation

Peter Arbenz
President

Wir dürfen mit grosser Freude auf eine erfolgreiche 50-jährige Zusammenarbeit zwischen der Schweiz und Bhutan zurückschauen. Viele haben dazu beigetragen, und mitwirken durfte jahrzehntelang auch Helvetas.

Tashi Delek und herzlicher Dank:

- Der Bevölkerung Bhutans für ihren Einsatz zur Verbesserung der Lebensverhältnisse und für ihren Willen, sich auf Veränderungen einzulassen
- Den Tausenden von Bhutanern, die neue Aufgaben übernommen haben
- Unseren Bhutanischen Mitarbeitenden für ihr Engagement und ihre Ausdauer
- Unseren internationalen Mitarbeitenden für ihre Professionalität und ihren Enthusiasmus
- Der Direktion für Entwicklung und Zusammenarbeit (DEZA) für die finanzielle und die inhaltliche Unterstützung
- Allen Gönnerinnen und Gönnern, und ganz speziell der Familie von Schulthess
- Und allen, die diese Erfolgsgeschichte ermöglicht haben.

Ein besonderer Dank gilt der Gesellschaft Schweiz-Bhutan für ihre Initiative und die immense Vorarbeit zur Herausgabe dieses denkwürdigen Buches.

Helvetas
Schweizer Gesellschaft für internationale Zusammenarbeit

Peter Arbenz
Präsident

C'est avec une grande joie que nous avons pu évoquer 50 ans de coopération fructueuse entre la Suisse et le Bhoutan. De nombreuses personnes y ont contribué et Helvetas y a participé au cours des décennies.

Tashi Delek, nos chaleureux remerciements vont à:

- La population du Bhoutan, pour ses efforts soutenus afin d'améliorer les conditions de vie et pour sa volonté de participer aux changements
- Les milliers de Bhoutanais-e-s qui ont pris en charge de nouvelles responsabilités
- Les collaborateurs bhoutanais d'Helvetas, pour leur engagement et leur persévérance
- Les collaborateurs internationaux d'Helvetas pour leur professionalisme et leur enthousiasme
- La Direction pour le Développement et la Coopération (DDC) pour son soutien financier et technique
- Les donateurs et donatrices, notamment à la famille von Schulthess
- Et toutes celles et ceux qui qui ont permis la réussite de cette belle histoire

Nous remercions également et particulièrement l'Association Suisse-Bhoutan pour son initative et l'immense travail préparatoire dans l'édition de ce livre mémorable.

Helvetas
Association suisse pour la coopération internationale

Peter Arbenz
Président

The list of project managers can be downloaded from
www.bhutan-switzerland.org/memories

216

The Swiss partners

Schweizerische Eidgenossenschaft
Confédération suisse
Confederazione Svizzera
Confederaziun svizra

Swiss Agency for Development and Cooperation SDC

The Swiss Agency for Development and Cooperation (SDC) is Switzerland's international cooperation agency within the Federal Department of Foreign Affairs (FDFA). In operating with other federal offices concerned, SDC is responsible for the overall coordination of development activities, cooperation with Eastern Europe, as well as for humanitarian aid.

The SDC carries out its activities with an annual budget of CHF 1.3 billion (2007) and a staff of some 620 people in Switzerland and abroad, as well as 1000 local employees. The Agency undertakes direct actions, supports programmes of multilateral organizations, and helps to finance programmes run by Swiss and international aid organizations.

www.deza.ch

helvetas

Helvetas was founded in 1955 as the first private organisation for development co-operation in Switzerland. Helvetas is a denominationally and politically independent association, supported by approximately 43'000 members, 40'000 sponsors and 16 regional groups.

The overseas programme includes the most varied development projects, which are implemented by about 600 local, and 40 Swiss staff members in 20 partner countries. In Switzerland, Helvetas focuses on awareness creation for development policy issues through information campaigns, the promotion of fair trade, and cultural events.

Helvetas is oriented expressly not only towards material needs or aims, such as improved living conditions, in-creased production and income or improved infrastructures. Equally important are immaterial aims – that is, social, cultural, and spiritual ones.

www.helvetas.org

society switzerland-bhutan

The Society's purpose is to further strengthen the friendship between Switzerland and Bhutan through:

- the Society's function as a communication and information forum which facilitates the insight into the cultural, spiritual, social, economical and political life of Bhutan and Switzerland;
- the exchange of knowledge and experience, as well as the training of professionals;
- the provision of background information and commentaries with respect to the media presentation of the partner countries of this Society;
- the development, promotion and implementation of projects and happenings which support the Societies purpose;
- the co-operation with other Bhutan Society's and, if appropriate, with other institutions and organisations; in particular, it endeavours to establish a sister organisation in Bhutan.

www.bhutan-switzerland.org

Epilogue

This book speaks about leadership, friendship and partnership. It carries a message about making development assistance effective:

Assist and support the innovative, enterprising, able ones to most effectively alleviate poverty. They will best help the weak and the poor.

Ernst Reinhardt

217 Thuenpa puen shi illustrates the concept of teamwork. The story tells how the elephant, monkey, peacock and rabbit combined forces to obtain a continual supply of fruit.

Credits

Photo credits

Ganga Ram Adhikari, SCAP Bhutan: 95, 96, 182
Natalie Beffa, Brig/CH: 88
Christian and Barbara Bigler, Aesch/CH: 102, 103, 104, 105
Traditional Dyeing Methods of Bhutan, 2002
Gisela Bonn: 9
Kunstreiseführer Bhutan, 1988
Martin Brauen, Bern/CH: 24, 25
Irgendwo in Bhutan, 1994
Christophe Chammartin, Lausanne/CH: 2
Jürg Christen, St. Gallen/CH: 133
Werner Christen: 142, 148
Edi Day, Zoo Zürich/CH: 40, 41, 42
Elio Della Ferrara, Chiuro/I: 11
Tiere der Alpen, 2000
Tashi Dendup, SCAP Bhutan: 94, 183
Chencho Dhema, SCAP Bhutan: 169, 170, 171, 172, 173, 174, 175, 176, 177, 206, 207
Dagay Tenzin Dorjee, SCAP Bhutan: 23, 181, 216
Leki Dorji, Thimphu, Bhutan: 10
Tandin Dorji, Thimphu, Bhutan: 145, 147
Marianne Frei, Zürich/CH: 93
Michael von Graffenried, Paris/F: 209, 210, 211, 212, 213, 214
Bundeshausfotografien, 1984
Armin Haab, Bhutan, Fürstenstaat am Götterthron, 1961, 1969
4 Apfelernte in Ha – es sind Gravensteiner
32 Ha – Ein Mädchen schaut den Kämpfenden zu
33 Ashi Kesang, die Maharani von Bhutan
37 Vom Ehrenzelt schaut die Königsfamilie den Kämpfenden zu
128 Wangdiphodrang, das Tor nach Ostbhutan
185 Die Pächter von Jigme Dorjis Gut in Paro beim Nachtmahl
188 Der Maharadscha spasst mit dem zukünftigen Diener seines Sohnes

Max Häberli, Zoo Zürich/CH: 43
Bernd Hartung, Agentur Focus, Hamburg/D: 89
Helvetas: 64, 74, 76, 166
Helvetas/Richard Gerster: 27, 202
Helvetas/Oswald Iten: 118, 162
Helvetas/Fritz Loppacher: 153, 192
Helvetas/Hans Maibach: 136
Helvetas/Walter Roder: 201
Helvetas/Gaudenz Tscharner: 48, 52, 127, 157
Helvetas/Dieter Zürcher: 55, 73, 138
Maria Känzig, Uster/CH: 106, 107, 108
Foto Klopfenstein, Adelboden/CH: 82
Fritz Loppacher, Weggis/CH: 30, 44, 73, 129, 151, 154, 159, 186, 187
Ursula Markus-Gansser and Augusto Gansser, Zürich/CH: 111, 134
The Dragon Kingdom, 1983
Fritz Maurer, Bumthang, Bhutan: 165
Kurt Meyer and Pamela Deuel Meyer: 7, 130
In the Shadow of the Himalayas: A Photographic Record by John Claude White 1883-1908, 2005
MEN Musée d'éthnographie Neuchâtel/CH: 110, 113
Martin Menzi, Thun/CH: 29, 69, 155
Peter Moser-Kamm, Bussnang/CH: 5, 18, 19, 20, 21, 22, 31, 46, 47, 49, 51, 53, 54, 57, 58, 77, 85, 87, 109, 115, 117, 119, 122, 123, 125, 152, 158, 160, 163, 167, 190, 191, 215
Erich Oberholzer, Thalheim/CH: 86
Bikram Panday, SCAP Bhutan: 203, 204, 205, 208
Ugyen Pem, SCAP Bhutan: 178
Hans Pfaffen, Chur/CH: 141, 143, 144, 146, 149
Ursula Pfaffen, Chur/CH: 3b, 61, 140
Claudia Pflugshaupt, Bertschikon/CH: 79, 80, 81
Ernst Reinhardt, Weesen/CH: 50, 56, 63, 75, 116, 150, 156, 161, 180
Christian Rohrbach, Wetzikon/CH: 90, 91, 92
Daniel Rothacher, Bern/CH: 59
Marie-Thé Roux, Sierre/CH: 134, 135
Karin Rüegg, Windisch/CH: 83
Ueli Rüegg, Windisch/CH: 65, 66, 67, 68, 70, 84, 112, 114, 128, 137
Felix Sigrist, St. Gallen/CH: 98, 99, 121
Fritz von Schulthess: 34, 35, 36, 38, 39, 45
Erinnerungen, III. Teil, Bhutan, 1982
Daniel Schwitter, Malans/CH:126
Guy van Strydonck: 26
Bhutan, un Royaume de l'Himalaya, Editions Olizane, 1984
Bal Kumar Thapa, SCAP Bhutan: 78, 184, 193, 194, 195, 196, 197, 198, 199, 200
Völkerkundemuseum Zürich/CH: 3
Textilien aus Bhutan, 1995
Markus Wild, Luzern/CH and SCAP Bhutan: 72, 168
Samten Zangmo, SCAP Bhutan: 164, 179
Dieter Zürcher, Uster/CH: 132

Maps

www.swissworld.org: 14, 17
Department of Survey and Land Records, Thimphu: 13, 16
TagesAnzeiger, Zürich/CH: 12, 15

DVD: Gross National Happiness in Bhutan.

Gross National Happiness means:
- Sustainable and equitable socio-economic development
- Conservation of the fragile Himalayan ecology
- Preservation and promotion of the traditional culture
- Enhancement of good governance

The DVD, produced by FAVACH / Erik Allgoewer in 2005 is a well structured and beautiful illustration of endeavours aimed at achieving these goals.